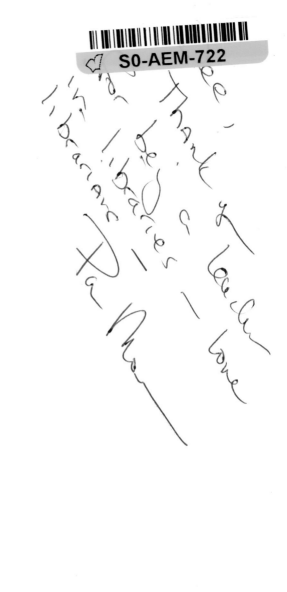

"An ambitious book! The authors aim to show reformers at all levels of schooling what and how we could and should respond to the demand that 'all children' succeed. Each chapter is filled with practical accounts of real life stories of teachers and students who aren't willing to comply and give up. Instead, the narrative of *Timeless Learning* demonstrates the power of democratized and collaborative progressive education designed for contemporary learners."

— Deb Meier, public school teacher for half a century, author of *Schools Belong to You and Me*

"Pam, Chad, and Ira have written a manifesto; they are not spouting blanket statements but rather revealing the intricate facets enmeshed in learning, teaching, and living. They are big dreamers and just as big doers, and their ideas and hopes are built from real experiences in walking the halls, breaking down walls, and hearing students and teachers alike. I've had the incredible fortune to spend time in conversation with these three, and this book is the next best thing."

— Stephanie Chang, Director of Educational Programs, Maker Ed

"A thought-provoking and insightful read highlighting the rapidly shifting landscape of public education and the fixes that we so urgently need in our public schools. Moran, Ratliff, and Socol have crafted a thorough and detailed walkthrough of how one of Virginia's leading school districts has charged full-speed into the progressive era of education. This book serves as an excellent reminder of how far we've come from the comparatively primitive classrooms of the industrial era and gives a front-row seat to how America's public schools are embracing a new world of pedagogical possibility, and rethinking what it means to learn."

— Julian Waters, youth educational provocateur and aspiring policy maker

"Schools do not transform. School administrators, teachers, and staff have to personally transform in order to cocreate individualized, meaningful learning journeys with every student. The authors with radical transparency share such a journey – a 'learn by doing' journey of overcoming financial restraints, physical space, fears of the unknown, and resistance to change by inspiring, trusting, and enabling teachers and students to cocreate the learning that will better prepare students for the Smart Machine Age. This book will capture your mind and your heart; it is an inspiring and practical read!"

– Ed Hess, coauthor of *Humility Is the New Smart: Rethinking Human Excellence in the Smart Machine Age*, Professor of Business Administration and Batten Executive-in-Residence, UVA Darden School of Business

"Maker Learning is about providing students with opportunities to explore ideas that are personal to them. We give them a voice when we allow them to identify and create solutions to problems that are pertinent to their lives. Pam, Chad, and Ira have worked with the members of their community to create schools that support processes and spaces that provide fluidity in addressing the learning needs and desires of all students, and adults. Backed by a body of knowledge and direct experience, the words on the pages of this book will be an inspiration, as they provide ideas for establishing learning constructs for the learners of today and the future."

– Lakeysha Washington, Principal, Benjamin O. Davis Middle School, Compton, CA

"A must-read book by three of America's leading public school educators. Socol, Moran, and Ratliff paint a picture of what learning must and can look like in the twenty-first century, and how to transform outdated schools into places of powerful student-centered engagement and learning. An inspiring, rich narrative from the front lines of K–12 education. Bottom line: If they can do it, so can you!"

– Grant Lichtman, author of #EdJourney: A Roadmap to the Future of Education and Moving the Rock: Seven Levers WE Can Press to Transform Education

"This book is the enactment of modern-day progressive education in Virginia and the shining example of how school and district leaders are an essential factor in the development of systems and dispositions that support youth and adults in becoming their best selves. It should be required reading for any educator interested in empowering teachers and students and investing in the future of public education. After years in the classroom, in schools, and in leading school districts, these exceptional educators share their blueprint for designing learning spaces for youth to own their learning and cocreate knowledge with teachers. At the heart of this blueprint is the belief that teachers and students should cocreate learning environments that are meaningful for them."

– Jessica Parker, Director of Teaching and Learning, the Exploratorium

"The single most important challenge our country faces is how to transform existing schools to prepare children for their futures. This remarkable team has done exactly that, advancing learning outcomes for kids in every school in a district that reflects the full spectrum of socioeconomic circumstances. Read this book and treasure it for the insights and pragmatic advice it provides!"

– Ted Dintersmith, author of What School Could Be and executive producer of Most Likely to Succeed

"Contemplating the visionary tool kit in *Timeless Learning*, one is shaken up, the mind is opened, and we are offered an open space to prepare for the critical evolutionary leap our schools must make. The authors provide an illuminating X-ray-like analysis of what has gone before, where past academic trails have led, and their clearing away and innovating forward in confidence breaks down walls to construct new open spaces, foster real world learning and promote an education our learners want and will need underpinned by a deep, palpable cherishing of *all* our children. A *must-read* tool kit for twenty-first-century learners of all ages."

– John Hunter, CEO, World Peace Game Foundation

"To prepare students for a bold new world we need to fundamentally rethink learning. The authors not only provide a compelling case for needed changes to the function of schools but they all have played an integral part in implementing transformative practices at the classroom, building, and district level. If you are interested in how to put theory into practice, then this book is for you."

– Eric Sheninger, Google Certified Innovator and Adobe Education Leader, and Thomas C. Murray, Director of Innovation, Future Ready Schools

"The authors challenge constraints often cited as barriers to contemporary progressive education. In their work to integrate innovative technologies, teaching practices, and learning environments they show how systems thinking and strategic design can lead to learning opportunities that were inconceivable a decade ago."

– Richard Culatta, Chief Executive Officer, ISTE

Timeless Learning

HOW IMAGINATION, OBSERVATION, AND ZERO-BASED THINKING CHANGE SCHOOLS

Ira Socol
Pam Moran
Chad Ratliff

JB JOSSEY-BASS™
A Wiley Brand

Published by Jossey-Bass
A Wiley Brand
One Montgomery Street, Suite 1000, San Francisco, CA 94104-4594—www.josseybass.com

Jossey-Bass books and products are available through most bookstores. To contact Jossey-Bass directly call our Customer Care Department within the U.S. at 800-956-7739, outside the U.S. at 317-572-3986, or fax 317-572-4002.

Wiley publishes in a variety of print and electronic formats and by print-on-demand. Some material included with standard print versions of this book may not be included in e-books or in print-on-demand. If this book refers to media such as a CD or DVD that is not included in the version you purchased, you may download this material at http://booksupport.wiley.com. For more information about Wiley products, visit www.wiley.com.

Library of Congress Cataloging-in-Publication Data
Names: Socol, Ira, author. | Moran, Pam (Pamela R.), author. | Ratliff, Chad, author.
Title: Timeless learning : how imagination, observation, and zero-based thinking change
    schools / by Ira Socol, Pam Moran, Chad Ratliff.
Description: San Francisco, CA : Jossey-Bass; Hoboken, NJ : John Wiley & Sons, 2018. |
    Includes index.
Identifiers: LCCN 2018011226 (print) | LCCN 2018014921 (ebook) | ISBN
    9781119461685 (epub) | ISBN 9781119462231 (pdf) | ISBN 9781119461692 (cloth)
Subjects: LCSH: Educational change. | Project method in teaching. |
    Student-centered learning.
Classification: LCC LB2806 (ebook) | LCC LB2806 .S584 2018 (print) | DDC 371.2/07—dc23
LC record available at https://lccn.loc.gov/2018011226

Cover Design: Wiley
Cover Images: Background image: © antadi1332/iStockphoto; Photograph of children by Ira Socol

Printed in the United States of America

FIRST EDITION

F10001874_070318

Pedagogy 101

by Alan Shapiro

Suited (I thought) and tied,

earnest as the day was very long,

I taught them when to be still,

why they needed to listen,

where Columbus was born,

how to answer textbook questions

and what the similarity was

between my decrees and their grades.

Sitting at bolted desks

while flies rambled on tall windows

they taught me when to shut my mouth,

why I needed to hear,

where they were coming from,

how to question textbook answers,

and what the difference is

between schooling and education.

18 April 1999

with permission from the estate of Alan Shapiro

Contents

Acknowledgments

None of our work would be possible without our professional colleagues who have worked tirelessly to enable the open and authentic learning that liberates our students. They are teachers and principals, assistant and deputy superintendents, bus drivers and cafeteria staff, department directors and computer technicians, learning coaches and network engineers, custodians, and more.

We also have learned much from the children who inform us of what matters to them. We have learned the power of listening to their voices. Our kids tell us in every way that their relationships with teachers and their peers matter. They want learning that makes sense. And, they want to actively participate in learning experiences fueled by their questions, curiosities, and interests in and out of school.

The educators and learners of Albemarle County Public Schools have courageously taken risks, many over decades, to create pathways to timeless learning for the young people we serve. We never fail to notice the educators who collaborate and work tirelessly before, during, and after school to make sense of today's learners' needs. When everyone believes in their power to make a difference, it does. Education is about everything children see, hear, and experience, and they are indeed fortunate to be surrounded by fabulous educators in our district and beyond.

In addition, each of us owes deep debts to people who were transformative in our professional lives. We appreciate Professor Ed Hess of the Darden School of Business who has kept us focused on social-emotional competencies such as empathy and that how learners learn is core to preparing young people for life in today's world. And, to Ted Dintersmith for shining a light on the need for deep change in American education. We value that he has shared our work with communities across America.

Pam: I'm grateful to my career mentor, the late Dr. John English, who inspired, taught, and coached me to see children as the priority in every decision. He defined progressive education through his leadership. And also to former superintendent Kevin Castner who said in the face of No Child Left Behind, "We need to keep passion in our classrooms"; from that, Design 2004 was born giving life to our division's work to empower learners. I am so appreciative to my husband, Jon, and son, Jason, who have grown up with me in the world of education. They gave up family time every day so I could participate in a career to better the lives of children and the educators who serve them.

Chad: I would like to thank three mentor educators for believing in me and giving me opportunities that many in their positions wouldn't consider: Tom Fitzgibbons, for my first job in public education. Your professional mentorship changed the trajectory of my life. Spencer Chang, for teaching me the value of character and humility. You made space for the important things and remembered not to take the rest too seriously. Pam Moran, for your tireless dedication to the mission, your ability to draw out the best in those around you, and the patience and unconditional love that sometimes requires.

Thank you to my wife and life partner, Cay Lee, for your perspective and support. None of this would be possible without you. To my brother, Jeff, for trailblazing and always having my back. To my parents, Joe and Linda, for instilling a passion for learning and trying new things. You gave me the confidence and freedom to explore. I owe my optimism and bias toward action to you.

And to the best teachers of all, my two children, Spencer and Maya. Every day, you inspire me to be a better human.

Ira: I thank my mother, Ruth Socol, whose open, multiage classroom in the 1970s demonstrated what an elementary school could be. And the late Alan Shapiro, who made education possible, and the late Cleo Cherryholmes, who made postcolonial thinking real. I also thank my family: Jill, my wife, for her constant support, patience, and love, and James, my son, whose brilliance in his interaction with technology and the world is a constant inspiration.

We also thank our professional learning network that makes itself available all hours of day and night to share resources, answer questions, challenge thinking, and connect us with the world's educators.

And we value our Wiley editors, especially Pete Gaughan, who have been with us all the way through the journey.

Please connect with us on Twitter!

Ira Socol @irasocol
Pam Moran @pammoran
Chad Ratliff @csratliff

Foreword

Children are, or should be, at the center of education because ultimately they are reason for the very existence of educational institutions. But unfortunately, children are too often forgotten in discussions about education. Adults involved in education too often don't see children. They see curricula. They see standards. They see test scores. They see timetables. They see technology. They see battles over funding policies. They see math and reading wars. They see fights over public schools. They see disputes about teacher unions. They see everything about the operation of schools except for the very reason for which schools exist: children.

Timeless Learning is a book that directs our attention to children. The authors implore us – everyone involved in education – to see children. They share their lessons about learning to "be much much better at seeing children."

When we are good at seeing children, we recognize that they are diverse. They arrive at our schools with different talents, passions, skills, knowledge, relationships, dispositions, attitudes, and experiences. Each and every child possesses a jagged profile of strengths and weakness. Each and every child has something that is worth celebrating and developing. Each and every child has a dream that is worth realizing. Each and every child has unique needs that we can help meet.

When we are good at seeing children, we understand that all children are first and foremost human beings before they are students. All children have the universal human right of self-determination. All children need respect, autonomy, to love and be loved, and opportunities to create value for others. All children deserve to be treated equally in schools as adults.

When we are good at seeing children, we accept that all children are natural-born learners, although they may be interested in or good at learning things that we may not value. All children are curious and creative. They want to explore, experiment, and express. They are naturally motivated to learn new things for genuine purposes. When they are not engaged in what we want to them to learn, we need to question ourselves rather than blame them.

When we are good at seeing children, we know that schools exist to serve the interests of children, not the other way around. Curricula exist to provide children opportunities to learn, not to limit their explorations. Standards exist to guide the development of learning opportunities for children, not to judge their worthiness. Tests and assessments exist to facilitate children's learning, not to shame and label them. As a result, we are never to allow children's learning to be dictated by curricula, standards, or tests.

Timeless Learning is a journal of three brave educators who embarked on a journey to learn to see children better. In this book, Ira Socol, Pam Moran and Chad Ratliff honestly document their exciting, exhilarating, and emotional journey to "a future destination in which all children will thrive in school because of their diverse interests, range of background experiences, and identities – not in spite of their differences." They see themselves as humble learners and fallible humans, so they don't hide their frustrations, their stumbles, or their struggles, nor do they hold back their happiness, joy, and excitement along the way.

In many ways, Pam, Ira, and Chad are ordinary people. They reflect on their own experiences as students and realize that they were drastically different. Each of them had their own good fortune and bad luck with their own schooling, just like everyone else. What makes them extraordinary is that they took their reflections many steps further. When they became educators, they realized that they had the power to make changes, to make schools a better place for children like them. Then they went beyond the realization and took actions.

Their actions took place in an ordinary public school district, which suffers from the same suffocating test and accountability educational policies applied in all American schools. They faced the same challenges of inertia, resistance, and the legacy of an outdated education paradigm as change-seeking educators in schools all over the world do. They had the same concerns and anxiety as every change maker has: the lack of guaranteed success and acceptance of the planned changes. They understood the risks; they learned from others; they prepared themselves; and they took actions. They took "rapid, yet deeply considered actions to change the educational system we have inherited."

But the actions, they knew, were not a one-time fix that would solve all the problems once and for all. Instead, the actions – any actions for that matter – will solve some problems and create others. Thus once actions of change are taken, the change maker has embarked on a never-ending journey of change actions. The authors knew that their "desired state is a world of opportunity and success for every child, but the path to that desired state is a very long, very difficult climb."

Timeless Learning is not a cookbook, although it contains plenty of recipes for a stimulating meal. Nor is it a prescriptive roadmap, although it provides abundant tips about traversing the difficult terrain of educational transformation from experienced travelers. As I read it, this is a tale of morally driven individuals who want to right the wrongs in education that they experienced. They do not want to see more children suffer from schools that are ostensibly institutions to help them. More important, they want schools to see the children and serve them well.

This is a critical time for education. The human society is going through an episode of tumultuous changes. Political instability, widening economic gaps, environmental degradation, rising racial tensions, growing nationalism, and rapid technological changes are all working together to affect the future world our children will occupy and we (at least some of us) will retire in. This future is extremely uncertain. It is impossible to get our children ready for a future so uncertain, thus the popular idea of readiness such as college and career readiness and future readiness is as absurd as it is popular. Our children cannot be ready to walk into the future premade for them. They have to create this future. Whether they can make their future (and our retirement) peaceful and prosperous depends on what we do in schools today. And what we do in schools should begin with seeing the children. Keep in mind the questions that guided the journey of Pam, Ira, and Chad:

What do you see when you look at your school?
What do you see when you look in a classroom?
What do you see when you watch children in the playground, or
    on a street, or in a park?
What does learning look like?
What does growing up look like?

Yong Zhao
University of Kansas
East China Normal University

Introduction
How We Came to See Learning and School

What do you see when you look at your school? What do you see when you look in a classroom? What do you see when you watch children playing in the playground, or on a street, or in a park? What do you see when you watch teenagers gathered on a corner? What do you see when you see two boys wrestling? Or three teenage boys pushing each other? What do you see when you watch two 14-year-olds trying to escape your gaze so they can pay attention to each other?

What does learning look like? What does growing up look like?

In the end it all comes down to knowing how to see. To understanding what we are seeing. And, to putting what we learn from our effective vision into action for our children.

Though this book will cover many topics, the primary lesson design we've created is one that we hope will continue to push us and our readers to become much better at seeing children. Once we are able to see clearly what is happening with children in our schools and outside of our schools, we will then be on the path to learn how to take rapid, yet deeply considered actions to change the educational system we have inherited.

We begin by describing what compelled us to each come to our work to change education. Although we are different leaders and we represent different background experiences, we share a passion for changing the vision of schooling as it existed yesterday and even as it exists today.

Ira's Story

Ira's realization of why he is here, doing the work he is doing now after a lifetime of trying out careers designed to be of help to others from victims of crime to victims of homelessness, began with his realization that all of victimhood starts in childhood, sometimes under the guise of parenting or teaching or both. This is one small part of his story from another book that represents a bit of who he once was and who he still is in some ways. It's what keeps him coming back to work day after day when it would be far easier to do something else, stay home, or hike a mile on the Appalachian Trail. He comes back because he believes if he can make one kid have better days than he had as a kid with dyslexia, it's all worth it. He knows this because his own early life experiences took him down paths that were catastrophic for him. This was his life before a high school teacher saw the potential within him rather than his deficits:

My days were changing. Falling back into the Special Education pattern of elementary school. Resource rooms and the tower. Tests and analysis. Broken only by avoided classes and sports practices. Football in the fall. Basketball in the winter. Baseball in the spring. I didn't make much of an impact on the football team, though I got to alternate at halfback bringing in the plays. But I mattered to basketball and baseball, as a point guard and a catcher, and those coaches – I suspect – were the adults who fought to keep me more or less in school. I probably went to a few classes. Though if I did I sat in the back and avoided contact with education whenever possible. And it was easy to do this because an uneasy truce was settling in between me and the teachers. They didn't bother me and I didn't bother them. Even when good, wonderful, nice teachers thought they might "get through" to me, thought they could help, I couldn't allow it. My image was all I had left and my image demanded, if not full-time insolence, at least total nonparticipation.

Drift set in, as it has often tended to do, at least since the structures of the school day were introduced. Not all the time – of course not. There are weeks, months, seasons, once in a while whole years of lucidity and tremendous accomplishment. At least by the scale with which people like me are measured. But those winning streaks alternate with two other time signatures, the crash and the drift. The crash is both self-explanatory and at least has a definite ending of sorts. I'll admit it is not an ending you look forward to; even the most suicidal person, having leaped from a rooftop, must fear the moment when he strikes the pavement no matter how much he seeks what is on the other side. Also, I have always been clearly aware of the crash when I'm in that stage, which makes it different from the drift. In the drift I am disconnected from most things, though not from assault and pain. In fact, in the consciousness vacuum that defines the drift, touches both physical and emotional become assaults, and pain is magnified to remarkable proportions. In this drifting time, I wandered the floors of the school chased by everything: The hum of fluorescents attacked, the noise of feet in the corridors struck like hammers to the skull, the smell of old chalk dust choked. The voices of teachers cut into me. The slam of lockers punched me. No amount of ingested alcohol, THC, or nicotine could quell enough of the hurts to allow me any comfort. (Socol 2007)

Chad's Story

Born and raised in the foothills of Virginia's Blue Ridge Mountains, Chad wasn't exactly a teacher-pleaser in school. In fact, he worked harder at avoiding schoolwork than at doing it. He figured out how to game the system, maximizing time out of class and minimizing the effort needed to get by and graduate. This effort trajectory (or negative effort trajectory) continued into college, where he spent far more than four years clumsily collecting undergraduate credits.

Fortunately, while on this roundabout tour of colleges and universities, he ran into beloved former teacher and coach, Tom Fitzgibbons. Tom, now principal of the high school in the urban center of Chad's hometown, offered him a teaching assistant job in the alternative education program. The class was housed in a church basement. The neighborhood was one of the city's toughest; the students, some of the area's most traumatized. There, Chad became a protege to legendary wrestling coach Spencer Chang. Something changed. This work wasn't about chasing a grade, chasing a paycheck, gaming a system. Chad wanted to do more than skate by. He wanted to change the world – through education.

What had been a sleepy but economically vibrant city was now a tough place to find a job. The middle-class life of Chad's childhood had become scarce. As once-bustling textile and furniture companies shuttered at the whim of capitalism, unemployment rates soared to among the highest in the nation. The crime rate followed, and Chad began to lose students to both sides of the gun.

Today, Chad is a father. His children attend great public schools where educators care about them first as children. He knows they can receive quality learning experiences inside and outside of school. But every day, he asks, "How might we create a lasting commitment in public schools so that *all* children thrive?"

Chad has seen the results of a school's focus on passing tests rather than on supporting young people's full range of needs. He has seen the results of students consigned to a dominant teaching wall rather than engaged in agency-building work. However, he has also seen what happens when kids are provided multiple pathways to learning, when they are given room to design, create, make, engineer, and build, and to have ownership in their own learning.

For some, schoolwork that values creativity, teamwork, logical reasoning, and entrepreneurial thinking is an enhancement. Even worthy of tuition. For kids who feel little hope, this can be a lifeline.

For nearly a decade, Chad continued teaching and coaching, struggling against the culture of a depressed city. The local paper featured his students for their accomplishments both in and out of the gym. It also spoke of those who lost their lives or were incarcerated. Hopes and dreams fled on the heels of factories and jobs. Community and entrepreneurial spirit were relegated to the streets in the form of gangs and drug deals.

Years later, following a screening of Davis Guggenheim's documentary film *Waiting for Superman*, Chad penned a letter. He has since returned to working in a school, but he holds this experience close. Still learning, always using today's work to inform tomorrow's, he plans to stay the course.

To Delvin, Tyre, Nick, Josh, Lynwood and Anthony, Chad, Anthony E., Cornett, Jason and Tasha, Steven and Dominique, Shavon, and those whose names are unreleased:

I think of you guys often. You were in one of my classes, on my teams, and in my programs at some point during the near-decade I worked in your high school.

But I failed you.

You weren't one for whom I advocated much beyond my scheduled time. I didn't go to your home to tell your mom or grandma I believed in you. I didn't ask you to come to my room during my planning block so you could do your homework in peace. I didn't ask you to eat lunch in my office to talk about college, the world, your potential, or to simply stay out of trouble.

And I didn't collaborate with your other teachers to unearth your hidden talents and discover common challenges. I didn't teach you how to navigate the system of schooling. I didn't connect you to key community members to be there when I couldn't. I didn't tell the staff to let me know each and every time you slipped. I didn't introduce you to my wife down in the English department so you'd have another place to go. I didn't accompany you to the police station when you got in trouble.

I simply didn't do the things for you that I did for others who faced the same challenges.

It wasn't a deliberate choice – I just ran out of time. And, ultimately, I ran out of physical energy and emotional stamina. Knowing I had the ability to make a larger impact on your lives, which perhaps could've altered the path of self-destruction upon which you traveled, also made it hard to sleep at night. I finally had to take a break from education.

I've since returned and am working in another district. I'm not in a classroom anymore, or even in a school building, but I often think about getting back "in the trenches." I happened to spend some time as a substitute principal for one of our elementary schools. There, I met a young fellow that reminded me of you. He was troubled and angry.

I made a few calls to get him some support both inside and outside of school, but, as with you, I felt largely powerless. When I walked out of that school one afternoon, I cried.

I cried because I know.

I know that regardless of how hard we try, or how much we care, or how high we get his test scores, this child's future is vulnerable. Maybe it's naive to think that we, as your educators for a short time, can help navigate the perils of poverty. But I believe, with all my heart, that we must try. As the old adage goes, "If not us, who? If not now, when?"

I promise that I'll never forget you and what you taught me. And I'll always fight like hell to provide the best educational opportunities for every student. You'll never know the madness of educational policy propaganda and political ideologues throwing garbage in the path. You remind me that it's worth pushing through. Lives depend on it.

Pam's Story

Pam was a good student. She nailed down good grades and finished at the top of her class. She read not just proficiently, but extraordinarily. Unlike Chad, she played the school game well. Unlike Ira, she never struggled because of a disability that became a weapon used by teachers against him. Like both of them, she questioned even as an elementary student why school was a home for some and a war zone for others.

Pam has spent more than four decades in public education observing and learning from some of the best educators who have ever taught. Along the way as she navigated her own professional journey from teacher to administrator she came to believe the burning question of her career is "Why do some educators continue to evolve and change over time and others do not?" As a superintendent, she now knows that the question she began to ask as a relatively young administrator is not one just for individuals but also for schools and districts. She has also learned that change doesn't start with wholesale mandates from the superintendent's office but rather by gathering educators together to explore what Simon Sinek calls the Golden Circle of Inspirational Leadership. As Sinek says the journey of deep change "starts with why" (Sinek 2009).

In a decades-past dissertation, Pam attempted to answer the question of "Why do some change?" by asking teachers why they made changes in practice. She found some simple, and some complex, answers. Highly successful teachers identified as changing instructional practices over time appear to have some characteristics in common. First, they believe they make a difference in the lives of learners they serve. They engage in critical inquiry to make sense of learners' needs – what we once referred to as *kidwatching*. To continue to realize their efficacy over time, they seek out critical friends with whom they can reflect upon the challenges of reaching every learner and from whom they can gain insight into what to do when they aren't connecting a learner and learning. They are willing to try new approaches to support individual children. They exhibit an internal sense of control and an inherent belief that they can impact student success by making changes in how they work with young people. And even in 1997, these highly efficacious educators believed that engaging young people in authentic, real-world learning would support them to construct relevance and meaning in their lives.

In many ways, the characteristics of the teachers profiled in Pam's dissertation represent what she has come to see as the timeless wisdom of educators who have created pathways for all young people to find their way on a journey of lifelong learning. She realizes that the best teachers educate young people for life, not school. Such teachers are far more interested in children taking joy in learning with them as they navigate through life than they are in whether their children pass other people's standardized tests. They know that motivated learners will continue to pursue their interests and passions across the vast wastelands of rote content learning that becomes increasingly irrelevant across time as we move farther from it. Such teachers understand the power of dialogue and debate about the big ideas found in science and history and the literature of authors who challenge the status quo. They know that children's curiosity and questions will propel them into deep inquiry about the world in which they live. They believe in the power of children who design, create, build, and make by drawing upon the expertise of adults and peers around them as they explore and sample the vast curricula of life.

Pam has watched over decades as individual teachers, school staff, and district leaders worked hard to build a variety of plans to improve learning consistent with what the best educators have always done to create environments where young people actively thrive as learners. She also has seen such efforts fail across time despite the thickness of once-common three-ring binders of goals and strategies, ubiquitous and exhaustive required professional training, and pages of evaluation procedures designed to improve and make standard effective teaching and administrative practices. She's come to the conclusion that there is no recipe for the secret sauce of change that will result in less random and more consistent superb learning opportunities for children in our schools. In fact, every time she hears "scale up" or "standardize anything" as it relates to learners and learning, she cringes. Such efforts are the antithesis of what educators must do to create healthy, vibrant systemic learning experiences for the children we serve, a perspective gained listening to educators over the years and which Pam believes is illustrated in the timeless voices of three teachers she interviewed and observed for her dissertation (Moran 1997).

Conboy, an elementary teacher, found that encouraging children to see themselves as helpful members of a learning community created a culture in which children learned to support each other as learners, and when connected in a multiage community, intentionally supported children to develop deep agency for their own learning and to communicate their thoughts to others. In other words, she purposely created situations in which children's voices mattered:

> I expect them (the first graders) to be actively engaged in whatever it is that's going on and I expect them to be helpful to each other. Helpful in a way that is not giving the other child the answer, but being there to guide them. I have third graders come in and work with my first graders and that's been working beautifully. In my first grade classroom now, the biggest thing I want to have people see is that these kids are figuring it out; they are figuring out how to read, how to write, do math. Those are the most important things to me. I am really proud of these kids because they have worked hard and come a long way. Some of them did not even know the sounds that letters make, and now they can put down any thought that they want on paper in a way that somebody could read. (Moran 1997, p. 93)

Like Conboy but from a different perspective, David, a middle school teacher, reflected on the importance of children learning much more from him than simply passing tests. In his work is reflected his belief that schooling is about children developing confidence in themselves, and becoming people who will find success not just in school but, most importantly, in life:

> To relate an incident, the day I decided I wasn't going to use a textbook anymore – first I started the day as if it was going to be normal, read out of the book. I was even doing the round robin crap, where each kid would take turns reading. So we started that, and of course they were all kind of sinking in their chairs, and then I had them stand up and drop their books on the floor. Then I told them to jump up on top of their books for ten minutes . . . Then we put them on the shelf and that was literally the last time I ever

used a textbook. It was sort of a cold turkey thing when I made
the decision that I was going to turn the corner and do something different . . . I feel like I've gotten to the point where I feel
like content is secondary to enthusiasm and interest . . . so what
I've evolved into, I'm purely project oriented now. We just go
from one project to another. My students pick a topic of interest,
research it, plan activities, and teach a lesson to elementary children. Before that we did Rube Goldberg mouse traps to illustrate
energy changes and energy transfers . . . that room was a mess.
I had my band saw in there and my drills, it looked like a shop.

I feel like there's this contradictory thing with testing. On
one hand you want everyone to be successful and yet you'll only
define success with one measure. Now maybe that state test is
going to be such a low basic test. I think a student I'm talking
about (who will struggle with the test) will be a successful human
being and if I'm really successful I'll get him to a point where he
will read out loud to his class . . . So that he will also read to his
children when he has children . . . I'm on them a lot. You have got
to read to your children. And that is not in the curriculum. Part
of what I think is incredibly important is to teach them how to
be parents. They're going to be parents . . . How do I assess that?
(Moran 1997, p. 186)

Finally, Diane, a high school math teacher, identified reflective practice as essential to her growth and development, even
including her students in the feedback loop so that she could
learn what worked or did not work for them as learners. Engaging learners in the instructional design to assess user experiences
supported learners, with Diane, to find connections between
math teaching and math learning, and learners were provided
opportunities to develop critical analysis skills well beyond hon-
ing their capability to solve math problems.

Every time I do something with the kids that's new, I'll make
notes about it. Did this work? Did it not work? If something
doesn't work real well, you sit back and think was it for the right

reason that it didn't work, like lack of preparation, or was it because it just wasn't relevant for what the kids were doing? I'll ask the kids. What would have made it easier for you? They're the first ones who will say, "If you do this again, try such and such." You have to listen to the kids. If you don't it's a nightmare. (Moran, 1997, p. 134)

These three teachers' interviews in the late twentieth century separated by a distance of nine grade levels reflect what many today refer to as twenty-first-century learning skills. They valued collaboration, communication, critical thinking, and creativity as an end in mind far more related to life's learning than school learning. Pam once said to Ken Kay, chief executive officer of EdLeader21, that twenty-first-century learning skills are really any century learning skills, and what differentiates the four Cs of collaboration, communication, critical thinking, and creativity in the twenty-first century from all centuries before is the power of technologies to rapidly accelerate the potential of human intelligence to solve the grand challenges that humanity faces today and forever forward.

As Pam looks back on her career in education, the idea that there is some definable skill set of teaching and learning in the twenty-first century that differentiates excellent teaching today from excellent teaching of the past seems absurd. What isn't absurd is that we have an opportunity to connect our profession to the journey of educators across time who understood that when young people and their teachers engage together in pursuit of learning for life, they create an edu-ecological system that thrives even as it evolves. In creating such a system, today's educators go back to the best of our roots in the earliest teachers who understood that learning occurs in many spaces, from caves to campfires to watering holes. The tools we use and the curriculum we learn shift across time.

However, to accomplish learning in today's world teachers and their learners must use a continuum of old and new technology tools to design, build, create, make, and engineer learning.

Neuroscience research is clear that engagement of the mind does not happen when forced to sit in rows, facing a dominant teaching wall, and rooted in space and time by the "cells and bells" model of the twentieth century. Today we know that this compliance-driven teaching favored some, left some behind, and drove many out of our schools, regardless of compulsory education. The history is clear. Schools of the twentieth century were designed to fail students. The current need is apparent. Schools of the twenty-first century must be designed so that all succeed.

When Pam visited the Pentagon with a class of fourth graders and teacher John Hunter from our district (his World Peace Game and documentary film went viral after a 2011 Ted Talk), she had no idea what to expect (Hunter 2011). The children had been invited with John to speak with everyone from policy makers, generals, and communication staff to the then Secretary of Defense Leon Panetta. They shared in all-day sessions what they were learning from playing the game, whether reading *The Art of War* or negotiating climate change policy across nations, just one of the challenges they must address over weeks of work within the experiential global community simulation game (S. Tzu 2005). What has stuck with Pam from that day years ago were words from a Pentagon policy wonk who commented that he wished more schools would teach children how to solve grand challenges with all the creativity and critical analysis they can bring to the task. He commented that in this day and age the world has neither standardized problems nor standardized solutions. And as John said to Pam on the school bus trip heading back to school that evening:

> Children show us what they can do when we remove anything from in front of them that might get in their way as people. They come to us as experts in something already. We need to use those strengths and build on those strengths. (Moran 2012)

To be contributors to educating children to live in a world that is increasingly challenging to negotiate, schools must be conceptualized as ecological communities, spaces for learning with the potential to embody all of the concepts of the ecosystem – interactivity, biodiversity, connections, adaptability, succession, and balance. These concepts have become a lens through which we consider and understand the schools we observe and what makes learning thrive in some spaces and not others.

In this book, we have created a map of what we believe are the processes necessary to move from schools in which content-driven, adult-determined teaching was the old norm to new learning spaces and communities in which context-driven, child-determined learning is the new norm. We believe we've seen and experienced enough success in the work we do in our own district and with educators in other districts to write this book. We aren't offering any recipes for success, but rather simply processes that we believe can help others take the big ideas from the best of those who have studied education across the millennia and put big ideas into practice. We often end presentations by saying to audiences, "Go back to your schools or districts and tomorrow, change something." This isn't a random comment. We've discovered that the statement "a journey of a thousand miles begins with a single step" (L. Tzu and Laozi 2008) accurately captures our mantra "change something."

Every journey has to begin somewhere. We each can pinpoint key moments in our own lives from our experiences with our own teachers, colleagues, and mentors that generated an epiphany that caused us to change something. In Pam's dissertation, the excellent teachers she interviewed all could point to those moments as well. As you dig into this book, we warn you that it's not a book for the educationally weak at heart to read, for we believe in provoking your thinking, challenging your beliefs, arguing with your assumptions, and pushing you to sail beyond the horizons in your willingness to take risks.

We write this because we believe every child matters. In every district. In every school. In every classroom. What we believe matters isn't captured on standardized tests written by people sitting in rooms far from your learners. What we believe matters isn't rewarded by rubric scores and student progress ratings on teacher evaluations. What we believe matters isn't captured in data-heavy and narrative-poor reports to school boards or parents. Instead, what we believe matters can only be assessed through kids who keep coming back to school because they see learning as worthy of their time and engagement. How will you know when school matters to kids? They will tell you through their work beyond curricula, in what they create and share with the world, in how they treat each other and what they do to make their communities a better place for others, and in their pursuit of learning not as mandated but as they desire.

Resources

Anderson, Robert. 2006. "Another No. 3 to Have His Own Night." *Roanoke Times*, 28 April. http://www.roanoke.com/webmin/sports/another-no-to-have-his-own-night/article_3bcb3aee-171b-56bd-aa81-ff89854dc479.html.

Hunter, John. 2011. "Teaching with the World Peace Game." https://www.ted.com/talks/john_hunter_on_the_world_peace_game.

Moran, Pam. 2012. "World Peace Game: No Standard Problems – or Solutions." A Space for Learning. 25 March. https://spacesforlearning.wordpress.com/2012/03/25/world-peace-game-no-standard-problems-or-solutions/.

Moran, Pam. 1997. "Some Do and Some Don't: Teachers Who Changed Their Practices." EdD diss., University of Virginia School of Education.

Sinek, Simon. 2009. "The Golden Circle." https://www.youtube.com/watch?v=fMOlfsR7SMQ.

Socol, Ira. 2007. *The Drool Room*. Derry, Ireland: River Foyle Press.

Tzu, Lao, and Laozi. 2008. *Tao Te Ching: The New Translation from Tao Te Ching: The Definitive Edition*. Edited by Jonathan Star. New York: Penguin.

Tzu, Sun. 2005. *The Art of War: Complete Texts and Commentaries*. Boston: Shambhala.

1

All Means All: Cherishing Children

There are so many chances to intervene. To stand up and
protect, or to look into the shadows which surround your
school's grounds and corridors, and find the child, teen,
young adult, who needs to know his or her value . . .

— Ira Socol (2010)

PAM: Every day educators make a thousand decisions. I think
about what drives decisions all the time and I have a
short checklist of one question: "How will this decision
benefit all children?"

IRA: Every school system in our nation, and most in the
world, was developed as segregated, and not just
racially. Consider "gifted" classrooms, "honors" courses,
even robotics clubs. Then look at in-school suspension,
at the classrooms with the most rote learning, the most
worksheets. You will see they are divided by race, by
class, and by disability.

CHAD: And that's why we have to make the case that every-
body needs enriched, engaging experiences; and it can't
be about competition for such experiences. It's got to
be about finding the exceptional talents, virtues, and
interests of every kid. When we create an environment
in which kids find some sort of passion that ignites a

15

greater interest in coming to school, that doesn't necessarily mean they're going to be in direct competition.
They might. But, we need to get out of this notion that
for my kid to be successful, your kid must fail, or be
held down in a compliant way. That's a bigger problem
to solve really. I think that maker education, as simple
as it may sound, could be just the key pathway to that.

Paths to Equity and Access: The Grand Challenge

Educators respond to all kinds of forces that lead them to make
decisions that don't benefit *all* children. If you're the parent of
one of the 10% of the kids who are in experiences that will get
them, by today's standards, ahead in high school, accepted at
Harvard, and then into a professional job, then you do not want
school to change. That alone puts enormous pressure on educators to maintain the status quo.

Homework, grades, schedules, leveled courses, ability grouping –
all are strategies that teachers today inherited from their parents'
teachers. We know from experience, data, and research that
these practices work against all children getting access to full
and rich curricula, engaging experiences, challenging work, and
even relationships with adults who matter. School reforms of the
twentieth century created different educational experiences for
what our parents' generation referred to as the "haves and have
nots." Over time, parents, educators, and community members
have become comfortable with that model.

The cultural biases of those in power, and yes, the desire to
preserve privilege, have filtered out both an interest in change
and reasons to change, so the structural consequences of schools
created by past generations are seldom challenged, even today.
Neither are the implicit biases that impact the way we see kids.
These biases have played out in schools so that those identified as
high performing or gifted have been entitled to special and more
interesting learning experiences than those identified as needing
extra assistance. And, extra assistance often translates into the
mind-numbing work of drill and practice.

Creating paths to equity and access for all children remains the grand challenge of public education in America. We can name all the problems and we can generate an endless list of solutions. We also know that educators can do little to nothing about home and community poverty. What we can control is what we choose to do more of, or less, in our learning spaces to give us the chance to notice children, to see their faces, hear their voices, find their strengths, and help them know their own value. This doesn't happen by chance. Rather, these are outcomes of school communities that focus on leveraging resources to authentically engage learners, not just to provide rich opportunities but also to insist on children getting access to opportunities that challenge their curiosity, stimulate their urgency to seek knowledge, and encourage their interests, questions, and passion to learn more. This is our life's work.

> It's my time to git it, and I won't be late
> I said it's my time to git it
> So I stepped up to the plate
> Let's make the world a better place
> With no mistakes
> Where every race can come together
> At a growin' rate
> Let's celebrate
> Let's jus' show and elevate
> So one day I can make it to Heaven's gate
> I got a lot of questions for God
> I can barely wait
> Ever since I was born I knew I would be great
> Cuz
> I have a dream . . .
> *– Kolion Troche, 2016 high school graduate*
> *and rapper (Moran et al. n.d.)*

The decision in our district a few years ago to support two librarians in creating a very inexpensive sound studio in their library (at first just old desktop computers and a basic sound board) created a new pathway for teens to write, perform, record, and produce their own music. Teens from all walks of life found their way into the studio. Kolion was one such teen. When he enrolled in one of our high schools, Kolion, a Brooklyn native, was fresh out of the juvenile justice system, and headed to a high school placement. Most people would have bet against this 17-year-old's odds of staying out of trouble. However, when he walked by a newly constructed space in his new high school, a music studio connected to the school library, he made perhaps one of the most important decisions of his life. He wandered in and asked, "What's this space?" The teacher – young, a minority, and wise beyond his years – connected with Kolion and invited him to join in the work of nascent studio musicians.

Kolion wasn't on a path to graduation at that point but he did have a love for rap music, and inside was a poet ready to be unleashed. In November, the principal indicated that he was working hard, but the barriers of state tests and verified academic credits seemed insurmountable. Pam crossed her fingers, hoping he would make it to the winter holidays. He did. Days became weeks and learning seemed to become timeless for him. He came to school early. He stayed late. He wrote rap lyrics for himself, for friends, for his biology class. By May, he had one state test left, earth science which was a ninth-grade course. On a sunny day driving in her car to and from schools, Pam got a call from the principal's office. She listened, then pulled off on the side of the road, palpable joy coming into her car from the other end of the line. Kolion's voice. The principal's voice. He'd made it. He would walk in June. He had found his voice, and in doing so, changed his trajectory from being on the verge of dropping out to graduating from high school. Pam says now that she knew whatever the investment that had been made in creating the music studio – and it was small even in our advanced versions – was worth every dime when she saw Kolion poised on stage, waiting to hear his name called to come forward and receive his diploma.

Equity provides resources so that educators can see all our children's strengths. Access provides our children with the chance to show us who they are and what they can do. Empathy allows us to see children as children, even teens who may face all the challenges that poverty and other risk factors create. Inclusivity creates a welcoming culture of care so that no one feels outside the community. We've all seen that children are not impossible challenges, but their needs can challenge a teacher's capacity to serve them well. And we've learned, along with other progressive educators, that we must willingly search our values and make decisions differently if we believe that every child matters. In doing so, we come to cherish all our children.

The "Insurgent Mission" to Create "Habitable Worlds" of Learning

Kolion was no magic student. No magic intervention or remediation programs existed to pull him through. He made it to graduation because he found a mentor with an "insurgent mission," a teacher who chose to "upend the status quo" as he connected with kids to change what learning opportunities in high school could become (Zook 2016). In discovering his passion for writing and performing rap music in a school that made that not just okay but promoted it, Kolion found a reason to keep coming back to school every day to connect with peers, diverse teens united through their voices, agency, and influence in their school community. Indeed he found his way as a learner. We are fortunate because we have Kolion's and many other learners' stories to share. Their stories give us hope for a different future, a progressive future, where school is much different than it has been for more than a century.

> What I've seen the most change in was that students were encouraged in their participation in the studio to understand the person across the table from them. If you have that student who wears the pants with the holes in them and the earrings and the tattoos and he may be an outsider to someone who wears a fitted cap and

baggy pants and a hoodie. They share so much in common but yet
through appearances they seem so distant. What a program like
this does, from what I've observed, is that it puts them in the same
room and it allows them to speak a common language because
their language is not their fashion or their group of friends or their
family background; their language is music, it's words, it's writing,
and – it's sound and it's fluent. What it does is create a connectivity between them. And, literally I've seen it demolish barriers between individual students, between teachers and students,
between teachers and teachers. I've witnessed that and I think
Kolion can attest to that same thing. He's experienced that and
he's become a role model on his own just because he's become an
example of not succumbing to the stereotypes that are so relevant
and strong in our society right now. (Moran et al. n.d.)

We share stories of children, adolescents, and teens all the
time, for it is through their voices that we challenge educators
with whom we interact in our district, state, nation, and around
the world. We challenge them to consider their own beliefs and
values about the young people who are required to occupy our
learning spaces for up to 13 years – 180 days a year, five days
a week, about seven hours a day in school, and into the night
and weekends as they take work home. And many of the educators we work with can tout fantastic tales of bootstrap successes
among graduates not unlike Kolion.

Sadly though, the social, political, and economic narrative
of schooling in the past has been grounded in a "soft eugenics"
belief that while some children have the capacity to become
whatever they choose to be in life, others do not. This plays out
in the decisions that educators make, often based on decontextualized data and confirmation biases that stem from immersion
in traditions of education that did the same to us. Even if lip
service is given to words such as equity, accessibility, inclusivity, empathy, cultural responsiveness, and connected relationships, schooling today is still far more likely to support practices
from the past that have created school cultures in which none

of those words define who educators really are, no matter what they aspire to be.

Consider how the "habitable world" concept developed by Rosemarie Garland-Thomson, Emory University researcher and professor, sits at the core of the philosophy of educators who developed and now sustain the structures and processes of schooling that impact young people such as Kolion (Garland-Thomson 2017b). Garland-Thomson views public, political, and organizational philosophy as representative of one of "two forms of world-building, inclusive and eugenic" (Garland-Thomson 2017a). Unfortunately, often it's the soft educational eugenics philosophy that is most often expressed in practice, if not in words, across the nation's schools rather than the creation of habitable worlds that are inclusive of all learners.

When children lacking the privileges of growing up in middle-class, mostly Caucasian families enter school, they often are sorted and selected into remedial programs, sometimes labeled as disruptors, and excluded from the normative culture because of cultural differences (Hammond 2015). This sets the stage that schools become increasingly difficult for children of color and poverty to successfully inhabit, worlds they may choose to leave as soon as legally possible to find a place where they can negotiate different life choices even if by measures that may challenge social norms. What does it say about schools that young people might not consider their learning communities as habitable worlds? No matter the source of data, educators know that familial opportunity gaps lead to school achievement gaps that have become established story markers of predictive demographics (Decker 2017). To change the story, we must change the narrative of the schools we build for learners.

The decisions we make at every level of the educational system create a narrative that often refutes the belief that we truly value all children. Our urge to use averages to describe the state of children in our schools – below, on, or above level – works against young people such as Kolion. Kolion isn't an average young person. No child is. If we want our schools to be learning spaces that reveal the strengths of children to us, we have to create a bandwidth of opportunities that do so. That means making decisions differently, decisions driven from values that support equity, accessibility, inclusivity, empathy, cultural responsiveness, and connected relationships inside the ecosystem. Those are the words representative of habitable worlds, not words such as sort, select, remediate, suspend, or fail.

> The solution, the way decisions are best made, lies in empowering teachers and students to make choices. Any systemic or institutional decision made for "all kids" or "most kids" or based on quantitative research will – guaranteed – be the wrong decision. Any decision based in "miracle narratives" will be at least as bad. We are not discussing "the average child" or "the average dyslexic" (neither of which exists), nor are we going to base policy on the exceptional case. Instead, we will "solve this" by making individual decisions with individual students. (Socol 2008)

From a Good Idea to a Learning S-Curve Culture

Kolion's story illustrates a counternarrative to the common organizational philosophy that if it's not in the strategic plan, staff should not be doing it. The addition of music studios in a school library didn't start with a strategic plan. It started with two librarians who identified the challenge of getting more kids who never step foot in a library to see the school library as a useful space. From that point, Chad and Ira began to work with the principal and the librarians to make changes in the library. The principal had given permission in a prior year to convert an old storage closet and two old desktop computers into a tiny music recording studio. The librarians and the principal fell in love with the idea of incorporating a larger music studio into the library. They also realized the importance of looking to teens to tell them what they were interested in doing in such a space. The librarians gave up their office and storage space, and the music studio was born. As a result of that initial invention work in 2011 by librarians, thriving music studios now exist in all high school libraries in our district.

Sometimes visitors to our schools ask Pam some version of this question, "How does ____ fit into your strategic plan?" She always answers first that the district has a robust strategic plan, and the strategic plan certainly supports applications of innovation work. Her key words, however, to visiting administrators capture her philosophy that when good ideas emerge, don't wait to capitalize on them because students don't always have time to wait on us:

> What we don't do is let a strategic plan get in the way of doing work that helps us invent something that we haven't done before. I think that's a really important philosophical difference because I've had superintendents say to me, "Well, we have a lot of good ideas like maker education that are out there, but it's not doable in our strategic plan right now."

In Chris Zook's book *The Founder's Mentality*, he speaks to the role of the founder inside a company who often times distances him- or herself from continued nurturance of a team's original insurgent mission (efforts to upend the status quo) and that distance often leads to a company growing stale (Zook 2016). Pam feels that drift to staleness herself on some days, and it's usually when she senses decisions are being co-opted by our urge in education to be controlled by external forces, adult conveniences, or those who hold tight to the status quo. Supporting the explorers, the pioneers, and the settlers is critical in the initial phases of change, but once staff move past the euphoria of initial change startup, that's when the hard work begins. When everyone settles into change routines, they tend to lose that early momentum. Sustaining momentum comes from understanding when an organization's learning S-curve is flattening and the time is right to resource a positive inflection point in that curve (Kahan 2012).

To that end, Pam took what some might consider a risk during the height of the recession era to use capital funding to turn libraries into learning commons with spin-off spaces that inspired teens to design, make, and hack, advancing the district's vision of all students being engaged and inspired as learners. The music studios created a new inflection point that encouraged change agency among other teachers and building administrators. This led to a variety of connected initiatives including interdisciplinary core coursework, build-out of mechatronics labs, experiential learning, inquiry, 1:1 device rollout, and modernization of learning spaces. And, through these changes, available learning tools, space design, and contemporary pedagogies have spread across the district. As a result, the culture of learning has shifted from a more traditional one-size-fits-all "sit and get" model to multiple learning pathways grounded in project work, choice and comfort, making, Universal Design for Learning, instructional tolerance, connectivity, and interactive technology applications.

The evolution of learning culture is the most critical work educators need to do inside schools today. Culture reflects community values and school culture remains a relatively compliance-driven system even with our best efforts to change that. The only way to change culture is to constantly create situations in which people together respond to the question "Why are we here?"

To borrow the term *last mile* from the telecommunications industry (Bartolic n.d.), the last mile work of educators to include all children in our learning communities won't happen without adults exploring their own biases, reaching deep to find empathy for children who sometimes don't engender that, understanding that accessibility is a right and not an option, and being willing to address equity even though it means giving up a share of resources that educators feel are owned through the entitlement of privileged past practice. A former superintendent, Kevin Castner, used to say that our district isn't a system of schools, it is a school system. This means working together to collaboratively solve challenges. Kolion's success in his last year of high school belongs to all of the community, not just his school or his teachers. Seeing learners like Kolion not as impossible challenges but as members of the full community is a critical insurgency that is essential if "all means all" is to become reality and not just educational rhetoric.

All Means All: Fostering a Pedagogy of Equity Inside and Outside the District

Educators also can learn from Kolion that while he did, in the end, pass tests and classes to graduate, even more importantly, he taught members of the school community, including the School Board, to see him not as below average but rather as a unique individual with a talent that would not have been seen without a continuum of opportunities. We have learned from our young people's stories that it's not just that educators provide access to opportunities, but rather it's their strong advocacy for individual children that makes real the value-laden meaning of the words – equity, accessibility, inclusivity, empathy, cultural responsiveness, and connected relationships.

To turn those words into reality in schools, educators must learn to braid decisions and resources together to create inflection points so that continuous growth and development occur. That does not happen by chance. In our district, for example, that's been done with preschool programming. Federal, state, and local funds are leveraged each year across the program to be able to get as many kids in pre-K seats as possible. It's also happened with the use of multiple sources of funding – e-rate, capital improvement, operational, and state tech funds – to finance projects that allow all students to move from guaranteed broadband access only inside our schools to, through a significant strategic investment by the district, having that service available inside their homes and apartments. Keeping the needs of young people, from children to teens, at the center of adult decisions means using resources differently to effect changes essential to contemporary learning.

Staff in our district must simultaneously attend to both the microlevel mission of building a community of learners and learning one student at a time and to the macrolevel vision that "all learners excel, embrace learning, and own their futures" (Albemarle County Public Schools n.d.). This means attending to the importance of resourcing change at both individual and community levels. It's absolutely critical that leaders understand and respect the role that humans play in the change equation. How, otherwise, are leaders able to find people who can envision how to leverage resources to grow the invention and innovative work needed to help all young people not just dream but act to pursue those dreams?

For example, an S-curve inflection point moved our work closer to a last mile solution a few years ago when staff leveraged resources to open a pop-up makerspace for children and even adults in a local barrio. That same community became the first that the district's tech department powered up with free Wi-Fi access for students so their school laptops actually functioned in their homes, not just in class. Making the connection from the pop-up makerspace to broadband access represents a "walking the walk" investment in equity work writ small and large. It's also a statement of how we cherish all children, regardless of who they are and where they live.

At the microlevel of beliefs and mission, educators must work to ensure every child knows their voice matters, they have agency in making choices and decisions, and they can be responsible for their own learning. Learners who have that level of control can influence their own lives. They also can influence people around them. They can influence their community and benefit others. Kids who believe in their own efficacy likely will be kids who, even when confronted with a teacher who is less contemporary in their pedagogy or who assigns work that learners don't really like doing or want to do, will still persist in pursuit of their own goals.

Young makers, such as children served in the popup makerspace, have shared when they create they feel a sense of control, agency, and some influence. We hear from children that when they find meaning and value in their work, they are more likely to be able to push through challenging situations. Their sense of self becomes valuable. When learners have a sense that they have value and their learning has value, they believe they can get where they want to go in life. It's why we philosophically believe kids who embrace learning are more likely to both own their learning as well as to excel (Albemarle County Public Schools n.d.). This comes from the kind of work kids do; first, creating ideas of what they want to do and then getting a chance to form, with their hands, those ideas into reality in our schools. As Chad says, "that's progressive education made real."

Traditional power brokers in education, on the other hand, often promote, advocate, and support an educational model that sorts and selects, promoting interesting, rich learning for just certain students. Chad spoke to that in a discussion with Jessica Parker, former director of community and learning with MakerEd.org, noting that progressive educators can't let their commitment to progressivism get co-opted by those who have in the past dominated the educational hierarchy:

> For example, teachers last year were participating in a Twitter chat and a teacher who indicated she worked with gifted students tweeted that making should be only for gifted programs because that's where the pioneering work for new educational models should reside. There are ten different problems in just that one tweet. First, if somebody believes in that kind of elitism it's a problem. Education has a history of allocating enriched opportunities to only the kids who don't need traditional schooling. Bright kids, which typically means privileged kids of educated parents, under the guise of "enrichment" are taken out of regular classes and given learning opportunities that are cooler, better, more enjoyable to do, because the idea is they're smarter by birth. This sends an immediate message to all kids that regular class sucks. The smart kids don't need to do something that sucks. Then educators use strategies to try and fix kids who aren't achieving like the gifted kids. They double block classes. They force students into summer school which means a kid is labeled as the worst kind of worst student. (Parker and Ratliff 2016)

What education has done literally to almost all kids now, everywhere across the country, is communicate through its structures that if a learner can't do the work in class, we'll give that student twice the amount of English and math in a school day, more by far any other content area, which includes science and social studies – and particularly any sort of art or physical education. That's called double blocking. Kids in remedial classes find themselves doing twice as many worksheets, listening to twice as many lectures, and taking twice as many tests because a single block of math and/or reading didn't work. So, once again, educators double down on compliance-driven schooling. That's the design of the institution – it's not conspiratorial. This exists publicly as the strategy of choice if a student is struggling in school. Significant literature and historical research document how and why this was set in motion a long time ago. President Woodrow Wilson (Wilson 1909) and then Ellwood Cubberley (Cubberley 1919) from Stanford both basically said in the early twentieth century that we only need a small group of people to get a liberal education, and a much bigger group to forego the privilege of a liberal education. Unfortunately, for many people today that's still okay. But it's not okay with us.

The district mission to create an inclusive community of learners and learning is no longer limited to just what we do in our own schools, but rather has expanded to influence equity and access beyond our schools. This has occurred through purposeful connectivity of our educators and learners with others across our district's 25 schools as well as to other states and even countries. Our efforts are different and unique here because educators are working to convert a public school system that over years and years wasn't designed for what we are doing now to empower children. We're working – against rules and excuses – to convert an institution to a progressive model of education grounded in an "all means all" philosophy when it comes to every child participating in rich, experiential learning.

For those, like us, who are committed to the insurgent mission of creating habitable school worlds for all children through progressive education, we also know that addressing equity and access can be accelerated with strategic partnerships and that we can't limit our work to the boundaries of our own communities. A small grant from the Battelle Foundation, an international health and science research nonprofit, helped fund purchase of equipment in the district's makerspaces and support for professional development (Bragg 2016). When Chad built the partnership funding proposal for this project, he also included strategies to connect work he was building out in our district with support for a school in a higher poverty district in Virginia. With Battelle's support for this partnership, two of our district's maker teachers packed up a van with maker resources and drove five hours to help another school community implement maker work. After spending an evening with the superintendent, the next day the teachers co-taught with a teacher from that middle school, doing activities with her kids, and Skyping back to our district so their kids could share work with our kids. The superintendent in that district wrote a post about the experience in his local newspaper in which he said that this was the best professional development he'd ever seen (Gearhart 2016).

What's Possible: Systems Thinking as Change Process

We have rejected the mass standardization of learning that has dominated schools for decades. Doing this work means that educators must confront personal and professional beliefs and values that hold students back and penalize those who come to us from families with fewer resources, less education, and insecurities emanating from stressful situations. They also cannot simply admire the problems we face, and, at best, create strategic plans full of tactics and programs, or, at worst, give up on kids.

Ira asked this question recently: "Isn't social justice just a question of how do you make it happen?"

In response, consider that resources are mostly there but decision makers must be willing to change the way they use them to support kids. We look for opportunities to do that all the time. As Ira has said about architectural renovations, staff have to take what's already there and figure out how to improve space for kids. For example, the area at one high school that Ira helped recon-ceptualize as the makerspace today at one point had been the wood shop. The shop had, sadly, been taken out of the school during the late 1990s in response to pressure from state testing of core curricula along with school capacity needs. Walls were built to divide the shop and use it as regular classroom space.

Ira and the facilities planner discussed a variety of ways to restore that space for maker work, but the solutions involved removing very thick walls that held up the second floor. And so, staff went with what was possible. A glass garage door was dropped in to get light in the space. A bridging area was added so eventually there would be a connector with what's now a CAD lab. This work represents a systems thinking approach by a staff team who work together on innovation projects. Chad uses career and technical education (CTE) funding as a match to access resources from building services and facilities planning staff. Ira supports with our system's technology resources. They work in a joint effort to leverage resources together to ultimately answer the question "What can we do?"

If Chad says, "I can cover the costs of mechatronics equipment because it aligns with CTE at the secondary level," then Ira may say, "Okay I will cover tools for makerspaces at the elementary schools." Instead of seeing barriers such as perceived constraints of funding streams or siloed departments that can be used to make excuses for why a project can't be done, staff here see opportunities for what's possible. This doesn't mean that staff operate outside of fiscal rules. Federal CTE money is used exactly as it is intended to be used, but staff add in local resources and supports to ensure projects are robustly funded. If federal CTE funds can't pay for architecture, then a facility need gets solved a different way. Too often, what people will do is to use the law, policy, and regulation as a barrier to change instead of saying "How can I help you figure out how to do this if it's going to benefit the kids?"

Our goal is to make responsible decisions, but always while keeping our kids' needs in mind and with the desire to engage them in meaningful learning always as the driver. Our district staff often find themselves figuring out how to support teachers who have innovative ideas that will pull in more kids as active learners through their passion, interests, and curiosity. We've said yes to adding beehives to our school grounds, offered support to student drone builders and pilots, found a way for kids to exhibit their work in a community-wide Hustle Showcase complete with an evening of student rap performers, and helped fund a coop with nests for a flock of chickens in an elementary school courtyard. We don't discount that as long as there are state tests, teachers must attend to standards. However, if educators cherish children, that means they're always looking for ways to connect with, accept, support, empathize, and value every single child, no matter what.

One example of what it means to cherish children by authentically supporting their interests occurred a few years ago with a middle school project that resulted in kids building rolling tree houses in one of the district's cafeterias. The kids wanted to redesign the cafeteria as a dining experience. However, they didn't want to build the booths that the adults wanted. They wanted to build tree houses. The project faced potential constraints that could have created significant barriers to the middle schoolers achieving their goal. Instead the School Board's attorney helped staff figure out how to support the tree house project by taking a couple of actions that kept staff coloring inside the lines of essential safety rules. He said first that the structure needed to be inspected and any recommendations for changes required by the inspector must be made. Second, school staff needed a plan to ensure that learners were taught to use the structure safely. But he didn't say, as he easily could have and as might happen in many school systems, "That's a liability. Take it down."

Equity and Opportunity

If we want to have an inclusive community, equity and accessibility, a sense that every child matters, and that children's individual diversity adds value to our schools, we have to constantly look for ways to extend opportunities that engage all our young people. Schools have to change, and that starts with valuing each child, trusting in them, and not treating them as if mistakes are a life sentence. Building those tree houses sent a message to the kids that their sense of mission, their voices, and their agency was important and valued. In realizing their interests and passion, they could see their influence on adults.

So how does a public school work towards equity without seeming to be unfair to the people who are providing funding and support? Those with wealth control the community agenda, many of the resources, and, ultimately, jobs. It is a fine line and, truly, nobody is anywhere near solving it. In school districts that try to pool PTO contributions, for example, there are often threats that wealthy areas will secede from the pool. In others, attempts to please the upper and middle classes result in programmatic segregation – with gifted programs and AP classes looking very different from the rest of the school.

But the need remains urgent. "I see the incredible pain that it causes educators working with kids in poverty day after day," Ira says. "We have a principal who spent 10 years as a principal in our highest poverty schools. I've known her a long time now and I've seen how that's hurt her. I see what it does to teachers, and I know we have to find ways as a nation to solve this." If we cannot create ways to support those who work in schools of at-risk students, we obviously will fail to give those children what they need. And what they need is abundance of opportunity, which we can sometimes give without adding a lot of money. All we need to do is understand how capable all kids are. However, as we pursue a mission of all means all, if we don't truly cherish all learners, our children will not succeed, no matter our words.

"Kids in poverty don't come to school knowing less," Ira repeatedly writes, "they know different" (Socol 2016). If we prize that "different," we take our first steps toward equity.

Educators in our schools work hard to find the strengths within individual learners and their own communities here, as do others in progressive districts across the nation. Empowering young people occurs along different pathways, and we see that happen in our small rural schools. As an example, when children who bring a maker mindset from their own country homes and farms get the chance to build in school with woodworking tools, their teachers bring joy and a sense of accomplishment and winning to a group of kids who have never had it before.

We empower kids in many other ways, too. A few years ago, one of our elementary librarians in a high poverty school worked with a group of kids in Guatemala who were even poorer than our poorest children are. Our kids helped to design a reading bus for them. That gave them a real sense of agency and power in the world. That helped the kids, and it helped the teachers too. In progressive educational work, teachers see all kids as competent, capable people. Who doesn't believe that all children deserve to be cherished?

Your Own Learning

Provocation
The educational reform movement advocates of the 1980s and 1990s pushed hard for the standardization of curricula, instruction, and assessment. Over time, subtle degradation of the teaching profession in communities across the nation that had traditionally placed educators on pedestals led to political outcries to do something about the deterioration of education in public schools. By the late 1990s, politicians on the left and the right came together to press for reform, basing their points of view on results from international assessments such as TIMMS and PISA tests along with media-incited coverage of poor conditions of schools primarily in urban settings such as Chicago, Detroit, Philadelphia, Los Angeles, and Washington, D.C.

Their response? The high stakes accountability mandate, the federal No Child Left Behind Act of 2001, eventually passed into law, ultimately impacting every teacher, classroom, and learner in America's public schools. This charge to close gaps by adopting an "all means all" philosophy was underpinned with the loss of local and state control and sanctions from the federal government for schools whose students did not make "adequate yearly progress" to reach 100% proficiency by 2014. Here's where K–12 public education had landed by 2014, according to Anya Kamenetz on National Public Radio as she shared perspectives from her discussions with colleagues in the education field:

> "At least in the academic community, it was well known that 100% proficiency wasn't going to happen without gamesmanship, and the amount of improvement that was needed in some states was not plausible," says Morgan Polikoff (education professor at the University of Southern California).
>
> In response, he says, schools gave more and more tests to prepare students to take the state tests. They practiced "educational triage," focusing more resources on students who were just below passing, to the detriment of both higher and lower achievers. They classified more students as disabled to get them out of taking the tests. In certain cases, they cheated . . . As the years passed and the "adequate yearly progress" targets grew, he says, more and more schools in more and more states fell into the category of "failing" – 50 percent, 60 percent, even 70 percent. "By setting up an unattainable target, states stopped paying attention," says Polikoff. They just gave up. (Kamenetz 2014)

After reading this first chapter, "All Means All: Cherishing Children," and the information provided in the **Provocation**, do you agree or disagree with the premise that schools have failed to educate all children? How would you defend your argument to someone who disagreed with you? In your opinion, can all children be successful as learners? How would you measure success? What needs to change to create learning communities where all children are cherished?

Structured Inquiry

In the last decade, educators, parents, and politicians began to consider that a commitment to "all means all" did not, or could not, mean *all* if the sole measure of competence happened to be high-stakes tests. As schools' lack of adequate progress according to federally approved criteria became apparent in middle-class communities, parents who felt their schools were just fine became concerned that their children were being overtested and overstressed by the requirements of the accountability czars in Washington. This led to a backlash against standardized testing and prescribed curricula.

As mostly middle-class parents pushed back against state testing, stories of educators leaving the profession because of high stress, the publication of teachers' scores by name in some mainstream media outlets, and cheating scandals in high-stakes, high-pressure school environments led educators to increase their challenges to NCLB accountability measures. Sometime around 2010, it appeared that the nation woke up, took a look at its schools, and began to see that the federally reinforced structures of twentieth-century schooling had driven the passion for learning from classrooms, had eliminated joy in the pursuit of curiosity and interests, and had discouraged the belief that teachers make a difference. Parents didn't like hearing from children that school was boring or watching as their children's disengagement rose and their creativity dropped. Something seemed to be missing from almost every school.

How might you find out what's missing from learning in your district, school, or classroom? If you perceive nothing is missing how do you know that? Take time to reflect out loud with a friend or write your thoughts about whether deep, meaningful learning occurs for all kids where you work. Who gets to engage in deep learning, to find their passions, and to be joyful in their work? Who gets challenged with interesting questions that push thinking and emotion? Who gets time to work on meaningful projects? Who is cherished and how do you know that?

Reflective Pause
In some places today, "all means all" is being redefined as more than simply all kids, regardless of their demographics, special

needs, or geographic location, passing other people's tests. Paul Reville notes that:

> We have a batch-processing, mass-production model of education that served us very well if we wanted to achieve a society in which we were sending a lot of people into low-skill, low-knowledge jobs. But for high-skill, high-knowledge jobs in a post-industrial information age, we need a very different system. (Walsh 2014)

Does *all really mean all?* What changes to the system do you think are needed to overhaul it from one that sends kids into a future of low-skill, low-knowledge jobs or even no job at all? Why would you make those changes? Make a list of your priorities for change. Which create a more personalized learning environment rather than a one-size-fits-all approach? Reflect upon a change that you can personally implement in your own setting.

Take Action: Four Actions to Create Paths to All Means All

1. Collective efficacy, according to John Hattie, has the greatest impact of any educational strategy on learners' performance. Identify or build a peer network that collectively can support your work to guarantee access and equity to rich and challenging learning experiences. This could be a Twitter chat, a critical friend in your school or another school, or a mentor.
2. Seek all the sources of information you can find on how children perform in your class, school, or district. Spread those in front of you and figure out what kind of assessments dominate kids' work. Become an advocate for learners becoming engaged in their own assessment reflection process. Ask kids for feedback, and you will get points for informing your own learning.
3. Pick a couple of learners you know who are struggling in your school. (It doesn't matter if they are in elementary, middle, or high school.) Observe them in class, hallways,

and the cafeteria or on the playground. Record what you notice about the learners. Reach out to talk with each of them. What questions might get at their sense of why they struggle? How might you invite them to ask their own questions of you? How can you use this information to inform your own understanding of what it means for all learners to be cherished?

4. Identify a barrier to learning success that exists in your class, school, or district that defeats the *all means all* philosophy. This could be a barrier of time, furniture, technology, or adequate resources. It might also be a barrier created by rules or norms. Identify three strategies that you can use to advocate to take down that barrier. Make your work to eliminate barriers for kids a message to others about your own values and beliefs.

Resources

Albemarle County Public Schools. n.d. "Vision, Mission, Values and Goals." Accessed 6 August 2017. https://www2.k12albemarle.org/acps/division/planning/Pages/Vision.aspx.

Bartolic, Igor. n.d. "Last Mile – the Ten Types of Connections." *The Best Wireless Internet.* http://thebestwirelessinternet.com/last-mile-connection.html.

Bragg, Michael. 2016. "$30K Grant Helps Students with Hands-on STEM." *Daily Progress,* 1 April. http://www.dailyprogress.com/news/local/k-grant-helps-students-with-hands-on-stem/article_114763c6-f86b-11e5-abc1-23c0a991e085.html.

Cubberley, Ellwood. 1919. *Public Education in the United States.* Cambridge, MA: Riverside.

Decker, Stacey. 2017. "U.S. Education in 2017 in 10 Charts." *Education Week,* 20 December. https://www.edweek.org/ew/section/multimedia/us-education-in-2017-in-10-charts.html.

Garland-Thomson, Rosemarie. 2017a. "A Habitable World: Why We Should Conserve Disability." ABC. 21 March. http://www.abc.net.au/religion/articles/2017/03/21/4639875.htm.

———. 2017b. "Eugenic World Building and Disability: The Strange World of Kazuo Ishiguro's *Never Let Me Go.*" *Journal of Medical Humanities* 38 (2): 133–45.

Gearhart, Rex. 2016. "Students Need Applied STEM Learning for Future." *Bristol Herald Courier*, 15 May. http://www.heraldcourier.com/opinion/editorials/students-need-applied-stem-learning-for-future/article_adbaea64–1a55–11e6-ba32-c79c94933601.html.

Hammond, Zaretta. 2015. "Is Implicit Bias Racist?" Teaching Tolerance. 1 June. https://www.tolerance.org/magazine/is-implicit-bias-racist.

Kahan, Seth. 2012. "To Make the Most of Innovation, Find the Right Inflection Points." Fast Company. 1 October. https://www.fastcompany.com/3001655/make-most-innovation-find-right-inflection-points.

Kamenetz, Anya. 2014. "It's 2014. All Children Are Supposed to Be Proficient. What Happened." *National Public Radio*. http://www.npr.org/sections/ed/2014/10/11/354931351/it-s-2014-all-children-are-supposed-to-be-proficient-under-federal-law.

Moran, Pam, and Ira Socol, with Chance Dickerson and Kolion Troche. n.d. "Transforming Learning Spaces and Students in the Process." ChangED. Accessed 30 July 2017. https://www.jackstreet.com/jackstreet/WCHG.DickersonTroche.cfm.

Ratliff, Chad (interviewee). "Access and Equity in Maker Learning." Interview by Jessica Parker. Unpublished, May 4, 2016.

Socol, Ira David. 2008. "When to 'Give Up.'" SpeEDChange. 9 June. http://speedchange.blogspot.com/2008/06/when-to-give-up.html.

———. 2010. "It Gets Better." SpeEdChange. 18 October. http://speedchange.blogspot.com/2010/10/it-gets-better.html.

———. 2016. "Kids in Poverty Don't Come to School Knowing Less. . . ." The Synapse. 21 April. https://medium.com/synapse/kids-in-poverty-don-t-come-to-school-knowing-less-792f724530ef.

Walsh, Bari. 2014. "Getting to 'All Means All.'" Harvard Graduate School of Education. Accessed 5 August 2017. https://www.gse.harvard.edu/news/uk/14/10/getting-%E2%80%9Call-means-all%E2%80%9D.

Wilson, Woodrow. 1909. "The Meaning of a Liberal Education . . . : Address Delivered January 9, 1909, Before the New York City High School Teachers Association." New York: High School Teachers Association of New York. https://en.wikisource.org/wiki/The_Meaning_of_a_Liberal_Education.

Zook, Chris. 2016. "The Key Traits of Great Founders." Founder's Mentality. Accessed 6 August 2017. https://www.foundersmentality.com/2016/10/24/the-key-traits-of-great-founders/.

2

A Little History: Why We Are Here

IRA: I get frustrated every day. We've accomplished so much
        here, but it still isn't . . . it isn't right for kids yet. Not
        everywhere, and it needs to be right everywhere. For
        every kid. We know that just one bad experience in a
        kid's day becomes that dominant experience, and we
        know that at-risk kids are the most likely to get caught
        in negative experiences, even here.

CHAD: The problem with being a revolutionary within is that
        you're accountable. You're responsible. You go keynote
        somewhere and you walk away and what happens
        doesn't happen on your watch, but here we've got
        [almost] 14,000 kids, and if something goes wrong and
        people follow the power cord, you're the one holding it.

IRA: . . . or Pam is.

CHAD: [laughs] . . . Yeah, true. But, this is the thing: When
        you are in the system you can actually change things,
        but at the same time the system constrains you. And
        honestly, the constraints are often how we see ourselves
        in the system.

IRA: Thus the frustration. We talk about "urgency triggers"
        regarding student needs. I struggle—we all struggle—
        with how to respond when things "aren't right yet."
        We don't have the freedom of the outsider, even
        though we have the power of the insider.

Schools of the Past: Designed to Fail

For too long, schools have been considered *places of teaching work* rather than *spaces of learning ecology*. In our many hours spent walking and talking through schools, we've seen both. We've visited big schools, small schools, urban, suburban, and rural schools. We've explored American schools of the North, South, Midwest, and West Coast, and even schools across Ireland. We've observed high schools, middle schools, elementary and primary schools, private and public alike. The smallest served 12 students; the largest, almost 4,000.

It's become clear to us what differentiates schools isn't size, location, demographics, or test scores. Those factors matter most to people who evaluate schools as they were defined and designed well over 100 years ago. As we've spent time with educators and looked deep into schools, we've found their similarities and differences are less a matter of policy and more a matter of philosophy. And, it is the choice of a progressive or a traditional philosophy of learning that most differentiates individuals and school communities.

In our observations, we've discovered that educators with a bias toward the child—those who embrace children's engagement, happiness, agency, and strengths—share a core belief that the essential role of school communities is to empower children through a multitude of learning pathways. Such progressive educators support children to develop life competencies through a wide bandwidth of democratic and experiential learning opportunities in both formal and informal settings—projects, maker learning, collaborative exploration of interests, technologies of all kinds used to produce learning, and exhibition of learning to authentic audiences. These educators speak with conviction about the value of knowing children as individuals rather than focusing on the data inherent in traditions of scientific management. They do not represent the norms of educational systems developed over decades through "cells and bells" structures, direct instruction, and bell curve expectations. In short, they work hard to free the child from the shackles of the compliance-based system they're trapped in.

In our daily efforts to make sense of how schools work, we researched and studied educational history, discovering that twentieth-century schools were set up as institutions literally designed to fail learners (Postman 1969). Over time these school communities formed behaviors, values, and norms that to this day present barriers to progressive efforts to change the purpose of modern-day schools. What might have evolved into organic, humane centers of childhood and adolescent learning and growth rather became places where, year after year, children were sorted, selected, and systematized into decontextualized batches, all moving along the assembly line. This one a success. That one a failure.

To change the deliberative purpose of schools as they *have* been, as they too often are, here we have conceptualized school systems through frames of relationships, connections, interactivity, interdependence, and adaptability. We have come to believe that to catalyze progressive education, educators collectively must exhibit an "insurgent mission"; one that empowers school communities to challenge and replace mechanistic, hierarchical traditions that distance the people running the school assembly line from each other and from the children they serve (Zook and Allen 2016).

Our homes, communities, indeed the world, need the natural assets our children bring with them as learners, and which they often lose over time on the assembly line. We see no actions as more important in schools than developing, supporting, and reinforcing our children's sense of agency, the value of their voices, and their potential influence within their own communities.

That is why we are here.

Culture as Reflection of Learning Ecology

In our work we've each, independent of each other, developed relatively congruent philosophical frames for what it means to educate and be educated. As we came together along with other leaders, inside and outside of our district, to support progressive educational practices, we found that our work resonated with this description that Alan Shapiro, James Gaddy, and Neil Postman used in a proposal to the school board and community to open the alternative public high school program that Ira attended. We believe that their 1970 proposal still today provides the foundational philosophy of what learning can be when the focus is not on school but on linking processes of inquiry and discovery to contexts for learning:

> In other words, we are assuming (1) that learning takes places best not when conceived as a preparation for life but when it occurs in the context of actually living, (2) that each learner ultimately must organize his own learning in his own way, (3) that "problems" and personal interests rather than "subjects" are a more realistic structure by which to organize learning experiences, (4) that students are capable of directly and authentically participating in the intellectual and social life of their community, (5) that they should do so, and (6) that the community badly needs them. (Postman 1969)

More than any other factor, a school community's culture will determine whether its inhabitants thrive or fail. The culture, in turn, represents the ecology of each school. That ecology is crafted not just by every space, not just by every in-class and homework assignment, not just by the schedule, not just by the grading system, but also through every word spoken or shown to every student, by every teacher's tone of voice or facial expression.

It was certainly that way for us as children. One of us successfully navigated school in one of the poorest rural counties in the Deep South. Another escaped from the classroom whenever possible in a small, blue-collar Virginia town. And the other unsuccessfully crashed on the shoals of a northern urban school in an old city of artists, blue-collar workers, and New York City commuters. Despite vast differences in our experiences, our locations, our schools, and our families, we've discovered that we had much in common. We shared the pressure of growing up in schools designed to apply the law of averages—a design that needed to fail some, and needed to send a few to college. We were the bell curve generation, and we represented the cardinal points of that cultural curve.

Some community members continue to memorialize America's schools of the past just as some envision the white picket fences and stay-at-home moms idolized in 1950s television as being a time when life must have been more perfect than today. They characterize childhood schools as places where everything that was right with America bore fruit. They are wrong. America's schools have never been any more picture-perfect than the *real* families of the fifties were. Those schools lacked diversity. Children were bullied by peers, and corporal punishment was not just accepted but expected. Many teens failed and dropped out. America's schools were considered failures when the space race erupted onto the covers of *Life* magazine (S. Wilson 1958). We forget that our past was no educational rose garden.

IRA: While Pam attended segregated schools in rural South Carolina, I began my student life in segregated schools just outside the Bronx. We all went through schools "back in the day" and we know that "golden days" myth is nonsense.

PAM: Didn't you ask that one night on Twitter?

IRA: Yup, I asked which were the "golden days"? The *Tom Brown's School Days* days? The *Blackboard Jungle* days? The *Rebel Without a Cause* days? The *To Sir with Love* days? Maybe the *Fast Times at Ridgemont High* days? No answers. The fact is that when people describe a great "school" experience they talk about one teacher or one coach or one class. But almost no one describes the school system, of any time, as "great."

In fact, in the early part of the twentieth century America's schools were designed to minimally educate menial laborers for factories, mills, mines, sweatshops, and farms. Woodrow Wilson described the function of schooling best when he said:

> We want one class of persons to have a liberal education, and we want another class of persons, a very much larger class, of necessity, in every society, to forego the privileges of a liberal education and fit themselves to perform specific difficult manual tasks. (W. Wilson 1909)

Our nation's school teachers were recruited in the early twentieth century to teach so that young people would fulfill Wilson's stated mission. They would become compliant, bell-schedule-driven workers. They would not question authority. They would find no inspiration for themselves or learners in Robert Browning's words, "Ah, but a man's reach should exceed his grasp, Or what's a heaven for?" (Browning n.d.)

Instead, students of the early 1900s fell out of schools to enter a workforce still populated by children. The 1920 high school graduation rate of 20% speaks to the "success" of a first-to-eighth-grade program designed to sort out 80% of children. The climb to a 50% rate by 1940 had more to do with the Depression limiting job opportunities for teens than any change in schools (Swanson 2010). And, though our goals for kids have certainly changed over time, and we speak about every child succeeding, our schools have changed little since before World War II: the same classroom shapes, same schedules, and same ways of dividing kids.

At the same time that America's schools were being shaped by the factory work of the Machine Age, the leading educational progressive John Dewey challenged the assumptions of the early twentieth century and the scientific management beliefs exemplified by the work of Ellwood Cubberley, educator and dean of Stanford College of Education (Trachtenberg 1986). Dewey envisioned another path for learning:

> The teacher is not in the school to impose certain ideas or to form certain habits in the child, but is there as a member of the

community to select the influences which shall affect the child and to assist him in properly responding to these. Thus the teacher becomes a partner in the learning process, guiding students to independently discover meaning within the subject area. (Dewey 1897)

A progressive education is designed to enlighten and empower, as both John Locke and John Dewey believed (Gibbon 2015). Principles of progressivism are timeless pathways that support children to take their place in a democratic society by engaging them actively. This can only happen when educators see value in understanding childhood as they support cognitive, social-emotional, and physical development, and foster empathy and relationships.

Social and economic levers such as equity divides or workforce changes can be morphed by school district staff into formal school language that supports progressive educational principles that many label and believe are important to developing contemporary life competencies. However, we've noticed in our work that labeling and formalizing the work often waters it down. We shy away from using what can be called the "bandwagons" of the big national organizations. We think of those as pop education. It's the must-read list, the must-attend conference, the must-listen-to keynoter. Unlike people and books and conferences that come and go, educators are challenged as they always have been to make sure progressive work such as contemporary maker learning, the latest surge, continues to move forward, and is, indeed, timeless.

For radical and deep change to occur, progressive education can't be a point in time. It can't be just tinkering around the edges of change. It can't be characterized as the latest fad. The scary proposition to us is figuring out how to somehow define our work but not define it too specifically, because if we do, at that moment it becomes a piece of history located on a timeline of educational fads or phases. The moment it becomes that, it's no longer living and pliable. And if you can't make the current work a pliable facet of the larger progressive educational philosophy, then it'll die, and we can't let that happen this time around. We can learn from history.

The philosophical frame for learning that John Dewey proposed in the early twentieth century could have taken America's schools in a different direction, but in the conflict between social and economic construction, economics and, of course, war efforts won out. Schools became their own educational version of the Machine Age driven by measurement, assembly-line curricula, "cells and bells" design, and obedience by classroom management and corporal punishment. Schools became "cults of efficiency," pushing children, teachers, and administrators farther and farther apart, each generation of educators selected for their capability to ensure compliance within the hierarchy. World War I and then World War II drove America to fully embrace the efficiency model, as if Henry Ford's assembly lines hadn't been enough. The progressive concepts of natural learning, the slower, less efficient, more patient education embedded in Dewey's model, hit a seemingly evolutionary dead end in public schools by the middle of the twentieth century (Giordano 2005). By 1950 almost all that was left of Dewey's work were suburban classrooms with sinks and doors to the outside, even as Cubberley's efficiency model permeated philosophy, policy, and practice within almost all of the nation's schools:

> Our Schools are essentially time- and labor-saving devices, created by us to serve democracy's needs. (Cubberley 1919)

Public Schooling Redefined by *A Nation at Risk*

Yet, something worked within the system. Despite the push toward compliance in the classroom, America became the most creative and inventive nation in the world. Why? Despite downsides to the factory model, schools were under local control and inside them an ecological system emerged that allowed for diversity. The kids who could soup up hot rods in auto body class exuded cool. Sports and other extracurricular activities were the norm.

Field trips to big, important cities gave kids often confined to their own community a chance for exposure and exploration. College had not yet become the preferred destination for most. Being a dropout wasn't the worst thing that could happen to you. And unions in the North provided pathways to middle-class success, particularly after World War II.

Inventiveness among people was rewarded within the greater community, and attending school was a social event, not just an academic must-do. Classes of children cross-pollinated what they knew and who they were—until ability grouping, course leveling, and mile-wide, inch-deep curricula became the norm. Teachers, mostly women, were some of the smartest people holding jobs in the country. They had been top achievers in their own high schools, attended normal schools and colleges, and brought a sense of nurturance to their work, the hallmark of being surrogate mothers to their communities. Perhaps these teachers also brought something else. In the late 1950s and 1960s, some felt the pull of the social disruptions of the time. Creative teachers— "subversive" teachers, in the words of Neil Postman and Charles Weingartner—began to deconstruct classroom experiences and assignments, giving children the time and space to break free, a push toward a different ecology of schooling than the impending standardization of the 1980s Nation at Risk reform movement would bring (Postman and Weingartner 1969).

Within the educational system, over decades, educators have been forced into riding waves of political and cultural currents sweeping the nation. Today, education may be one of the most political things we do in the United States. Education, indeed, feels more and more like a fight to control the future. As political, economic, and social forces impacted schools from the twentieth century into the early twenty-first century, a pendulum effect of curricular and program changes thrust educators and children back and forth with each swing. The Cold War. Sputnik. New Math. Assassinations. Civil rights movements. Title IX. IDEA. Open schools. USDOE. *A Nation at Risk.* Outcome-based education. Personal computers. The National Governor's Conference

of 1989. The swing from left to right and back again finally led
to the federal No Child Left Behind Act of 2001. Looking back
in time, it's easy to see how and why the swings of reform kept
coming one after another, each more entangled than the last
with the politics of culture and the economy.

During the last half of the twentieth century, schools began
to change, becoming more filtered, standardized, and program
driven. The subtle shift to question the efficacy of educators
began to surface in media. What began in the late 1950s when
Life magazine coverage of Sputnik led to crisis comparisons
of schools in America with those in the USSR, slowly built
momentum as American supremacy in business and global
power was challenged (S. Wilson 1958). Educational companies
marketed their resources, from achievement tests to filmstrips, as
"teacher-proof." When American industry seemed to crash on
the shores of the OPEC oil embargo in the 1970s, the "cult of
efficiency" doubled down and training to manage by objective
became the administrative norm.

In the mid-1980s, the *Nation at Risk Report* accelerated public
concerns about schools and the scrutiny led to even more pressure
to standardize, program, and train towards a one-size-fits-all
factory model for schooling (National Commission on Excellence in Education 1983). Schools such as the Parkway School
(*Time* 1970) in Philadelphia and the 3 Is High School (Karpf n.d.)
in New Rochelle, New York, which had experimented with progressive concepts, abandoned them. All of these shifts combined
into a runaway train in the late nineties, leading straight into the
federal No Child Left Behind Act of 2001 (107th Congress 2002)
and most recently into the Common Core Curricular Standards
(now adopted by a majority of states). Students became overtested, lesson plans overprescribed, and teachers and parents
overstressed; all finally led to significant questioning of the federal government's role in education. In 2015, some of the burden
of federal education mandates were lessened and greater control
returned to states and local communities in the newly enacted
federal Every Student Succeeds Act (114th Congress 2015).

Reimagining Schools for This Age

Despite the more than century-long longevity of America's education efficiency movement, there is hope that this century's communities see the need to educate children differently than in the last. Once the dominant economic fuel of communities and drivers of personal opportunity, the mills and factories across America long ago shuttered their doors and silenced the assembly lines. Today, both changing demographics and the rising Smart, or Second, Machine Age, as described by MIT's Andrew McAfee, have emerged as dominant forces shaping society (DLD-conference 2017). Those who study trends and analyze future impact, entrepreneurs, corporate CEOs, and even some visionary educators, forecast significant workforce, lifestyle, political, and societal changes in the coming decades, potentially impacting not just the status of the United States as a world leader but every home and community in America. No one can doubt, if they are paying attention to just about any source of media, that we are in a state of flux. Educators can't ignore signs that doing the same thing we've done in classrooms for generations isn't going to help children develop the scaffolding they need to successfully build competencies; as Postman said, "not just life but actual living" (Postman 1969).

A different path is on the horizon, driven by the perceived diminishment of America as an economic power, the globalization of community through technology, and a rising desire among parents, teachers, and, of course, children, that schools be more than test-prep factories. Learning today can occur anywhere, whenever a person seeks to follow curiosities, questions, and interests beyond the walls of school. In an era of communications and information change that's even more rapid and profound than when American public schools first universally appeared (the 1840s) or when the system was refined (1890–1910), we find ourselves again at a turning point. Today, it's become a common debate when education is discussed whether schools will either adapt to the changes that surround them or cease to exist.

Regardless of changing political agendas, the Smart Machine Age and its impact on our homes, communities, and nations is here to stay. Educators must learn to see children as individuals again, to understand the implications of our children's world in which they can connect to information, each other, and expertise in the blink of an eye, and to understand that it's our relationships with young people that will keep them connected with us as educators—not our grasp of content information or capability to administer tests. We have come to the conclusion from watching our children and staff at work that the more we try to control our young people through the conventions of standardized public schooling, the more we lose them to other educational opportunities. Nothing exemplifies that difference our best designs for learning make for learners than when visitors come to find out about our work.

For example, a school team from an affluent northern Virginia suburb visited schools in our district a couple of years ago. Ira and Chad immediately noticed the team members were almost uneasy around the learners in a seventh-grade language arts class. They didn't know how to approach them because the kids were sitting in a variety of ways and working on different projects, some chatting in groups and some working individually. A 3D printer hummed in the background and the teacher interacted with kids all over the room. It was as if the visitors didn't know quite what to do without a teacher actively teaching, without a teacher controlling what might have appeared to them as a "mob" of kids.

When the visitors finally landed in the middle school's mechatronics lab, one sixth-grade boy was kneeling on top of a table sawing an old classroom chair apart to make a seat for a go-cart. He'd assembled a team of kids around him. They were all working on the project.

One of the visitors said to Ira, "Is that a classroom chair?" and all Ira could say was, "Well, not anymore." Then, the boy looks at him and he says, "Hey, Mr. Socol, this is December and I've only been in four fights all year." Ira fist-bumped him and said, "Good going, man. That's really cool." The visitors looked at this kid in horror. But, four fights for this kid was unbelievable given he had found himself in a fight almost every day in past years. Then the visitors asked the teacher running the mechatronics lab, a teacher completely surrounded with kids working actively with 3D printers, laser cutters, drills, computers, and table saws, "Well, how do you know the kids are working?" The teacher spread his arms and smiled, "Look."

The realization hit Ira that these people didn't know how to observe any of this. Many educators don't seem to know how to observe or interact with kids outside of dominant teaching wall classrooms. They don't know what authentic learning looks like. They're not taught that. Instead, their implicit biases don't even allow them to see what empowered and inspired learners look like in school. They see chaos in active spaces because the learners aren't seated in rows, listening to the teacher, working on work or screen sheets.

So much talent exists in children that doesn't get seen or heard because the potential of young people often is lost in our traditions of worksheets, repetitive motion tasks, and teachers standing at the dominant teaching wall. When kids tune out, passively or aggressively, because work has no context, little meaning, and makes no sense, we never see the strengths and assets of the full range of learners who are in our schools. Our national attempt to standardize learning has resulted in compliance or resistance rather than empowerment of young people as learners. And, in most cases, well-intended educators perpetuate this unwittingly. It's time to question assumptions. It's past time.

Most everyone who has attended public school has been taught to succeed through compliance. Parents want what they experienced. Teachers do work really hard, but often lack understanding of why the systems in which they work fail, over and over again. *The failure of the system is not the fault of educators.* They don't question desks in rows, bells and classrooms, or standing at a whiteboard all day because it's what educators know, what's been modeled for them, what they likely were taught in their education programs to do. Seldom has there been anyone around to ask these questions: "Why do we arrange ourselves this way?" "What beliefs lie behind the way schools are?"

The Problem of Standardization

Standardization, though we hate the word, does seem to work in schools. That's a dirty little secret. It mitigates the burden of responding to children in personal ways. It provides a benchmark against which we can measure our learners and ourselves. It makes sure that deviations from the mean are reduced to the greatest degree possible. It creates a sense that if we could just replicate successes, we could fix every school in the country.

Industrial societies and scientific modernists saw standardization as a way to guarantee universal success. The twentieth century pursued standardization for, essentially, good reasons, but we see its failure in so many cultural scenes—massive housing projects that became nothing more than new slums, repetitious suburban housing developments without variety or vitality, corporations unable to respond to customer needs. Today, in our schools, standardization fails our children, our communities, our nation, and our world.

The problem is that standardization becomes the antithesis of creativity in schools. There's no "follow the questions" inquiry or problem- and project-driven assessments in standardized classrooms. Covering the standardized curricula means rejecting the biodiversity of communities that have the potential to generate new ways of thinking based on their own unique environments. Those statistical norms that drive much of standardized practice seem to be built for mythical school communities, model neighborhood schools where we expect students to succeed in the same way. Using "teacher-proof" assessments and programs makes a lot of sense if the goal is one-size-fits all schooling. The programmed learning of today—moving through curricula paced to finish on time for testing and using filtered pedagogies designed to maximize standardized testing results—is just twentieth-century efficiency and effectiveness, carrot and stick, management by objective, modernized through contemporary technologies and infused with algorithmic monitoring systems.

But in our work, we have learned that no average human exists, no median community does either. And we have learned that human learning is messy and complex, and that childhood, especially, is very messy, and very complex. Authentic opportunities for learners to create, design, build, engineer, and compose cannot truly coexist within the standardization model. That's why tinkering around the edges, adding a "genius hour" to an otherwise unchanged school day, accomplishes nothing except to highlight all that's wrong with our schools for this century.

A school cannot change without system change. Nothing can. If a principal says "Our school is now going to be student centered and built around individuals" but the decision-making process does not change, the locus of control doesn't change, then the school won't change either. This requires a lot more than language, though language matters. It requires a lot more than intentions, though intentions surely matter. It requires more than understanding childhood and adolescence, though obviously that matters, too. What it requires, at the heart, is the will to truly change what leaders, what teachers, what adults do every day. This starts with how they function, how they make choices, and what they see.

Making Change

Pam doesn't define leadership in a hierarchical way because she believes in the power of a system of education that truly operates more like a web versus a chain. When an ecological model of education such as Neil Postman identified emerges in such a system, teachers realize the importance and value of their voices in helping to shape the work, and they come to realize the importance of learners in helping to shape the work with them. It's not by chance when she talks to groups of people that she often tells stories of maker work through the voices of kids she has come to know. They are as important, if not the most important, leaders in the whole effort to shift the way we think about learning from her perspective. It's led her to consider how leaders can get to know the diversity of children and staff and what their experiences are like within the system unless they spend a great deal of time embedded in the full environment of a school.

IRA: How do school leaders learn to walk schools? To hear children? To capture those voices and scenes as data? When I walk into a classroom I almost never watch the teacher. I watch the kids. You know what the teaching is like by seeing the kids.

PAM: You told me you watch the kids' feet first.

IRA: I do, but only if they're sitting at desks. Then I watch their feet to see if they're bored, nervous, restless, or asleep. But if kids are really working, doing active work that is their choice, that matters to them, all you really need to do is take that in, and start asking open-ended questions. Take the time to notice what's different from the norm.

While it's easier to keep doing what educators have always done, we all must look to that different path on the horizon. Changes happen when people become revolutionaries, and yet start defining themselves as being part of the system, rather than apart from it. Leadership for change welcomes the revolution and the evolution, the daily reinvention of practice that means a school is moving along with its students. Our inventive, indeed, revolutionary teachers working organically with kids, with principals, in their schools, are the ones who make progressive work go viral.

The twenty-first century world rapidly changes around our schools, and swirls around our children: smart machines, globalization, climate change, geopolitical conflict, and economic shifts. In our opinion, sustaining schooling as it has existed will not prepare our children for the world they will enter as adults. We educators all must focus on helping children become creative and empathetic problem-solvers. We must help them be ready for a world none of us can define, but that we all know will look nothing like the recent past.

Change in this time, though, has to come *without* a simple instruction manual. How do we prepare children if we don't know what we're preparing them for? Pam's kid, and Ira's kid, are both perfect examples: Both have great jobs that did not exist a decade ago. Chad's kids will work—well, no one knows. We can't focus on content anymore, or even specific content skills. For example, kids don't learn "keyboarding" anymore, they learn "text entry"—big keyboards, tiny touch screen keyboards, using fingers, using thumbs, dictating into speech-to-text, dictating into audio and video. Text entry isn't a "skill" to learn, it's a strategy for adapting to the tools in front of you—and those are changing at an exponential pace. As Ed Hess, author of *Learn or Die*, says when we chat the future and how we are responding as educators, "Learning how to learn is a far more important focus for curricula today than learning content" (Hess 2014).

Kids today need the chance to design, create, and communicate, all highly desirable competencies in this century. Our study of how children learn has led us to create maker opportunities as a pathway to contemporary experiential learning. Making to learn and learning to make can go in many different directions because the work is developed in the context of what children want to make. The path they take begins to drive their own connections to content they need to map to their learning. We see kids all the time who find learning becomes important to them through their maker work and that content suddenly starts to make sense. In doing so, they naturally experience social-emotional learning through empathetic design and collaboration with peers and experts.

Such young people learn to plan, test, research, and search for what they need as learners, building a sense of agency through their work. They learn to work within a democratic community, figuring out how they want to work together, individually, to share and to choose the paths they want and need to take. They serve as authentic audiences for each other and share their work with peers and the world. They have the chance to learn because they are curious, interested, and passionate; they exercise crea-tive, critical, and entrepreneurial thinking as they make in school cultures where equity and access is increasingly the norm, not the exception.

Organic Learning

There is nothing reductionist about this work, but we find that people often want us to reduce our work to its lowest common denominator because they need answers that are easy to com-municate and implement. Recently, Chad was talking about the problem he perceives with all the articles that people are writing these days and all the keynotes given in which the speakers are trying for a simple definition of the work, or they're trying to define "it." He tells the story of a writer for a popular education outlet who became quite frustrated because we won't define our very complex work in superficial ways.

This particular writer wanted us to share how we teach peo-ple to be makers. Because he didn't get the typical educational responses about professional development, outcome measures, and programs, it seemed to upset him that a recipe didn't exist and we didn't produce pat, easily quotable responses. He jumped on Chad, who said, "Dude, I'm telling you—you can't lead with that philosophy if you believe in this work." Chad refuses to define making as anything we turn into curriculum and tests. This interviewer probably ended up with four hours' worth of audio, but the whole meaning of our work was lost in the published article because the work is not reductionist. It's just not superfi-cial. It's not a program you can buy. It's not a test you can give to kids and report to the state. Rather, our work has evolved to an organic educational philosophy grounded in an open, rather than a locked-down, mindset about what constitutes learning.

We've found that no article gets it right. Even people who write with depth still struggle to get it right. Some people just feel the need to push for answers to how you raise test scores with making or how you assess it. People struggle to get past that this kind of learning can't be measured with efficient, quick-and-dirty tests. What our kids do as learners represents a context that's far more sophisticated than simply picking the right bubbles on a computer screen. Teachers dig deep into not just what kids are supposed learn but how and why they learn. They become "kid-watchers." That expertise is key to the success of learners such as Kolion in Chapter 1. It's hard for a teacher to develop that expertise who isn't embedded in this work and active in the reflective process of professional observation. No place is that observation more important than in middle school, a short time span in the life of a K–12 learner but a time of great change socially, emotionally, physically, and cognitively.

The Middle School as Case-Based Learning

Years ago, when we all first began working together, Ira wrote a couple of blog posts about redefining middle school. His perspective on this came after walking schools and reflecting on both the research and observations into how adolescents learn:

> The middle school is really just the junior high school continued, and that was always a bad idea. Kids stumble through a bizarrely carved up yet age-dependent curriculum, and nothing could be less appropriate. There is no age range with a greater range of individual skills no matter the birth date, and there is no age range where getting kids interested in school is harder. After all, kids, eleven to fourteen years old, have a million things, really important things, to learn—about themselves, society, life, their bodies, and almost none of those things are taught in schools. (Socol 2011)

In this post, Ira called for "project-based everything," and went on to describe in detail his proposal to drive middle school learning by maximizing authentic, contextualized curricula:

> So I want to divide the Middle School Grades—6, 7, 8—into 9 large, and 3 "mini" project-based experiences. Project-based

experiences that kids choose, completely interdisciplinary experiences. Kids would pick three 10-week experiences and one shorter experience for each year, and that is what they would do all day. Teams of teachers would join together to offer these options. It could range from building a *Habitat for Humanity* house to making videos to putting on *The Oresteia*. Or you could be restoring a 1959 Studebaker, writing scripts for vampire movies, or studying the planets. In every one, you can easily include language, history, math, sciences, foreign languages, physical exercise, music, art. (Socol 2011)

Through this kind of thinking, we first built microenvironments where this kind of work could happen with middle school kids. Chad leveraged early connections within the Maker Movement to build out mechatronics labs in every middle school, and those became the heart of our "maker" curriculum beliefs. Not because of the labs—because of the culture spilling from them.

Maker work is more than project-based learning; it is more than problem-based learning. It is, in Chad's words, "when we add content to student-created context," and it is central to true change because it switches the power to define the school experience from the teacher to the learner.

Unfortunately, the translation of making in schools can be quite superficial, such as the weekly or monthly "creative hour" model we sometimes read about (though if a kid gets an hour out of the week that inspires curiosity and creativity—that's a plus). Even though education books pop up all over the Internet that make this work look easy, it isn't. It's so much more than *10 steps* or *four kits* you need to implement a successful makerspace.

When makerspaces become a scheduled destination every couple of weeks for kids to work on activities that often are quite teacher directed, that's not what we are after in our work. Making is so much more when *it is the education*. The process is so powerful, and the results are so powerful, when the transformation is deep and we have teams of teachers working their butts off figuring out how to do this in their classroom. Today, we see great examples of real maker learning all over our schools: kids who are learning math and tool uses while constructing a dog house, sewing a pillow, or coding music with Sonic Pi.

Trust in Childhood: An Essential Teacher Disposition

Encouraging children to exercise the freedom to make isn't easy and it demands an openness to risk that teachers themselves must be encouraged to take. Educators have to take risks to trust in childhood. Many educators have been trained to think otherwise.

It truly is hard work to trust in kids and in childhood. It demands a reset of adult mindsets to set up situations every day so that children, adolescents, and teens get the chance to see their own learning emerge from their passion and independence, to be messy, to not finish some projects, and spend weeks working on others. Children live in a dual world of adults who can't wait for them to hurry and grow up and who simultaneously want to protect them from every possible fall, failure, or fracture. Our children's learning curve seems to be exponential until they're five, then they go to school, and it slows down. So reversing that model of teachers exerting tight control over environments, pace, and learning options is amazing to see.

For example, a kindergarten teacher at one of our schools has embraced a philosophy of trusting children. She's a veteran teacher, and she has this long, wide windowsill in her classroom. The kids will put their little chairs up there to look out the window, including rocking chairs. People tell her, "That's so dangerous." But she says to the kids, "If you rock too hard, you're going to fall off the edge and that's going to hurt. So, you don't want to do that." The kids have learned to police it entirely themselves. She doesn't have to say a word about it.

The kids, these five-year-olds, are making their own classroom. She also led a two-year, but totally successful, battle to evaluate every adult rule on the playground. Starting with, in her words, "No one ever died from twisting on a swing." You'll see kids going up the slide when her kids are out at recess. She says to kids, "You go up the slide without looking to see if someone's coming down—you're going to go down." Kids get bumped up sometimes.

She's worked to restore childhood and knows that occasionally children get bumps and bruises from exploring in their own way. Her perspective on risk challenges adults, parents and peers alike, who have been taught to be risk averse, litigation conscious, and rule bound. Her philosophy has begun to impact others around her, though. She believes that kids need to play, kids need risk, kids need to be kids. You can't bubble wrap kids. You see the kids in this kindergarten teacher's class with incredible confidence because they're learning to take risks by doing. It's the same confidence and determination you see when a two-year-old explores the world or an astronaut enters the International Space Station.

School communities today can do so much better for children than the schools invented by Ellwood Cubberley, and we've been fortunate to work with educators in communities that are doing just that. Our nation's future demands a change in the historical educational narrative of the twentieth century. We've seen educators in our district and across the nation fighting upstream to do the kind of work that's essential to get back to America's creative roots, the fuel of a past economy and the fuel of our future one.

If as a nation we believe that learning is critical to humanity, then lifelong learning should be the key goal for every learner we touch. And, if citizenship today means something different than it did 10 years ago as a rising tide of worldwide participation and communication unfolds, then we have to educate young people to enter a different mode of citizenship, one that is global in influence and connectivity. We also must educate our young people to not take our democratic way of life for granted. They must become versed in wading through media sources that in some cases have great credibility and, in other cases, are no better than the fake "Dog Island" websites their teachers use to help them learn to negotiate the Internet.

The lives of children have become complicated because the world is an agora, a marketplace of ideas, virtually and across most communities today from rural to urban. As adults they will need to negotiate the challenges created by all the changes that arrive almost daily on our doorsteps, courtesy of the rising tide of smart machines, virtual realities, 24/7 connectivity, and Internet space in which every human being with a connected device becomes their own media outlet, for better or worse.

Long ago at the beginning of the past century, we picked up one-room schoolhouses with one-room teachers and dropped them into the egg-crate schools we have today. Teachers still, for the most part, hold on to the idea that the classroom is a one-room schoolhouse. Educators of the nineteenth century morphed into twentieth-century educators who worked as separate entities who just happened to be located under the same roof.

Our narrative in chapters that follow will take you on a journey into classrooms, schools, and communities that see paths beyond the horizon, spaces where educators and young people are stretching their reach to exceed their grasp. It's their work that motivates us to share their stories, their dreams, and their realities with you. We intend to use their work and play to engage, provoke, and push you to not just think about possibilities that exist but to act on those possibilities in your own work and play as a teacher, administrator, parent, or young person.

Each story we tell represents educators who live and work in our schools and schools across America. These are stories of educators who every day consider each learner as worthy of their time. They are becoming a critical mass pushing back against mass standardization because they understand that each school is a microenvironment, unique because its inhabitants also are unique in their interactivity. They know that children learn well when opportunities exist to make learning vibrant. We give voice to their work, not claiming it as our own, but simply as transformational ventures that we are fortunate to experience alongside extraordinary people—teachers, administrators, parents, and children. Their work becomes the history of contemporary learners and learning.

Your Own Learning

Provocation

There is a tension between those who believe that stocking knowledge in the minds of learners is the only real purpose of education and those who see education as an opportunity to educate children less to remember rotely and more to activate learning from experiences and interests that involve problem solving, critical thinking, and inquiry. The movement back and forth between these two models, classically traditional and progressive education, results in little commitment to any real change that sticks because educators themselves have been trained into compliance so they tend to do as directed without questioning authority.

Consider the Wilson quote you read earlier: "We want one class of persons to have a liberal education, and we want another class of persons, a very much larger class, of necessity, in every society, to forego the privileges of a liberal education and fit themselves to perform specific difficult manual tasks" (W. Wilson 1909).

What do you believe is the purpose of education? Where do your own beliefs and behaviors come from? What do you really know about the history of how our educational traditions came to be? Why are you here?

What's your reaction to this? Not just your simple reaction, but also a deeper level of thinking about the structures that developed and became part of the psyche of the American public educational system, and which still drive structures of schooling in this century.

Consider launching into your I-search journal (in the cloud or on paper) to write down your thinking, to ask questions about which you are curious, your observations of your own classroom, school, or district philosophy of education in action.

Structured Inquiry

One way of looking at the history of the human group is that it has been a continuing struggle against the veneration of "crap." Our intellectual history is a chronicle of the anguish and suffering of men who tried to help their contemporaries see that some part of their fondest beliefs were misconceptions, faulty assumptions, superstitions, and even outright lies. The mileposts along the road of our intellectual development signal those points at which some person developed a new perspective, a new meaning, or a new metaphor. We have in mind a new education that would set out to cultivate just such people—experts at "crap detecting. (Postman and Weingartner 1969)

Really? Is the primary purpose of schools to create experts at "crap detecting?" If yes, how do we do that? If no, what *is* the primary purpose? How might you present your argument if you were asked to explain to a school board, "Why do we have schools?"

Reflective Pause

Ira says, "I always point out the kids' learning curve seems to be exponential until they're five and they go to school and it slows down." Chad says about maker work, "It's not a program you can buy. It's not a test you can give to kids and report to the state."

What would school look like if learning did not slow down? What kind of experiences in school creates exponential learning? What are the challenges and risks in teaching without a linear text, a scripted program, or standardized curricula? What do learners and teachers need from the system to mitigate risks and support stepping away from mass standardization? Are there, in your opinion, dispositions of educators that work for or against their success in progressive school communities? What evidence, information, or research do you have that confirms or refutes your reflections?

Take Action: Four Actions to Become a Better Observer of Learners and Learning

1. **If you haven't read *Teaching as a Subversive Activity*, it's time.** You can get it used or new, and you'll begin asking questions, considering and acting upon solutions to grand challenges. Postman and Weingartner believed change is constant in society but that those who work in schools simply filtered out any need to change anything about educating young people.

2. **Dare yourself to be a crap detector.** Take your cell phone and wander your classroom and/or your school. Capture as many images (keeping the privacy of individuals in mind) as possible that depict the learning work kids are expected to do. Take the time to study the pictures and describe what you think the learning vision actually is in your class or school. What values are present in your images? What if the images don't match the vision? What will you do next?

3. **Shadow a student all day—someone at risk preferably.** You might have to bargain with an administrator to do this or ask for assistance to cover the office if you are an administrator. Do this. Do the work the student does. Follow the rules the student follows. Take the tests the student takes. Be the student and at the end of the day, record your reflections.

4. **Spend time studying leaders in your school or district.** Education leaders are as different as people are. Ascertain what they see as the purpose of education based on their words and behaviors. Take an education leader out for coffee and get him/her talking about their work. Ask the question, "Is this a leader I want to work with?"

Resources

107th Congress. 2002. No Child Left Behind Act of 2001. H.R. 1. https://www.congress.gov/bill/107th-congress/house-bill/1.

114th Congress. 2015. Every Child Succeeds Act. S. 1177. https://www.congress.gov/bill/114th-congress/senate-bill/1177.

Browning, Robert. n.d. "Andrea Del Sarto by Robert Browning." Poetry Foundation. Accessed 26 July, 2017. https://www.poetry foundation.org/poems/43745/andrea-del-sarto.

Cubberley, Ellwood. 1919. *Public Education in the United States*. Cambridge, MA: Houghton- Mifflin.

Dewey, John. 1897. "My Pedagogical Creed." *School Journal* 54 (January): 77–80.

DLDconference. 2017. "Machine, Platform, Crowd (Andrew McAfee, MIT & Hilary Mason, Fast Forward Labs) | DLD New York." https://www.youtube.com/watch?v=6h2q0jml9g0.

Gibbon, Peter. 2015. "John Locke: An Education Progressive Ahead of His Time?" *Education Week*. 4 August. http://www.edweek.org/ew/articles/2015/08/05/john-locke-an-education-progressive-ahead-of.html.

Giordano, Gerard. 2005. *Wartime Schools: How World War II Changed American Education*. New York: Peter Lang.

Hess, Edward. 2014. *Learn or Die: Using Science to Build a Leading-Edge Learning Organization*. New York: Columbia University Press.

Karpf, Josh. n.d. "What Was 3Is?" Accessed 26 July, 2017. http://foody.org/3i/intro.html.

National Commission on Excellence in Education. 1983. *A Nation at Risk*. Washington, DC: US Department of Education. https://www2.ed.gov/pubs/NatAtRisk/risk.html.

Postman, Neil. 1969. "3I Program: Proposal." http://foody.org/3i/proposal1969.html.

Postman, Neil, and Charles Weingartner. 1969. *Teaching as a Subversive Activity*. New York: Dell.

Socol, Ira David. 2011. "A Middle School That Works." SpeedChange. 1 January. http://speedchange.blogspot.com/2011/01/middle-school-that-works.html.

Swanson, Christopher B. 2010. "U.S. Graduation Rate Continues Decline." *Education Week*. 2 June. http://www.edweek.org/ew/articles/2010/06/10/34swanson.h29.html.

Time. 1970. "Education: The Parkway Experiment." 20 March. http://content.time.com/time/magazine/article/0,9171,943213,00.html.

Trachtenberg, Alan. 1986. "The Art and Design of the Machine Age." *New York Times Magazine*, September 21. https://www.nytimes.com/1986/09/21/magazine/the-art-and-design-of-the-machine-age.html?pagewanted=all.

Wilson, Sloan. 1958. "It's Time to Close Our Carnival," *Life*, 24 March, 1958, 36–37. https://books.google.com/books?id=PlYEAAAAMBAJ.

Wilson, Woodrow. 1909. "The Meaning of a Liberal Education . . . : Address Delivered January 9, 1909, Before the New York City High School Teachers Association." New York: High School Teachers Association of New York. https://en.wikisource.org/wiki/ The_Meaning_of_a_Liberal_Education.

Zook, Chris, and James Allen. 2016. "Reigniting Growth." *Harvard Business Review*. 1 March. https://hbr.org/2016/03/reigniting-growth.

3

Change: Liberating Learners and Learning

PAM: In our society, we often see children characterized as if they are still toddlers incapable of negotiating risks and handling bumps in their paths or as little adults who just need to grow up faster. They are neither: They are children and they are both vulnerable and, in the vast width of their curious vision, they are brilliant. Even our high school kids – to quote one of our high school principals – are children, and they all deserve the time to be children. But let's understand childhood. Childhood doesn't mean helpless or even intellectually limited, it means inexperienced, but constantly growing. It is our job to offer children enriching experiences, to challenge their curiosity, and to surround them with love and resources. That's how children become what educators label as strong, creative, and committed learners. And, I've learned over the years that a child who spends a lot of time in remedial programs doesn't become that kind of learner.

IRA: We don't say "achievement gap" here, we say "opportunity gap," and that's because the only real difference between kids who grow up in poverty and/or isolation and the kids who grow up in wealth is opportunity – the opportunity to discover everything from vocabulary to intellectual argument to a range of foods to travel to a vision of what an adult can be. I remember as a young teen meeting a friend's parents – they were college professors, researchers. Before meeting them, I had no idea that profession existed. If you don't know something exists, you can't imagine yourself there. If you can't imagine yourself there you can't dream, search out, plan, and play. If you don't know about planes you will not work to become a pilot.

So here you will see all kinds of kids getting every kind of cool chance to find their passion as learners. We don't ask kids to develop "grit," we choose to surround them with whatever abundance we can muster. We don't choose adult comfort at the expense of children's. We choose to do what our kids need.

CHAD: There are really only two types of schooling, that which is meant to assimilate and oppress and that which is designed to enlighten and empower. The kind of learning you describe doesn't happen because it's mandated through policy. Policy doesn't drive practice. Policy drives behavior. When teachers shut the door, teachers do what teachers want to do, regardless of policy. Policy just serves as a carrot or a stick. If you don't change what teachers believe, you're not going to change what they do. So that's where my work to simultaneously focus on connecting beliefs with actions comes into play.

How Beliefs Begin

How do teachers' beliefs get formed? Researcher Mary Kennedy found that naive childhood schooling experiences form people's durable values and beliefs about what constitutes good teaching, and for teachers those early-formed beliefs "influence their thinking as they develop practices" (Kennedy 2005). That's how educators become conditioned to say "This too shall pass" when changes are proposed: Their early beliefs and images of school are firmly cemented into their actions as teachers.

Given well-documented challenges of significant resistance to school change, how do we get from classroom to learning space, from teacher to facilitator, from school to education? For decades now Ira has talked about "liberation." "Liberation Technology" and "Liberation Theology" – the educational kind, not necessarily the Catholic Church kind. Liberation Technology is about using the systems of education – the buildings, time schedules, calendars, furniture, and everything from paper to computers and phones – to liberate children to think, to dream, to imagine, and to read, write, research, communicate, and collaborate in ways that support them, not limit them. Liberation Theology is about beliefs, impacting both adult and child.

Ira has a fondness for provocative titles, and two of his early research papers, "Pushing Past the Missionary Position" (Socol 2008) and "Literacy (as) Tyranny" (Socol n.d.), attempt to bring ingrained, unquestioned belief systems about school out into the light. If school is about "saving" or "converting" children, with teachers seeing themselves as missionaries, the school and system will inevitably favor those born into the "desired state" – middle-class kids, kids without disabilities, white kids. If the school believes that certain paths are superior – reading on paper, doing math sitting in a chair, staring at the teacher – then those same already advantaged kids are advantaged once again. So school-as-we-know-it actually functions more as a religion, a sequence of unquestioned beliefs, than it functions as a rational system. And beliefs can't be changed just from the top down; the whole system has to begin to see things differently or change will create civil wars.

Yet, change in beliefs can occur. We see it in national attitudes toward things like gay marriage, or the foods we eat, or health care. In the national mood we often see the viral spread of ideas. When, through contemporary social media, a song, an app, or a game becomes popular, we know it immediately. At some point the phrase "to go viral" became a part of the social media vocabulary moving from simply a descriptor of a bad year of flu to how anything spreads quickly. Yet, while we have seen in our schools a practice spread through a grade level or department, or even down a hallway, we know it is not that easy in education to get deep, system-wide change.

Getting to Deep Change

Every educational leader eventually realizes that creating conditions for change, the conditions where an educational practice can go viral, are difficult. Education is a change-resistant profession. Yet, we have noticed that changes can happen quickly – and those changes can stick. Larry Cuban wrote a book with David Tyack, *Tinkering Toward Utopia,* that lays out how leaders get to deep change with staff – and how seldom that actually occurs (Tyack and Cuban 2009). The work that it takes to get deep change in the processes and practices of education often takes years longer than anyone might anticipate because whether working with children or adults, the shift from surface to deep learning takes time, commitment, and constant metacognitive processing of where to move next in the process.

What makes the difference? Within our schools and elsewhere we've seen failure to change despite the best laid strategic plans. We've seen bottom-up generated change despite administrative indifference. The impetus to change can come from any area of an organization and be initiated by a teacher, an administrator, or even a student. Change does not have to conform to the slow process usually expected. While we have many stories of how quick pivots to implement change have occurred, one in particular changed the way we use summer time for research and development of innovations, positive changes that advance the work.

A few years ago, Chad and Ira supported the process of creating a summer "Pop Up Maker School" in an impoverished Latino community. We had never pushed our summer programs out of our schools this way before, but an opportunity appeared. "Gloria [a Latino Community Outreach leader] walked into the office one day and said she had access to this double-wide trailer," Chad recalls, "and she wanted some kind of summer academy to support those kids. This was the week before school ended."

"It was too good an idea to let wait a year," Ira adds, "so we just said sure. Chad grabbed a teacher who needed administrative internship hours and offered him the role of academy leader. I asked the principal of the nearest high school if we could borrow furniture and computers. Then Chad pushed the whole 'Maker Camp' theory and we were off." In that moment, we had planned a popup maker camp that opened two weeks after the first conversation with Gloria. Its success changed our summer expectations permanently. The success was tremendous in not just giving children voice and opportunity but also by proving that change can happen through fast pivots in leveraging teams and resources, an entrepreneurial approach to supporting educational innovation and innovators.

Change can and should happen more quickly than it typically occurs in education if conditions are right. The trick is changing the conditions – avoiding becoming too procedure driven. We, of course, do use strategic planning, but we are not bound by a plan. In fact, we relish the opportunity to work in the sandboxes of invention and innovation because that's where strategic work and eventually operational sustainability of change begins. You just have to make sure that the sandbox is there, is valued, is inviting.

Too many times, we've seen important and serious work to design and launch a great idea to improve learning impeded by almost Soviet-like administrative adherence to a plan. The first lesson we've learned together is to climb out of the strategic plan box to see the world beyond our schools. The second is to accept that a sandbox is messy, and is always a work in progress. As Pam says, "Don't let a strategic plan get in the way of a good idea." Also, don't let initial failure, initial struggles, initial doubts, derail the idea. Those circumstances probably mean that we need to invite others to play with us, think with us, and struggle with us. Keeping structures open to constant flow, feedback, and change is essential.

This kind of thinking inside a school system leads to a shift in culture that enables change by making sure changemakers feel valued and protected, and it is a culture change that means new ideas strike teachers as compatible with their vision and mission. Education need not be defined by a pendulum swing back and forth between progressive and conservative philosophies and practice. It need not be that slow metronome of status quo where nothing really ever happens except occasional tinkering around the edges of the status quo. Instead, deep and progressive cultural change becomes a shared dynamic belief in childhood opportunity, a belief system that can be articulated and shared between generations of educators.

Driving Change: Moving from Education Policy to a Liberation Philosophy

Educational dialogue takes place at three levels: philosophy, policy, and practice. Policy is the political manifestation of a philosophy that defines the purpose of schooling. Practice is rooted in and driven by one's own philosophy within the context of policy. Most people give little thought – if any – to the cultivation of a philosophical foundation, so their practice defaults to and is driven by their own prior educational experiences. This means the vast majority of public school teachers are traditionalists without even knowing it – or questioning it.

"The very first thing Ira ever talked about to our teachers was colonialism," Chad says, with Ira noting, "Most didn't understand a word." "It's Virginia," Pam adds, "I think they thought you were going to talk about the Jamestown colony, or those hats in Williamsburg." "The only impact I had that day," says Ira, "was while sitting in that chemistry classroom, I asked, 'Does anyone here have furniture like this at home?' I guess that began our Choice and Comfort Pathway." And yet, as Chad finishes the thought, "Postcolonialism is an essential part of everything we do now. It's an unseen mover."

Liberating adult learners begins by showing people why and how schooling can be different, and how that difference can change our calculus of winners and losers. But you cannot show people by projecting slides on a screen, you must find and reach that one person who in the face of dissonance will change and then connect with others to bring them along. It's almost as if change can only occur one person at a time to get the fundamental philosophical shift essential to deep change in practice. A leader can't impose and certainly can't mandate agency. Just the notion of that is ridiculous. Leaders first have to know people as individuals. Then, leaders must give educators the autonomy to think about challenges to their beliefs. That begins with understanding how the beliefs we hold dear about schooling were formed and even became elemental in the DNA of education.

Our public schools began with a missionary function. Faced with a flood of non-English-speaking, and most problematically, Catholic, immigrants in the 1840s, states across the United States began rapidly expanding the nascent public education system (Wagoner and Urban 2013). The political purpose was to "decatholicify" the largely Irish immigrants. To teach them English. To teach them the King James Bible. To teach them the "Protestant work ethic." To make them "Americans" (Boers 2007).

The purpose from there on was largely the "melting pot" idea, the "forging of America." Whether it was perceived as missionary conversion of the immigrants and lower classes, or as a system of social reproduction – the preservation of the society's existing order, or even as a system of opportunity – offering all a chance, schools ended up looking the same, a random assortment of content delivered wrapped in a behavioral modification system.

The "colonial" issue, in a nutshell, defines opportunity gaps. For example, in traditional British colonialism, the English child raised on the estate in Essex, with parents speaking "the Queen's English," begins that "race to the top" halfway there. This child knows the language, the rules of rugby, the proper way to drink tea. The child growing up in Derry or Bombay, Lagos or Port

Elizabeth, comes with differing languages, differing sports, differing eating habits. If school is about that British language, those British customs, and those British manners, the children from "the colonies" begin way behind. Unless that kid from Essex falls asleep under a tree, as in *The Tortoise and the Hare*, and has no one to wake him up, it is simply inconceivable that the colonial kids will ever catch up. The best they can hope for, if they run all their lives, is to be second-class Brits.

Similarly, here and now in the United States the child raised in Scarsdale or Greenwich or Santa Barbara, or schooled at Sidwell or St. Ann's, begins the race more than halfway there. They know the language, the rules of classroom play (including how to bully), the proper way for a parent's note to excuse them from work or school itself. And if they mess up, they most likely have the resources to escape any trouble. The child living in poverty who attends school with Sophia or Finn, or Emma or Asher, knows how to navigate city streets, often how to function on a highly adult level, often how to be their own caregivers, how to communicate in a wide range of circumstances. But they do not know what that first group of kids knows, and if they get into trouble they are on their own, and if they are abused, people may joke about it. So unless the kids in Scarsdale or Greenwich or Santa Barbara, or at Sidwell or St. Ann's, fall asleep under a tree for years, the best these postcolonial kids can be, if they run all their lives, is second-class Americans.

Seldom do educators get challenged to consider colonialism as a frame for compliance-driven education, but when they are presented with this the responses can be difficult. There are many educators who firmly believe that "conversion" – say, making over young African-American children so they wear white shirts and ties and learn to speak like their white teachers – is the best path for the life success of those children. But some respond to the idea that educational reform simply perpetuates school models that were specifically designed to oppress someone. Progressive leaders must constantly ask, "How do we get people to a place where they recognize that philosophy, policy, and practice all can be tools of learning liberation or oppression without saying it?"

When we've engaged with people who wrestle with the idea of education as a tool of learner oppression, we've often seen them react to that with a "Wow!" in a moment of realization. Such realization puts educators on their own learning path. After that what they need are the support and resources to make changes in practice that move them to open up different pathways to learning. As educators consider their own potential role in captivating contemporary learners' curiosity, interests, and passion, they must come face to face with the question of why they should create environments of divergence in learning opportunities rather than environments of compliance.

Looking for the American Dream

When Pam was a young administrator, she was trained to observe in classrooms for specific "look fors" by the educational rock star of the time, Madeline Hunter. This led to the number one goal of her district's plan, to manage by objective. Train. Observe. Leave. As she observed she worked from a checklist that narrowly defined the walls, floors, and ceiling of what teachers were expected to do every day of the school year. Was there an objective written on the chalkboard? Could students tell the observer the day's objective for what they were learning? Was there a beginning, middle, and end to the lesson? Did the teacher have a span of control over the class? How were students reinforced for correct responses? Did the teacher call on students by name? Were students gazing out the window, drumming on desks, or paying attention? How often did the teacher circulate during the lesson or teach from the same spot? What evidence was there that the teacher monitored and adjusted the lesson based on student responses? Was there a written lesson plan that included key elements of the Madeline Hunter lesson design?

Pam remembers meeting with teachers to go over the expected look fors and to schedule a time to visit and watch teachers teach a lesson. She walked into classroom after classroom and spent full class periods with her checklists looking for those things that were considered important to see. She owned a grey paper book filled page after page with hundreds of look fors, each page listing variables of effective teaching from questioning to classroom management. She was taught to record narrative of teacher talk and student responses, to code teacher language, to draw the classroom in rows and hash mark teacher interaction with individual students, to check, check, and check again items off of the list. Then, she would walk away, meet with the teacher to conference about the observation data and never visit again until another year had passed. She says today that she knew nothing much would change as each teacher went back to their status quo and she went into the next room. Here's what she discovered in her own words:

"The more I learned about observing scientifically, the less I saw in the classrooms I visited."

This was clinical observation in 1984.

For decades, in education the typical "demand curve" that forces change in many other sectors has been disrupted by the fact that education's true customers, the students, have little to no say in their future; they have no voice and no economic clout. Students today are caught between the two opposing forces that coexist in public education: the urge to sustain the status quo and the desire to change. Both are controlled by stakeholders who bring internal and external pressures to bear upon the organization we label as "school". In the typical world governed by "supply and demand" such pressures cause change to occur in response to the needs of those served by the organization. In schools, however, the needs of those served, students, often are the least of that which is considered. Thus the tendency of schools to stasis lies unchecked.

Schools were designed in the early 1900s to fill factories with compliant workers who stood ready to follow directions, assemble widgets, repeat the motion, and work until they retired – or died, whichever came first. Most found that life in the tracts surrounding the factories offered some sense that they had found the American dream. There was never an intention in the early to mid-twentieth century that most students would graduate from high school and certainly little intention that high school graduates would go to college. Those were the unwritten rules of education. Then, the world changed.

The *A Nation at Risk* report pointed to the need to reform – to change – public education (National Commission on Excellence in Education 1983). This report along with the 1966 Coleman Report and the research of Ron Edmunds from the late 1970s generated a whole generation of research into what came to be known as the Effective Schools Movement (Lezotte 1992). Effective school research that focused on school correlates spawned effective teachers research and administrators were taught to look more scientifically at improvement of schools (Gursky 1991). School leaders entered into an era of training to develop education leadership and management skills. This philosophy of scientific management led to new bureaucracy, more paperwork, and new systems to manage data.

Nothing much changed that benefitted learners and learning.

If the education reform models of the last century did not have much impact on creating the schools that children need, what does? It begins with liberation, changing the way educators philosophically run schools based on a different set of core values and beliefs about what's most important in the learning process. From volumes of research, there's significant reason to question pedagogies that society, parents, and educators hold dear, for example, transmitting information to be memorized. Many of the pedagogies of the twentieth century lack effectiveness in accomplishing what those who use them intend to do – help learners learn. Instead, pedagogies that some refer to as teaching wall practices continue to dominate today's classrooms holding many children, year after year, passively in place at their desks. In our own study of contemporary learning, however, we are redefining and reimagining today's schools, finding pathways along a progressive trajectory that deemphasizes the basics of the twentieth century along with the compliance strategies designed to educate young people to work in the factories of their great-grandparents' workforce.

We've learned that teachers today face many of the same challenges that their earlier generation peers faced; the challenges of children who live in generational poverty, or children of immigrants who speak no or little English, or children born with disabilities that impact their learning. However, the homes, communities, and workforce today's children will enter will be very different than those of prior generations. Societal norms are shifting. Demographics in the nation are creating minority-minority communities, ones in which no clear majority dominates.

And, the Smart Machine Age of the twenty-first century is impacting the workforce differently than the Machine Age of the twentieth century did. These changes press today's teachers to see the value of different ways of organizing space, using accessibility technologies, and advantaging instruction through a culturally responsive lens.

A teacher who works in a school with kids who maybe speak 60 different languages – a school that serves as an international refugee center that enrolls kids who have really never been in a school building before – once said, "I had to teach some of the children to pee in the toilet and not in the drain on the floor. That's step one. If we're lucky, they speak a language that's already spoken in our community. If not, it could be languages that do not even have a written form." She also reflected, "Teachers have to trust the kids and be patient enough because the kids will learn what they need, and recognize they're just going to do it in a different order and need different paths."

That's an important statement to consider given the mass standardization of America's schools. How many times have you observed in a school and noticed that most learning comes through a one-size-fits-all program? For years, the solution of choice to most educational challenges has been to buy a program in a box – or with today's educational technology, workbooks on a screen. Then someone, often a consultant, provides decontextualized, cursory training to teachers on how to use purchased resources. After instructing with such materials, teachers collect reams of data from tests they use to prepare children for assessments of information that will be quickly forgotten. Then the teachers, in turn are evaluated with compliance-driven account-ability systems to track their performance, often sourced from vendor alleys that dominate national conferences. Our own conversations with teachers, observations of children, and tracking of societal, workforce, and demographic changes has led us to question everything about today's schooling.

What if, instead of trying to replicate procedures and structures that have lacked effectiveness, we were to explore how to identify multiple pathways to enrich learning through interesting user experiences that attract children rather than push them away from the work we believe is important to learn as well as the work they want to pursue as learners? How might we free our educators to explore possibilities grounded in a purposeful, collective efficacy to ensure that every child develops their extraordinary learning potential and also finds magic in their pursuit of curiosity? How do we do that with disciplined inquiry? What do we learn and how do we use what we learn to inform the system's work?

Flashes of Genius Are Everywhere

How might we capture Jim Collins's genius of the "and" in building cognitive knowledge and competencies as well as ensuring children develop emotional, social, and physical health life readiness (Collins 2001)? How do we avoid Collins's tyranny of the "or" that created a narrowly defined twentieth-century education reform movement that has dominated schooling since the 1980s, the dichotomy of vocational education or college prep, state standards or child-determined curricula, direct instruction or instructional facilitation, and so on.

As captured by Collins in *Good to Great*, top leaders understand that movement forward is often created, in the moment, from flashes of genius that may originate from any person in the organization. Such leaders positively regard diversity of thinking as it aligns innovation with the core beliefs and values of the organization. Providing opportunities for genius to emerge is critical for children and the adults in both user experience and interface. This occurs when progressive educators take the time for kidwatching learners, particularly children who don't con-form to school norms, and find where their strengths may lie. Then, such progressives willingly take risks to try new ways to connect learners with different paths to learning. Collins first identified this kind of serendipitous approach as a frame for suc-cessful leaders who discover new and viable solutions to old prob-lems because they look beyond traditions and encourage taking risks. We believe, like Collins, that when everyone in an organi-zation is freed to innovate, the more likely that the organization will align its action and eventually its flywheel will not just turn but fly (Collins n.d.).

> Visionary companies make some of their best moves by experi-mentation, trial and error, opportunism, and – quite literally – accident. What looks in retrospect like brilliant foresight and preplanning was often the result of "Let's just try a lot of stuff and keep what works." (Porras and Collins 1994)

This kind of serendipitous approach has played out in our creation of one of the district's summer research and develop-ment labs, the CoderDojo (a multiweek-long K–12 multiage cod-ing camp). We borrowed the CoderDojo model from its origins in Ireland, a social entrepreneurial start up that began with an idea in 2011 and action to implement by an 18-year-old high school student, James Whelton, and business entrepreneur Bill Liao (CoderDojo n.d.). When Pam and Ira visited the Tipperary Insti-tute and watched Irish children, age 6–18, working together on a Saturday morning to learn to code, they saw far more than kids using technology. It was an epiphany about community learning and the shifting role of children and adults in the CoderDojo process, a space where all learners are teachers and all teachers are learners.

Inside our experimental model, there is, as the saying goes, method in the madness. We've walked with colleagues or along with site visitors to observe in the summer in a school library or learning spaces where we are running the CoderDojo, and we've pointed out that if we really listen, we'll all hear a vocabulary that's incredible from kids who are gathered all together in multiage spaces to learn code. It's a language they all can speak regardless of their nation of origin and as they code they learn to communicate together, to learn English or other languages with each other. The teachers work alongside learners and it's not unusual to see a child explaining how to use a tool to a teacher.

Running a variety of summer programs that engage learners in progressive learning experiences gives our educators and learners the chance to design, make, build, and iterate. From what seems to work in the summer settings, we then can transfer what we learn from their research and development into the regular school year. We have learned from this work that children need control in their environment, choice in how they learn, different options for locating themselves comfortably in space, and trusting relationships with adults and peers if they are to become learners with voice, agency, and influence.

While our nation needs more young people growing up to become proficient programmers, computational thinking in the world of the CoderDojo offers so much more. Children learn math concepts that are significantly beyond the scope of standards specified by the state. We've watched our youngest children come to understand algorithms and vectors in the context of designing games in Scratch, a coding language for children developed at MIT (Scratch n.d.). Older children have used HTML to create their own websites or write original music in Sonic Pi. Girls and boys equally love the challenge of learning to automate gizmos and art projects they've designed and activated with Arduinos, batteries, LED lights, and so much more. They've become researchers, writers, poets, artists, authors, STEM specialists, musicians, historians, and readers. They collaborate and work individually. They help each other. Age is less of a determiner of expertise than deep immersion in work the kids are driven to accomplish.

We've learned from our CoderDojo observations that children are not by nature disengaged in school nor are they passive learners waiting to have a teacher tell them what to do or how to get an A. They are passionate, active, inspired, interested, intentional learners who design, create, problem-solve, and finish work. Discipline problems and labeled handicaps disappear. They want to come to school in the summer. They don't say they hate math, and maybe that's because they aren't graded on right or wrong but rather are driven to keep coming back until they make their programs run. Adults are in the room, building relationships, asking good questions, making connections, referring to others who might be able to help or to sources they can access. The adults are never the sage on the stage and even take a lower profile role as guides on the side as we watch students experiencing Collins's "genius of the and" in their development of literacy, numeracy, *and* the 4 Cs of critical thinking, creativity, collaboration, and communication (Kay 2011).

People around the world agree the first step of literacy is accessing complex vocabulary. Kids in the CoderDojo learn the complex language of coding and content as they work together. All of a sudden they are looking for information to access that, in many cases, is far more sophisticated than their labeled "reading level." All the rest, motivation, success, new skills, and knowledge, comes after kids have a reason to want to be able to read for understanding and meaning. As they work in the CoderDojo, the adult master facilitators and the Teacher Fellows who are there to learn how to teach using experiential paths see kids becoming more facile with complex vocabulary. The learners and adults working together illustrate the tagline we use to explain what progressive philosophy means operationally. This tagline, *trust in children and childhood*, grounds us in our work to build the capacity of all our educators.

Trust in Children and Childhood

Unfortunately, many educators in schools across the United States have been trained to not trust in the natural ways that kids learn. And they seldom get a chance to see what learning looks like outside the constraints of a hundred years of factory-model schooling. That's why we have purposely shifted professional learning from being one-size-fits-all events or "sit and get" classes into authentic adult learning experiences that move progressive curricula, assessment, and pedagogy into the learning spaces that our teachers and learners inhabit together. This occurs through both learning technology integrators and instructional coaching positions, full-time, nonevaluative teachers who work directly with teachers in schools. They engage as models, coplanners, and coteachers who make progressive philosophy tangible in the work learners accomplish. These educators are pros at asking questions, finding needed resources, and providing one-to-one professional development. Most importantly, they are relationship builders.

However, we realized that this model of teacher-to-teacher support by itself would not move the district to spread adult learning across the system as fast as needed. We knew that making a progressive philosophy go viral would take years and it would take multiple paths to accomplish.

Opportunities such as the summer CoderDojo model and our maker summer schools have created a new inflection point for learning. Instead of separating adult learners into their own rooms, we've also provided opportunities that blend adult learners into the same learning spaces occupied by our children. By changing the way we resource and structure summer opportunities, we've changed how we cross-pollinate our most progressive work back into the school year. What we've also learned is that if we don't have a commitment to "R and D," then the kind of invention we want to encourage among educators simply won't happen easily during the regular school year – if at all.

As we evolved summer school opportunities from mostly providing basic intervention for students required to participate because of failing state tests to a continuum of enriched experiential learning options, we've seen our learners become active participants and collaborators with adult learners. We've flipped remedial summer schools into maker camps. We've added a high school design, maker, launch entrepreneurial experience for high school students to recover credits. Along with CoderDojo, these summer opportunities create a path for adults to work in "low stakes" learning environments to practice a progressive teaching philosophy through application of our Seven Pathways concepts that support transformation of learning through use of interactive technologies, connectivity, choice and comfort, P-based learning, universal design for learning, instructional tolerance, and maker-infused learning (US Department of Education n.d.). When students work with master practitioners in our summer environments, teachers who also are in learning mode are working side by side with students and master teachers to try out new technologies and strategies. We expect them to experience both successes and failures as they take risks to try out new ways of working with young people in less structured, multiage communities than found in the typical school environment.

The key to this model comes in the luxury of time spent trying out new tools and instructional approaches while kidwatching to notice how learning works in a progressive space. Time spent debriefing in teaching teams during the summer creates a different kind of dialogue about learners among the teachers. They see students who struggle in traditional classrooms exceeding expectations as they exercise the opportunity to choose projects, work collaboratively or alone, and bring their own interests into the work. It does not mean that the standards we must address as public educators don't matter. They do, even in summer learning. However, teachers who get the chance to see what children who come with disabilities, stressed family backgrounds, limited English language proficiency, and even high academic capabilities can do when we unleash them from the constraints of school begin to see that they too can change the parameters inside their classes during the regular school year to incorporate more choice, more P-base learning (projects, problems, and passion work), and more maker opportunities into their work with children.

What really jumps out at us when we work with teachers and listen to them talk is that liberation of their own growth and development means that they often see themselves starting over as educators. Imagine being a middle school English teacher who opens the door to considering that coding isn't much more than a step away from writing poetry or narrating stories. When given the chance to make sense of code, she finds with children that the conventions of writing bring a deeper sense of connectivity to both the logical unfolding of code as well as to building the beginning, middle, and end of a story.

Cheryl, though a highly experienced middle school teacher, willingly takes risks to consider how technologies can expand the potential of middle schoolers to see themselves as designers, authors, makers, and experts in finding the knowledge they need to solve big challenges. She is one of many explorers of an educational frontier who helps figure out the potential of new approaches such as how access to a 3D printer can amplify students' creativity and critical analysis in the language arts classroom. She's figured out by watching students that simple replication of "off the Internet shelf" predeveloped code to print an object isn't what inspires her students. Rather, it's when they design and then code to create their own artifacts that makes learning come alive. Her learners are not just engaged learners but, more significantly, they are inspired learners. As she has worked with other teachers and the children who participate in the "R and D" experiences at the CoderDojo, she has helped connect learning innovations to schools all over the county.

Through research and development summer opportunities for professionals such as Cheryl, teachers find when students love the work they are doing, the need to intensify control through pedagogy and lock down their movement and questions with classroom management becomes unnecessary. They realize that children of any age working together can learn so much more than when they are age-based in grade levels. They see children who falter in traditional teaching situations become learning stars when given opportunities to choose their own pathways to agency. And, they realize they can walk back into their own schools and change their own practices. They can trust kids. They can support parents. They can see the power of caring for kids. They learn that even if some children aren't surrounded with the love of society, as France or Finland or even preindustrial societies do, they begin to see the differences among children, cherish the differences, and note the strengths, not the deficits.

Your Own Learning

Provocation

Russell Ackoff of the Wharton School and W. Edwards Deming, two gurus of change processes, conversed in the early 1990s about the broken system of education and how the waves of reform have changed little because "the system cannot understand itself" (Ackoff and Deming 2011)

> The prevailing style of management must undergo transformation. A system cannot understand itself. The transformation requires a view from outside – a lens – that I call a system of profound knowledge. It provides a map of theory by which to understand the organizations that we work in. . . . The first step is transformation of the individual. This transformation is discontinuous. It comes from understanding of the system of profound knowledge. The individual, transformed, will perceive new meaning to his life, to events, to numbers, to interactions between people . . . Once the individual understands the system of profound knowledge, he will apply its principles in every kind of relationship with other people. He will have a basis for judgment of his own decisions and for transformation of the organizations that he belongs to. (Deming 2000)

This is a challenging idea to consider – how we transform educational management. We don't discuss these kind of quotes in our daily work. However, we all believe if we don't engage in deep metacognition about our beliefs and understandings, we will not effect lasting progressive changes in education.

Deming developed his theory while leading the reconstruction of the Japanese economy in the 1950s. As a result of his work, Japan became a dominant economic power in the world by the 1970s. Some believe that his focus on participatory democracy in the workplace was a hallmark of progressive economic development. His philosophy was based on real experience in a culture very different than ours, and it influenced America's industrial sectors in the 1970s and 1980s.

Deming believed that to change the system, leaders must understand what he called a System of Profound Knowledge (Deming 2005):

- **Appreciation of a system:** Understanding the overall processes involving suppliers, producers, and customers (or recipients) of goods and services
- **Knowledge of variation:** The range and causes of variation in quality, and use of statistical sampling in measurements
- **Theory of knowledge:** The concepts explaining knowledge and the limits of what can be known
- **Knowledge of psychology:** Concepts of human nature.

Imagine rewiring these elements of the system into schools through your lens as an educator today. Visualize how our educational system might transform if we ourselves developed profound knowledge of the system since "the system will never understand itself."

What would be different if educational systems were transformed? For learners? for those who teach? for you?

Consider launching into your Isearch journal (in the cloud or on paper) to write down your thinking, to ask questions about which you are curious, and record observations of your own educational landscape. What would it mean if we did indeed understand the system in which we work?

Structured Inquiry

Chad, Ira, and Pam have all struggled with change in our own work as educators. We come from very different background experiences and generations. As you read our words, consider these questions:

What is your own philosophy of practice and how did you develop beliefs, values, and a point of view of what education, real school is?

What do you see as the unwritten rules in your school or district? How might discussions of these become more explicit? How do you challenge the unwritten rules?

Reflective Pause

What's interesting or challenging about this statement of Pam's? "The more I learned about observing scientifically, the less I saw in the classrooms I visited." What does this mean to you?

Take Action

To lead individuals in the system (which could be a classroom, a department, a school, or a district) to begin to transform the system takes courage. To paraphrase W. Edwards Deming, this means starting not with others but with you. Taking action, in our opinion, begins with self-education. You cannot wait for others to plan for your own education. It's great when others offer you an opportunity to learn, but often those opportunities don't line up with your needs if offered at all. So what does it mean to self-educate?

Five Actions to Live as a Self-Educator

1. **Seek out others who are life learners as aspirational peers.** It doesn't matter whether you are a year from retiring or a first-year educator. Put yourself in charge of your own learning, because you can make a change in a short period of time that benefits the people you serve. Notice what your aspirational peers do. Listen. Ask questions, Talk with them. Hang out with them in social media and face-to-face. Participate in Twitter chats, schedule virtual face-to-face conversations, schedule coffee for time to talk, ask friends what's on their podcast or book apps, search online for other schools engaged in work you want to know more about and reach out to them to build a professional learning network.

2. **Read, listen, write** in the car (well maybe not write), at night when you can't sleep, on the plane, when you work

out. Share what you are learning so you inform the thinking of others, too. It doesn't matter if you feel you can't write or don't have experience. You have something to offer as well as much to learn. We've found that people who come to deep understanding of our educational system build an appreciation of systems thinking and knowledge of the system by consuming and producing content that offers context to their own learning and that of others. Become a person who does this even if you don't have time. That's a truth for every person I know. None of us has time – but there is no excuse for learning stasis, in our opinion.

3. **Get outside the box.** Spend time thinking of environments other than schools as educational systems – informal and formal. We know learning happens in coffee shops, restaurants, airports, hotel and college lounges, fitness centers, museums, libraries, community makerspaces, and so on. You can learn as we have about human motivation, attention, seating preferences, interaction, engagement and so much more. Life is learning and learning is life. We educate for life, not school.

4. **Become an aspirational peer for others.** Model self-education. Make yourself vulnerable by sharing what you don't know, your challenges, your mistakes, your gaps. And, share resources, connect people to each other, reach out to those you would prefer to ignore to engage them in conversation.

5. **Have a *bias toward action*.** We know many people who can talk the talk of progressive education. People also often have great excuses as to why they can't accomplish change in their own districts, schools, or classrooms. However, we have choices every day to make changes that can impact one child, one peer, one parent. As Ira says when he talks to educators who visit us to see our work, "Change something tomorrow." If you wait until the stars align, you may wait out your career for the right time to make a change. When you finish this chapter, record something you want to change tomorrow and then take action to make that change happen.

Resources

Ackoff, Russell., and Deming, D. Edwards. 2011. "A Conversation between Russell Ackoff and Edward Deming." Ackoff Center Weblog. 2 April. http://ackoffcenter.blogs.com/ackoff_center_weblog/2011/04/a-converstaion-between-russell-ackoff-and-edward-deming.html.

Boers, David. 2007. *History of American Education: Primer*. New York: Peter Lang.

CoderDojo. n.d. "About CoderDojo." Accessed 23 July, 2017. https://coderdojo.com/about/.

Collins, James Charles. 2001. *Good to Great: Why Some Companies Make the Leap . . . and Others Don't*. New York: Random House.

Collins, Jim. n.d. "The Flywheel Effect." Accessed 29 July, 2017. http://www.jimcollins.com/article_topics/articles/the-flywheel-effect.html.

Deming, William Edwards. 2000. *The New Economics: For Industry, Government, Education*. Second. Cambridge, MA: MIT Press.

Deming, William Edwards 2005. "A System of Profound Knowledge." In *W. Edwards Deming: Critical Evaluations in Business and Management*, Volume 1 (ed. J.C. Wood & M.C. Wood). Oxford: Routledge.

Gursky, Daniel. 1991. "Madeline!" *Teacher Magazine* 3 (2): 28–34.

Kay, Ken. 2011. "Becoming a 21st Century School or District: Use the 4Cs to Support Teachers (6 of 7)." Edutopia. October 16. https://www.edutopia.org/blog/21st-century-leadership-teacher-support.

Kennedy, Mary. 2005. *Inside Teaching: How Classroom Life Undermines Reform*. Cambridge, MA: Harvard University Press.

Lezotte, Larry. 1992. "Correlates of Effective Schools." *Education Week*. 1 May. https://www.edweek.org/tm/articles/1992/05/01/8school3.h03.html.

National Commission on Excellence in Education. 1983. *A Nation at Risk: The Imperative for Educational Reform (A Report to the Nation and the Secretary of Education United States Department of Education)*. Edited by David Gardner. CreateSpace Independent Publishing Platform.

Porras, Jerry I., and James Charles Collins. 1994. *Built to Last: Successful Habits of Visionary Companies*. New York: HarperBusiness.

Scratch. n.d. "About Scratch." Accessed 23 July, 2017. https://scratch.mit.edu/about/.

Socol, Ira David. n.d. "Literacy (a)s Tyranny." Scribd. Accessed 29 July, 2017. https://www.scribd.com/document/34962232/Socol-Literacy-as-Tyranny.

Socol, Ira David. 2008. "Pushing Past the Missionary Position: Educa-
    tion, Salvation, and the Attempt to Alter Teachers' Conceptions
    of Their Role." Scribd. Accessed 29 July, 2017. https://www.scribd.
    com/document/25224676/Pushing-Past-the-Missionary-Position.

Tyack, David B., and Larry Cuban. 2009. *Tinkering toward Utopia: A
    Century of Public School Reform*. Cambridge, MA: Harvard Univer-
    sity Press.

US Department of Education, Office of Educational Technology. n.d.
    "Seven Pathways of Educational Environments." Accessed 26
    December, 2017. https://tech.ed.gov/stories/seven-pathways-of-
    educational-environments/.

Wagoner, Jennings L., Jr., and Wayne J. Urban. 2013. *American Educa-
    tion: A History*. New York: Routledge.

4

The Education World Learners Want

CHAD: So as a parent of two children, ages 11 and 9, what
I know is that between what I could teach them if I
wanted, what they could get to on the Internet, what
they could learn through peers, and what they could
learn through family experiences – there's not really a
lot anymore that we need public schooling to impose
upon children in terms of content.

IRA: This is true for the middle and the upper classes, but
not for those in poverty. And public schools won't
continue if they offer nothing to the middle class,
which, obviously, has to pay for them. If public schools
vanish because they offer nothing to the middle class,
we drop back completely into the Social Darwinism
of the nineteenth century, with kids in poverty being
written off from the very start. This isn't a dark vision –
it's Detroit, it's Chicago today – where the schools still
exist but have fundamentally been abandoned.

CHAD: Right, and so here's a real "for instance" and an awak-
ening for me – as that middle-class parent – when
my kids come home from their public school, they're
interested in what they're learning, and they're newly
inquisitive about the world, more curious than even
the day before, and they really want to know more.

My son's teacher is fabulous, she's out of this world. I'll say to my son, "You should ask your teacher to talk about that because she's into it." And he'll say, "Oh, why would I do that? I can use YouTube." And I think for a second – now here's a kid who loves school and he comes home from school just full of joy. But, he also isn't limited in what he learns by the school, but he can be enriched by the experience.

Learning in This Century

To serve contemporary learners, educators should ask all the time: Are children in schools getting opportunities to be curious people? Do they get lots of opportunities to ask questions? Rather than having somebody spoon feed them the answers, do they get a chance to figure things out on their own, with their peers, through connected devices? Certainly the role of teachers in helping learners develop knowledge remains important because teachers are still part of the equation of helping kids get what they need for success – on all kinds of levels from social-emotional to cognitive learning. The structures of education were built, and those questions last answered – without ever asking children over 120 years ago when childhood was still barely defined, and adolescence was – intellectually – unknown. Now, emotionally, morally, philosophically, and intellectually we need to get everyone asking these questions again. And young people need to have a chance to answer questions about what makes for great user experiences as learners.

The conundrum for us today is not related to twenty-first-century anything because learners and teachers already are there and have been there. Instead, the grand challenge today is how to set up situations that allow contemporary learners to "search – connect – communicate – make" in a global culture of participation, an evolving paradigm in which "many to many" learning will be the norm and "one to one or some" learning will be the exception, regardless of what today's dominant educational hierarchy continues to think and value.

Learners live in a world with an ever-broadening continuum of options to seek and find experts and expertise, some flesh and blood and some in the form of evolving artificial intelligence, their learning potential advancing at an exponential pace. At no other point in history has there been greater accessibility to the world's knowledge and expertise than today. At the same time, at no point in history have educators been more challenged to sustain a human context to engage learners while also integrating all the potential of digital devices into their work with young people.

Despite technology advances, it's good news that the basics of how people learn have held constant over time. People learn through interaction with others, connecting their learning with stories, movement, and images, and by imitating real-life skills with support from expert mentors and coaches. As contemporary learners connect with experts and expertise both face-to-face and in virtual environments, they join a unique global learning and communication network that extends learning beyond the walls of schools. As a result, educators must design user experiences that respond to the needs of learners who enter our classes today already capable of teaching themselves, finding expertise to support their learning interests, and changing the context of school as the place where students go to learn.

This shift in how learners access learning today is exemplified in our district by the teen who taught herself how to construct "special effects" makeup from watching videos online and who now after graduation is off to the city to find work in the movie industry. We find this in the student who found himself constructing electronic music in a school's sound studio and now has a full album for sale in iTunes. It's reflected in the young woman whose empathetic soul led her, after her bus driver's death from a diabetes-induced foot infection, to design an Arduino-powered shoe insert sensor that is now in a patent-pending stage. It's embedded in a group of fifth graders who after learning about the Flint, Michigan, water crisis decided to create and place water quality sensors in their local water sources to ensure their community could become more aware of water pollution sources (Kjellstrom 2017). We've also watched this different world of learning to which learners are attracted emerge in teens who added beehives to their school grounds so they could study and contribute to global research on pollinators (Glover 2017). We also hear it in the stories our young people tell about themselves and their growing sense of the world in which they live as they design, make, and produce their podcast stations, rap and rock lyrics, spoken word poetry, YouTube videos, and websites. All of these exemplify how humans have always learned coupled with how humans today learn with new technologies that are only recently available.

"It is that prime shift, and we all know it's difficult," Ira says, as he tries to let teachers understand that the old system traps them as well. "Teachers are trained to be instructors. They usually enter the profession based on a vision from their own success in traditional schools. For administrators that's even more so – they have usually succeeded by following rules. And the only way to get to the change are to constantly ask those questions; What do our children want? What do our children need?"

The fingerprints and footprints of our young people's learning are all over our community and on the web. Our children use every resource they can to create the education world they want. We have to ask every day: What kind of schools will we provide in their world? As Pascal Finette, former chief heretic of Mozilla, once said, "The rising culture of participation combined with technology and power of networks will instigate the most fundamental change in human history" (Finette 2012). When we think about what learning – education – needs to become for today's and tomorrow's learners, we believe that the culture of participation Finette describes will unfold fundamental changes in how young people access and act upon learning opportunities over this next decade and deep into this century. We already see that in schools all over our district and across the nation. "My kids love school," Chad explains:

They love their teachers – but that moment hit for me that the utility of the teacher is fundamentally different. My son simply does not see his teacher as the expert in knowledge that he wants to acquire. He sees her as the organizer of a community in which he and his classmates might acquire knowledge and learn to use it.

Adults may argue about this – they do argue about it – but despite the historical victories of industrial education, the fundamental utility of school has now firmly shifted to the progressive educational ideal, what John Dewey wanted. Ira notes that

> kids know it, and if the adults in the school don't know it yet, kids simply subvert the structure. If they can't have their computers open to the world on the tabletops, they have their phones in their laps. If the class is the teacher-at-the-PowerPoint the kids are simply lost in other thoughts or chatting with their friends via their own technology. And if the adults don't get that and shift to strategies that synergize learning, the kids come home from school to middle-class parents and say, "school sucks."

The danger for public education lies in what happens when kids say that "school sucks" every day. Eventually a large percentage of the parents with resources will find another way to educate their kids. Take a look at the pressure on states to cut back on standardized testing. That pressure comes from middle-class parents who are communicating that the whole education reform-accountability model has sucked the life out of their children's classrooms.

We watch this happen every year – those who can exercise their options, the parents who can afford private school or to homeschool, leave if public schools are locked down and traditional. But those parents have rushed back when their local school embraces paths to connect their kids with challenging and interesting work – maker work – work based in the children's passions and interests. Those are real enrollment facts, and as we have built out better schools we've had elite private schools in our community talk about their need to follow our lead. We work every day on shifting toward where our schools must be.

While the rise of the Smart Machine Age changes the fundamental nature of learning in contemporary times, the study of how people learn and have always learned is of critical importance to adult learners in the education profession, the teachers who will continue to influence the structures and processes of schooling, education, and learning even as the technology evolves into ever more sophisticated tools ubiquitously available to adults and children alike. Indeed, as Professor Emeritus Edward Hess of the University of Virginia Darden School of Business notes:

> . . . the most vital skill for finding meaningful work and building a meaningful life in the Smart Machine Age will be knowing how to iteratively learn – knowing how to go into new situations and learn by trial and error. Iterative learning is not foreign to us. Trial and error is how we learned as young children. It is how, for example, many of us learned to ride a bicycle. We started with training wheels to avoid taking big personal risks. We learned by doing and adapting to the results. (Hess 2017)

Learning also will continue to be critically dependent upon the quality of relationships that adults create with young people. That feels unquestionably human. John Roepke predicted in a recent post for *EdTech Digest* that artificial intelligence will change the game when it comes to replacing some of the traditions of teacher to learner, freeing teachers to design more human-centered learning opportunities (Roepke 2017). Geoff Colvin, author of *Humans Are Underrated: What High Achievers Know That Machines Never Will*, wrote in an op ed post for the *New York Times* that empathy, creative problem solving in groups, and storytelling likely will be the human currency of economic progress in the Machine Age:

> These skills, though basic to our humanity, are fundamentally different from the skills that have been the basis of economic progress for most of human history: Logic, knowledge and analysis, which we learned from textbooks and in classrooms, are now

skills being commoditized by advancing technology. By contrast, the skills of deep human interaction address the often irrational reality of how human beings behave, and we find them not in textbooks but inside ourselves. As computers master ever more complexity, that's where we'll find the source of our continued value. (Colvin 2016)

Because of the changes rapidly emerging in this new phase of human history, the Smart Machine Age, educators must adapt to all the ways that technology changes the context of our learning environments, user experiences, and user interfaces. For example, "Jill Watson," the AI grad assistant (unbeknownst to students) who could answer college students' questions with 97% certainty with timeliness, represents a new generation of expertise that goes well beyond the Khan Academy or a Wolfram Math World (Noyes 2016). Interestingly, "Jill" was considered to be the best grad assistant available online to students at Georgia Tech and they valued "her" support so much she was nominated for a grad assistant award at the end of the year.

And, yet, there is an intangible, indeed a human element, that from our perspective will continue to define the need for human interaction in the learning equation. It's as Ira says, "an assurance that an adult will look a child in the eye every day, asking the intuitive and often unspoken question of 'Are you okay?' What are you interested in today? What would you like to make? How can I help?"

Adults matter. When we talk with young people they tell us over and over again that in their schools teachers make a difference in their lives, the principal sets the stage for the culture of their schools, and any adult with whom they connect from bus drivers to teaching assistants can be their mentor, coach, surrogate parent, or connector. Our learners love their tools. They keep them close 24/7. They see them as paths to community interactions that adults don't understand and to learning opportunities beyond anything many of the adults in their lives ever access. Yet, we know that learners don't see technology as replacing face-to-face relationships with adults. However, they also don't see the traditions of school structures as being one and the same as the traditions of teacher and learner relationships.

Julian Waters, recent high school graduate, spoke at the World Maker Faire Education Forum to the work inside our system to change the opportunities, experiences, and expectations of learning while we also seek to sustain the power of relationships among learners and adults in their education world:

> So many in our society are quick to criticize the system that public school students learn under, but equally strong in number are those who strive actively to change it. By promoting student voice, self-directed learning, and passion-centered projects in school, we're making a lasting difference for students in their secondary schooling and well into their future. Together, we can make the education of tomorrow . . . These are the kinds of changes that can stem directly from student voices being heard AND invested in . . . These educators, and these amazing new ideas and mindsets have transformed Albemarle County Public Schools into a school system where anything is possible and *where students not only experience education, but help to make it.* (Parker 2016)

Julian in many ways exemplified in his own high school experience how he as a student saw the education world he wanted and began to build it because of a principal, a new library makerspace, and the support of adults who encouraged him. Julian moved from describing himself as just an average student to becoming an inspired, high-performing learner through informal learning experiences in which he studied, designed, built, and iterated drones in a newly built makerspace and with the help of online expertise. With principal encouragement he took his passion for drones to the cafeteria, recruited a diverse community with a newly discovered interest in drone technologies, and started a drone club to build and fly drones. When called by a neighboring middle school principal, he accepted the invitation to teach middle schoolers about drones, and they began to receive mentorship from high schoolers with a shared interest. Julian went on to become a keynote speaker at the World Maker Faire, sharing his story – and announcing his candidacy for the school board after graduation. Julian is anything but average. He doesn't fit any profile of a graduate. His competencies are unique and unseen on a high school transcript. He is a citizen leader, scientist, and entrepreneur. He's also a budding politician.

Breaking the norms of high school were essential so that Julian could be seen as an individual beyond the bell curve averages of grades, discipline referrals, attendance, and SATs. His passion lay outside that of the traditional structures of high school. We would never have known Julian if we were wedded to those structures. How did we make the changes that allowed us to find Julian? We began by prototyping small, informal spaces that challenge the norm of what *going to class* means in school. We designed changes so that learners could access informal spaces for learning, shifting high school libraries to learning commons as a starting point. An old library storage space filled with media and equipment dinosaurs of 1999 became a makerspace in Julian's high school. Here, Julian found duct tape, foam board, Arduinos, and a rekindled passion for learning. He also found a learning tech integrator, a librarian, and a principal who encouraged, supported, and valued his interests and passions. The space is key. The tools are essential. Relationships are critical. All three interface to create a culture in which the Julians of our schools find their own agency, voice, and influence as something to be regarded not suppressed.

Julian's work in school represents the ever-expanding learning continuum that can be found in the virtual worlds of the Internet *and* the capability of local communities and place-based schools to open doors for learners that otherwise would not be available. When educational communities are open to options that expand possibilities for where, how, when, and what learners set out to learn, different paths to learning evolve almost by the month as result of new technologies, creating a democratization of access that didn't exist in the past.

Serial, the viral podcast whose Season I series told the story of a murder among Maryland teens, represents a seminal shift in how humans use the Internet to tell stories and how to pursue curiosity, inquiry, information gathering, and collaborative analysis (Koenig and Snyder 2014). That this "broadcast" engaged so many in interaction without the synchronous nature of traditional broadcasting demonstrated a new norm that allows work beyond and through the walls of schools. The overlapping conversations within face-to-face and virtual communities showed clearly how information is now shared, knowledge developed, and analysis evaluated and challenged.

The case of *Serial*'s protagonist, Adnan Syed, was reopened in 2016 because of the power of the global network to crowdsource reams of research for his law team, which eventually included – through the podcast's popularity – University of Virginia law school interns, who put it all together using new and old investigative methods to make a case on his behalf. The podcast series just caught the attention of the public – especially millennials – and created an online learning community that grew and grew with a level of crowdsourced research that remains unprecedented.

Ira spent hours talking with Pam and many others who wanted his "cop as detective" perspective on the Syed case and to find out what bothered or troubled him about it. Even as Ira speaks to how the police behavior in the case troubled him a great deal, he used the context of public engagement with this case and translated it back into what motivates human learning – the urge of the human mind to make sense of that which is not known and understood. However, in this case, what intrigued Ira emerged from the power of technology to generate a networked learning conversation from a very different media learning space outside of traditional learning places. It was as if you could see human thinking – the power of the brain times thousands of people – linking together similarly to a vast global computer network. The *Serial* podcast series and podcasting in general have led to a viral explosion of human inquiry, information gathering, and analysis engaging people who represented every demographic, educational background, and point of view.

How do audio stories connect with creating the schools today's learners want and need?

Audio, as a medium, for much of our lives has seemed like an antique medium. Today, however, it now is being reestablished as a contemporary medium, just as stories have dominated human culture for millennia. However, thanks to mobile devices, the audio medium today is totally portable and totally human. Ira has introduced kids to old radio dramas from the thirties, forties, and fifties, because they represent amazing examples of storytelling, especially for learners who have significant difficulties accessing print as he has had throughout life. Educators who mostly, unlike Ira, were good students in school miss that some kids work in a blind world where print can be inaccessible and learning becomes limited to the few things truly available to them. Those kids can be missed when educators tie themselves to an education world that worked for them and forget that it doesn't always work for others.

We also think that with a commitment to study and action, we can make the changes we need, but doing so means breaking traditions of what it means to learn in school. If we consider the numbers of people on Reddit and other social media who were learning together about law and the judicial system, the science of cell phone transmissions, the history of colliding cultures, and urban demographics from just that one series of podcasts on *Serial*, we can find in all the learning that occurred and the conversations it generated, the audio series created a new paradigm about what's possible for learners of all ages. Schools often ignore what's possible. As a result, educators are losing control of educating young people and many don't even recognize that yet.

The Road to Change Is Filled with Resistance

To understand the power we have today to make changes to advantage more learners, to give them the education world they want and need, it's helpful to know that resistance to new technologies and teaching strategies dates back to the early history of our public schools. This is nothing new and actually has been documented in recent research as to why professors in higher education don't adopt new strategies even when it would benefit their learners (Matthews 2017).

A book by William Alcott from the nineteenth century described the introduction of the blackboard and the slate to the classroom (Alcott 1843). The blackboard, as Alcott describes it, was impressive, but it was a new technology, and teachers were really afraid of it. It had taken, by that point in time, almost 30 years for blackboard/slate "technology" to get from West Point, where it was introduced after being brought to the United States from France, by Claudius Crozet, to the wall of the public schoolhouse (Phillips 2015).

That 30 years matches the similar gaps in moving film, radio, and television into classrooms, as well as the Internet moving from military applications to schools. And like those things, media that were designed for distributed creativity became one-way instructional devices in the classroom. The school blackboard was originally conceived of as a student collaboration space, where kids would work together. The slates were for individual children to use because, as Alcott pointed out in his 1843 research study, kids wrote more when they could erase more easily on slate than on paper. The slate board was the key to personalized learning in the context of learning in the mid-1800s. Alcott also spoke about teachers needing to let kids play with those slate boards. In words that parallel what we sometimes hear today from teachers, Alcott even noted his perceptions of potential resistance of educators of his time to allowing children to use slates: "But they are so liable to be broken, it will be said, as to render it expensive to parents to keep them supplied with them" (Alcott 1843).

The blackboard over time was corrupted into the dominant teaching wall and the use of slates as a technology of active learning was abandoned. This leads to the question how do educators come to adopt new technologies and the pedagogies to use them to engage learners?

As brilliant as film and then television were, and the opportunities for those technologies to revolutionize learning in the first half of the twentieth century, what we ended up with was the filmstrip, this horrible precursor of PowerPoint. PowerPoint is just an iteration of that 1950–1970 filmstrip. We have seen across our careers that when technology becomes tools to control and manage rather than to support and encourage learning, both teachers and learners lose potential to amplify deep learning. We have spent much time considering that schools can't get out of this horrible loop because educators keep trying to reproduce what's always been done in the past instead of looking at how people learn in the world today. It's why we have focused on how to ensure that screens on learning devices do not become a replacement for drill and practice worksheets, no matter how effective they are as a management or entertainment tool.

Consider the viral tech rage of 2016, Pokémon Go. Even as stupid as it felt to many older adults on a whole bunch of levels – the technology of augmented reality, which nobody's done enough with especially on this continent, offers incredible opportunities for learners to launch from their physical community into virtual communities. Immersive virtual environments become more sophisticated every day across a variety of formats. A fad such as Pokémon Go may stick around for a few days, months, or even years before children are attracted to the next generation of entertainment tech. In schools, being aware of specific fad tech that gets boosted up to our learners has become a skill set of value. When we look deeply, we often find the next generation of learning opportunities that come with tech fads.

Using portals of all kinds that go well beyond the social entertainment of Pokémon Go to connect to the world has become common. Young learners in our schools have gone underwater with a marine scientist on the Great Barrier Reef and participated in workshops with an archaeologist in a distant natural history museum. It's not unusual to see students paused in front of monitors in libraries watching webcam viewsheds from rainforests to megacities such as Beijing. One elementary school teacher annually sets up a link on the school website so children and their families can follow a real-time nest cam in the school courtyard of bluebird parents caretaking eggs to young fledglings.

From building Minecraft worlds of historical sites studied by our kids to creating their own virtual reality documentary videos, children move seamlessly between the physical environment, in which they cook, sew, hammer and saw, write, read, draw, sculpt, solve math problems and engage in sustained dialogue about past and current events, and virtual environments where they create, design, build, model, share, and explore.

Forward thinking doesn't always pan out in the moment, but we've learned that if we don't constantly push ideas beyond the horizon of known landmarks, we only will continue to affect incremental educational change in response to an exponentially changing world. The drive to sustain twentieth-century schooling has often resulted in new technologies simply being used by teachers to maintain status quo teaching strategies rather than innovating teaching strategies to take advantage of technologies to more effectively activate learning. Contemporary technology in schools, unfortunately, often represented a reductionism in the use of the blackboard, television, filmstrip, smart board, and so on to sustain passivity of students while maintaining the integrity of the teaching wall model.

However, we've learned from our own experiences when technology is used to promote conversation and debate, as in the *Serial* podcast series, or for students to create their own podcasts, virtual reality movies, games, or 3D-printed solutions, we see a substantive shift in learning power as teachers work with students to connect them to the global communication and learning network. We see this happening through our work to create interdisciplinary content, context through maker work and projects, and social-emotional relationships among learners to learners, learners to teachers, and learners to communities.

Explicit linkages among contemporary technologies, pedagogies, and curricula are essential to learning in the physical and digital communities young people inhabit today. The current youth generation, the phigitals as some reference them, has been born into blended communities that are unlike anything their grandparents, parents, and teachers have experienced

(Stansbury 2017). They have never known a world without the Internet or mobile devices. Their perspective on the world, shaped by the impact not just of the technology they use daily but in the context of all the ways in which technology shapes their access to learning, forces us to look differently as educators at how people learn today.

Change Comes in Many Forms

Contemporary learning doesn't happen by chance. As we work to seamlessly migrate learners into digital environments, we also work to strengthen their active engagement in physical spaces that provide them with choice, comfort, and connectivity as they construct learning. Moving students out of desks in rows and teachers away from the dominant teaching wall has occurred intentionally and represents broad team efforts to design user experiences that bring tools, curricula, and pedagogy into alignment as learners acquire lifelong learning competencies essential to success in homes, communities, the workforce, and as citizens. This work has formatively evolved from years of study and efforts to advance the work, some of which were successes and others not.

Chad often says that we can't consider pedagogical or any other educational change before we move past written policies to question the learning philosophy that has underpinned public education for a very long time. Current educational philosophy represents past questions that were asked and answered about the purpose of learning beginning in the early part of the twentieth century. Those questions led to a reform movement that moved students and teachers from one-room schoolhouses into the large factory schools we still have in most districts across the United States. The answers to questions posed in 1910 led to the philosophical frames for schools of that time and, over decades, educational policies followed that came to define the structures, procedures, and types of personnel found in today's schools. However, Chad asks, "Do the schools we have today still exist because school reformers keep asking and trying to answer questions that led to schooling circa 1910? And, aren't those the wrong questions for contemporary schools?" Instead of asking questions with a focus on past philosophical drivers of education, what if educators posed a different set of questions, such as:

What are the underlying societal phenomena that lead to this notion of a need for change for today's learners? and

How do we have the will to challenge educational assumptions that have existed for decades?

For example, on the periphery of contemporary educational discussions, one of the biggest questions being asked right now is: What's the utility of compulsory public schooling in today's world?

If you think about public school as a design, it is another version of technology. It also is an articulation of a block of one's life, a block of time. Schooling as we mostly know it is deconstructed in a certain logical order in terms of time, division by age, and, then in content to suggest what one must need to know. So, if the idea of that is okay, the utility of public schooling is roughly three-fourths – maybe not quite that much – of one's childhood. Not much has changed about the system of public education since the flip from one-room schoolhouses to comprehensive "cells and bells" schools that developed in the early twentieth century.

This system of public education still brings children into contemporary schools with an intention of doing something to them, hopefully something of value. We want to impose structures upon learners that result in their learning certain things that governments and communities consider most important to being a citizen in this country. Those with control over public education also want children to learn to behave in a certain way. We expect children, regardless of their background or experience, to adopt a certain set of norms that align hopefully with life success. For example, we expect children to learn to talk a certain way that's consistent with the dominant culture's norms. Yet, the whole notion of being polite and the way in which we're polite represent social constructs of an American culture based upon middle-class values of what has been a dominant white culture. We expect such norms to drive the work and behaviors of children even though, as educators travel overseas or interact with different cultures here in the United States, they know expectations for children can be radically different than those of white, middle-class America.

Though for a very long time educators have been responsible for transmitting the values and beliefs of our dominant culture forward from generation to generation, today these values and beliefs are being challenged as communities diversify and flip to minority majority or even minority minority cultures. Most importantly, unlike past generations that sought for their children to emulate the dominant culture in order to fit in, get ahead, and assimilate, we see some families challenging the norms, beliefs, and values of "old" America.

In sharing a perspective in discussions about progressive education, Chad has made the point that even though we like to pretend we're an open and free society, in reality, we're not. We're actually still relatively closed down to ideas that challenge the normative culture, especially in homogenous communities that still occupy mostly rural America. In school this plays out in the compliance-based work promoted to reinforce certain behaviors deemed appropriate along with the knowledge considered important to learn to ensure a societal status quo. We have counted on schools as a primary technology to transmit knowledge and values forward in our citizenry through structures, procedures, and personnel created by philosophy and policies of the twentieth century.

When you think about school today as a technology, consider that almost everyone has tools in their possession that allow them to connect not just to an Internet of Things but also to an Internet of ideas, knowledge, and resources. In such a world some are asking: What's the utility of school anymore? What if the education our learners want and need can be gained in spite of schools not just because of them? When Finette speaks to the power of the global communication network, he's talking about a system of learning and communication potential unlike anything the world has ever seen, a network that makes the printing press as an educational technology look superficial in terms of the significance of change it wrought.

What learners can access in many schools that still is limited to printing press technology pales in comparison to what they have access to outside of school with network technology. And, now that people can do much of the learning they need outside of school, as exemplified by a number of entrepreneurs who have achieved success without attending college or even K–12 school, perhaps being in school may be far less useful as a path to economic success than it was in the past century.

The Utility of School

So, let's get back to the question: What is the utility of school given what learners want in a learning world?

The real question is what do we need school to be? What type of society do we want to have, and what are the problems within it right now that we must address? And, ultimately, what is the relationship between our work to educate young people and the challenges faced by local communities and the world? There are no simple solutions to complex challenges but educators cannot ignore their role in determining the purpose of schooling. We cannot leave this critical work to the politicians, business community, and parents to do that for us.

Today is a period of social change that is in many ways similar to what we went through in the 1960s. There is a similar sense of angst, equality issues still exist, and a growing number of people are starting to recognize real problems, and they're open to progressive educational solutions that can in part address social needs such as equity and access. At the same time, there is always the other side who are afraid of progressive education because of its challenge to middle-class schooling norms.

If the utility of school is shifting to a progressive educational ideal in this century, then it creates a situation in society in which it makes sense to make the utility of public education one of a community. School becomes a community of learners. It's a community of people who want to learn, want to learn how to learn, and figure out with the teacher what it is they need to learn in society. It's a community connected to other communities. A key question as a school's utility becomes its role as working community is how might children and adults engage together?

That's what making does: It engages community members together. When a child or adult creates something, actualizing it so it matters in their own context, and perhaps what they've made also might have some sort of impact on society, whether it's in their own household, their own little world, their community, their country, whatever – they share what they've made with their maker community, a learning community. This is a basic tenet of progressive education: Learning across communities matters. When educational communities start working together, not just people face-to-face but connecting all over the world, children become part of global conversations, cultures, and teams that collaborate to solve big world challenges.

Making changes not just the utility of schooling but the purpose of school, moving school culture from one of compliance in learning and behavior to one in which a diversity of ideas and solutions is valued and behavior is less focused on compliance norms and more focused on responsiveness to community norms. When young people show what they can make or create in authentic ways, not just what they know in decontextualized tests, all of a sudden they take a much greater level of pride in what they're doing and in sharing their expertise with others.

Learner-Centric Assessment

To create paths to this kind of success means that assessment must look really different for children to show you what they can do, not just what they know. What assessment looks like ultimately determines what teachers feel compelled to do to set the stage for learners to learn. Assessment of K–12 learners has been shaped by two major forces in recent decades; the standardization movement led by federal and state governments and colleges and university entrance requirements. However, as progressive education permeates more and more schools, opportunities increase for students to show not just their surface learning but the deeper learning in which they've been inspired to pursue their own passions and interests through project-based learning, community action, and maker work.

We've been working to support learners to build digital portfolios and lead learning conferences with their parents. It's interesting to see kids trying to figure out what matters about their learning when they get a chance to showcase their work in more authentic settings. Colleges and universities are starting to line up to value this kind of student work as a different path for applicants to share beyond the transcript and SAT scores. MIT was one of the first ones out of the chute to say to potential applicants, "Give us a maker portfolio." Now 85 highly competitive colleges and universities have built a consortium to support an affordability and access initiative for high school students who otherwise might not have opportunities typically afforded to children of middle-class families. These colleges and universities have come out with a position that the common app can be supplanted, or at the least supplemented, by what they're labeling as a digital locker, in essence a digital portfolio (Scott 2015).

When learners can document their capability to work with other people really well, this fits within the skill sets that are needed in life. Teens who can show you that they can communicate in multiple ways and actually flex the way they communicate have a capability that will stand them in good stead in the workforce, community, and home. If a child or a collaborative team of learners makes a video to teach others how to do something, it needs to be spot on in terms of giving other people directions. Our elementary students sometimes struggle with directions when they're trying to teach others how to construct something, for example, that uses an Arduino. Recently watching fourth grade girls build a game using Ozobots they were programming, it was fascinating to observe them try to communicate to another group how to play the game.

These kinds of opportunities help children begin to learn the value of using precise language and using language in a variety of different ways to communicate. In turn this leads us to further questions:

When do learners get the opportunity to learn different communication skills and show audiences what they can do formatively over time?

How do they become active users of what Finette calls the global communication network?

How does every learning opportunity in school become a real experience in developing knowledge and competencies for life, not just for a class or course?

How do we build learning opportunities that learners want and need?

We know this. When life learning competencies come together through the creative juice of making or the passion-based projects formed from deep interests, all of a sudden kids value communication in a different way than if they're just expected to write to a writing prompt or respond to a multiple choice item. And, when learners can share their learning work and articulate coherently why it's important to them, that's worth its weight in gold.

Your Own Learning

Provocation

To understand why it's not twenty-first-century learning that's the real "main thing," we have to go back to our historical past, to understand more about the roots of desks in rows, worksheets, blackboards, multiple choice tests, bell schedules, agrarian calendars, classroom management, age-based classes, sorting and selecting groups, 100-point grading scales, and the cult of efficiency and effectiveness that's been the driver of the teaching wall as dominant place inside the room. Padraic Pearse, Irish poet, educator, and revolutionary, described the English "factory school" system being imposed in America and Ireland in the early 1900s as "The Murder Machine," a killing of the human connectivity embedded in how people have learned since prehistory (Pearse 1916). We are born to explore, to question, to play, to tell stories, to learn with others, to create and use tools to advance and build new ideas, new tools, new possibilities for humanity. Why and how we learn transcends centuries. What we need to learn changes by the moment.

Historian David McCullough and his perspective on history as moments of story, art, and inquiry inspires educators to consider how humans come to understand the purpose of learning in the context of rather than the facts of history. It's a truism that we learn about the potential and the pitfalls of tomorrow by understanding the past, for, as McCullough says:

> If we don't know who we are, if we don't know how we became what we are, we're going to start suffering from all the obvious detrimental effects of amnesia. (Cole 2003)

What do you see as the big questions that need to be answered regarding the functions of contemporary education?

In what ways does Finette's, Pearse's, McCullough's, and your own points of view on education intersect with or offer challenges to your own thinking?

What kind of world do you want? How are the things you do in your school every day moving our world toward what you want?

Consider launching into your Isearch journal (in the cloud or on paper) to write down your thinking, to ask questions about which you are curious, your observations of your own educational landscape, and what it would mean if the utility of school was redefined as a community and communication learning network rather than a location where children go for knowledge.

Structured Inquiry
Ira has written extensively about the influences upon the unfolding history and changes that have occurred in American education. He often says that the system we have was designed to fail itself and to fail the young people we serve. The five-part series he wrote in the blog, SpeEdChange, will provide you with a perspective that offers a deeper understanding of the historical context of education in America and from whence our current practices, now traditions, come (Socol 2010).

A key argument here is that we cannot expect all of our children to succeed if we continue to use the systems that were literally designed to fail 80% of children. Those structures include age-based grades, grade-level standards, multiple choice assessments, the division of time in the school day, and standard classroom management techniques.

What are the ways in which your school, and your classroom, limit opportunities for student success? How might we move from that contrived learning environment with concrete and unfair structures of class, schedule, time, curricula, pedagogy, and testing to one that disorganizes the organizational structures of Gutenberg-era teaching?

If you were designing a school from the ground up today, what would you see as the greatest challenge to educating children for life readiness?

Reflective Pause
Moving from the industrial model, compliance-driven educational structures we have inherited from the late nineteenth century, requires real shifts in curricula, assessment, and instruction if contemporary learners are to acquire the competencies they will need as adult family and community members, members of a workforce, entrepreneurs, and lifelong learners. Important shifts in spaces and technology uses, instructional tolerance, and school time are essential to building the range of communication, critical thinking, creative ideation, and collaboration skills required in this century. Huge changes in classroom management are fundamental to building the capability to read and write

analytically across cultures and media, and to demonstrate the complex mathematical understanding necessary to so many contemporary careers.

"School" must become a space – both physical and virtual – where learning is a constant cocreation of teachers and students. Where content meets the student where they are, demonstration of knowledge is performative in a global context, and inquiry – inside and outside of school – is based in the actual life of children, adolescents, and their communities' needs. This is the shift that allows us to finally move into the present and future, into the post-Gutenberg era. And it embraces a turning point in human information and communication as important as the invention of the printing press.

Why must we, all of us, actively lead our schools toward new forms of deep learning? How do we build the capacity – across faculty and leadership – for the rapid, significant change needed by our students now? What must all of us do, starting now and working continuously, to create a culture of learning innovation?

Take Action
How do we focus on possibility, getting the work done, getting past the "Yes, but . . . " that freezes so many schools in place? Where do we begin?

The Gutenberg era, and the education system created as a reaction to the technological inventions of the 1840s, defined information as "fixed print" and education as "write it, print it, read it, recall it." Our post-Gutenberg definitions are different: "search, connect, communicate, make." Those definitions require a learning revolution that supports the information, communication, and cognitive knowledge revolutions that have challenged us – individuals, organizations, governments, businesses, schools – for the past two decades.

After years of building this work in schools, in an exploration of the "why, how, and what" of integrating contemporary technologies, redesigned spaces, and transformed pedagogies into highly diverse school environments, we've found that contemporary learning will not grow from work in schools with limited populations or choice entry programs, but in public schools that welcome all students who come to the door. For we believe that shifting twentieth-century factory schools to deep learning environments is something needed by all students, and so these shifts must be accessible to all students.

Four Actions to Live as a Changemaker

1. Spend time with teens, adolescents, elementary children, and toddlers outside of school. Watch them in informal and formal learning settings. Ask them what interests them. What do they like to do? How do they learn about things they need to learn? What's important to learn? Even young children can talk about learning if you shift language and listen.

2. Walk and observe kids in class if you have permission. Walk with a principal and notice everything you can about how they connect with each other, adults, the furniture, technologies. Is the learning in any context that makes it real and of interest to kids? Does it make sense? What does the teacher do? What do kids do? What kind of choices appear explicit in the space? Are kids all doing the same thing with the same tools?

3. Write down what you notice and generate questions you have about what seems to matter or not in different learning spaces you observe. What needs to change to create a "many to many" network of communicators in a learning community versus a "one to some" classroom?

4. Identify what you would like to see more of and less of. Be clear in your journal writing or thinking about why. Think aloud with a critical friend about what you will do as a teaching peer and/or administrator as a result of your observations. Think small steps before actions.

Resources

Alcott, William Andrus. 1843. *Slate and Black Board Exercises*. New York: Mark H. Newman.

Cole, Bruce. 2003. "David McCullough Interview." National Endowment for the Humanities. May/June. Accessed 16 July 2017. https://www.neh.gov/about/awards/jefferson-lecture/david-mccullough-interview.

Colvin, Geoff. 2016. "Is Artificial Intelligence Now the Real Deal?" *New York Times*. 9 March.

Finette, Pascal. 2012. "The Participation Culture: Pascal Finette at TEDxOrangeCoast." https://www.youtube.com/watch?v=yJMnVieDfD0.

Glover, David. 2017. "Mr. Stanek's Bees." https://www.youtube.com/watch?v=iEZgg4cG61I.

Hess, Edward. 2017. "The No. 1 Job Skill Needed for the Smart Machine Age: Knowing How to Iteratively Learn." University of Virginia, Darden School of Business, Darden Ideas to Action. 7 February. https://ideas.darden.virginia.edu/2017/02/the-no-1-job-skill-needed-for-the-smart-machine-age-knowing-how-to-iteratively-learn/.

Kjellstrom, Willy. 2017. "The RIFFLE: A Stream Monitoring Project." https://www.youtube.com/watch?v=mt6cDi1yNEE.

Koenig, Sarah, and Julie Snyder. 2014. *Serial: Season One*. https://serialpodcast.org/season-one.

Matthews, David. 2017. "Anthropologist Studies Why Professors Don't Adopt Innovative Teaching Methods." *Inside Higher Ed*. 6 July. https://www.insidehighered.com/news/2017/07/06/anthropologist-studies-why-professors-dont-adopt-innovative-teaching-methods.

Noyes, Katherine. 2016. "These Grad Students Didn't Know Their Teaching Assistant Was a Robot." *Computerworld*. 9 May. http://www.computerworld.com/article/3067792/data-analytics/these-grad-students-didnt-know-their-teaching-assistant-was-a-robot.html.

Parker, Jessica. 2016. "Julian Waters on the Impact of Changing Minds." MakerEd. 7 October. http://makered.org/blog/julian-waters-on-the-impact-of-changing-minds/.

Pearse, Padraic. 1916. *The Murder Machine*. Dublin: Whelan.

Phillips, Christopher J. 2015. "An Officer and a Scholar: Nineteenth-Century West Point and the Invention of the Blackboard." *History of Education Quarterly* 55 (1): 82–108.

Roepke, Jon. 2017. "How Artificial Intelligence Will Transform Education." *EdTech Digest*. 24 April. https://edtechdigest.wordpress.

com/2017/04/24/how-artificial-intelligence-will-transform-education/.

Scott, Jaschik. 2015. "80 Colleges and Universities Announce Plan for New Application and New Approach to Preparing High School Students." *Inside Higher Ed.* 29 September. https://www.inside highered.com/news/2015/09/29/80-colleges-and-universities-announce-plan-new-application-and-new-approach.

Socol, Ira David. 2010. "Designed to Fail – Education in America: Part One." SpeEdChange. 25 September. http://speedchange.blogspot.com/2010/09/designed-to-fail-education-in-america.html.

Stansbury, Meris. 2017. "3 Things Schools Must Know about the Rising 'Phigital' Student." *eSchool News.* 31 May. https://www.eschool news.com/2017/05/31/schools-gen-z-phigital-student/.

---- 5 ----

Envision All Things Future

Welcome to Futurama II! Welcome to a journey into
the future – a journey for everyone today, into the
everywhere of tomorrow. Never has the world held a
brighter promise of things to come, or a greater need
for new resources for the tools and machinery of power
and mobility, for the building together of a road to a
new life of abundance and a greater dignity for us all . . .
                                        – John Herman (n.d.)

Thus opened the scripted journey through Futurama II, the
premier General Motors exhibition at the 1964 New York
World's Fair (New York World's Fair 1964/1965 n.d.). When fair
attendees went on a magical ride into the future as imagined by
the creatives, the designers, the inventors, the engineers of the
time, what they saw was not a vision of incremental change but
one that exploded the vision of people to see beyond horizons,
into deep space, under the seas, and past the technologies. The
exhibition didn't take people just to places they might see as
possible but into worlds of impossibilities made possible.

We wonder all the time about the impossibilities of
schooling that we cannot yet see. We ask that you join with
us in our exploration of what could be possible, not limited by
the constraints of the past or defined by the filters of those who
taught us to not see.

> Don't imagine a future that's insufficiently transformative.
> (Socol 2008)

IRA: Listen, I consider myself very lucky. I grew up in that
       moment of infinite hope. We'd have social equality
       and flying cars. The peaceful atom would give us clean
       power and good government would bring us a Great
       Society and we'd explore the universe. I saw *Futurama*
       as a young kid and watched *2001: A Space Odyssey* as
       a young teen, and so despite the dark present of my
       childhood – Vietnam, race riots, climbing crime rates,
       filthy pollution – I knew, I just knew, the world could
       be much better.

PAM: And now we expect so little. We doubt science, we
       distrust government, we settle, as they say, for bread
       and circuses – and if it's artisan bread and animal
       cruelty–free circuses, we accept that as change. In
       schools, as in all the other facets of society, we mistake
       tinkering with the edges as transformation, but trans-
       formation requires all parts of a system to change.

CHAD: We need to find that fire again. I'm younger and I think
       I grew up in a time of increasing limits. Television got
       better, but possibilities for life always felt constrained.
       The Internet appeared, but it is used to stoke fears more
       than it's used to imagine.

There is an unfortunate tendency in times of great technological change, and in the social upheaval that inevitably follows that
change, for humans to yearn for a future little changed from the
past. During the Industrial Revolution of the 1840s–1880s
the same false nostalgia dominated that many people feel today.
Many of the "great traditions" from the 1800s are ones to
which society still clings. Our vision of Christmas, our concepts
of hearth and home, and our perception of the classroom all
emerged in the Victorian era to soothe and hold culture as stable

as possible (Restad 1995). If asked today about the future, most people simply imagine better phones, larger TV screens, and cars that drive themselves – in other words, the past made safer and richer. We just do not imagine fundamental changes in our lives.

"I adored the 1957 Monsanto House of the Future; it was full of fabulous furniture, ideas for the future, and innovative, original design," wrote blogger Lloyd Alter. "OK, it was all plastic and sponsored by Monsanto, but they were cool then and as we knew from *The Graduate*, the future was in plastics. I was disappointed to learn that the new version was to be a 5,000 square foot McMansion that 'will look like a normal suburban home outside, but inside it will feature hardware, software and touch-screen systems that could simplify everyday living.' But I couldn't imagine how ugly and stupid it actually turned out to be . . .

"*We didn't want the (new) home to intimidate the visitors. We want the house to be real accessible to our guests,*" Disney designer Tom Zofrea [said as he describes making the home] a mix of Art Nouveau and Craftsman Style. (Alter 2008)

What Alter described in his post contrasts sharply with the future seen from those World's Fairs of 1933 in Chicago, 1939 and 1964 in New York, or 1967 in Montreal, where the fabric of our cities, the forms and locations of our homes, and even the jobs we imagined were transformed completely. The world imagined in those World's Fairs created a path to envision a future that was significant in its potential for dramatic societal, home, and workforce changes.

People coming to this vision from the sleepy 1950s were restless for radical change. And in that moment, the suburban John Dewey–inspired school took shape. From New York to California children moved into light-filled classrooms with rolling furniture, doors to the outside, and lots of display space for student projects (Wallenstein n.d.). Those designs became a mainstream norm of the 1960s – an "alternative" norm to earlier decades that now seems dangerous in an education world of shrinking possibilities (Reed 1981). Yet, the idea of all that glass and all those open doors today seems not just a security risk but also a source of distraction that takes children's attention away from the *work* of school. Contemporary teachers across America tape posters up to block student views of corridors, and face desks away from windows – literally preventing the world from reaching the classroom.

There is always tension between the way society is and the possibilities of what it could be. So, while today's Disney defines the future as having 11 digital picture frames above the mantle, and the window walls of Dewey's schools have been replaced with slits that block outside views, a growing group of North Americans are choosing to build mobile "tiny houses" and furniture megastore IKEA lets its potential customers tour 400-square-foot apartments constructed around gourmet kitchens. The microwave is much less important to our rising generations than dual convection ovens. Work laptops remain in the backpack while home entertainment – and work at home – is mostly done on our phones. The educational equivalent comes in "democratic schools" and the "unschooling" movement – true education change in the spirit of the Summerhill School and writers from John Dewey to John Holt.

Radical change engulfs our planet, and while some see their moment of liberation, others (including most institutional structures) shift into resistance mode. In some ways this resistance makes sense. With so much change, we seem to recoil from too much more. Even digital books threaten memory, real or imagined – curled up by a mythical fireplace, the smells of old paper and new ink mingling, the nuclear family awaiting the dinner that mom prepares. However, if the countercyclical approach Neil Postman and Charlie Weingartner discuss in the seminal education read of 1969, *Teaching as a Subversive Activity*, makes sense, then now is the time to dream our biggest dreams because technologies and global relationships can make them possible.

The Countercyclical Narrative: Getting Past Incremental Change

We often wonder about the purpose of education as it has been – an institution charged with transmitting the values of a dominant society – and the possibilities that Postman and Weingartner envisioned that "schools should stress values that are not stressed by other major institutions in the culture" (Postman and Weingartner 1969). This countercyclical trajectory of thought pushes us to consider, if we were constructing an educational World's Fair for this century, how might it showcase what's impossible for most to envision as the futuristic learning spaces, technologies, and culture of learning that our children and their children will need and want?

Even many parents, unable to break out of the zones of what they have known, want little more than the schools of their own youth. That's certainly true of the cab driver who shared his story with Pam one evening. Born and educated in the most rigid of Ivory Coast schools, he describes to her spending hours each night as a student memorizing homework to avoid the "teacher's stick on his back." Yet in his narrative, he makes it okay to get that same homework load for his own six-year-old child enrolled in a charter school, even as he worries about his son having no time to play. It's also true of the university professor in Virginia who believes that it benefits his 16-year-old to take as many advanced placement courses as possible, despite the filling of every waking hour with excessive homework and even though research shows that more homework doesn't equal better learning – or even better test scores (Dell'Antonia 2014).

Educators may tinker within the system, even alter the structures a bit, but when you walk into the schools of today, they in general do not represent any significant transformation towards an imaginative future. Rather, it seems that the more society reveres educational change, the more schools seem to stay the same. Educational structures that bind education so tightly to the values stressed as important to major institutions and society often limit potential to envision schooling as never before dreamed possible. To counter the urge to sustain the status quo in schools, we ask all the time, "How do schools change society?" If communities believe that renewal of the existing social contract with educators will get our young people the education they need in this century, then schools must lead the way.

In truth, our educational dreams today are insufficiently transformative. After all, despite all the money thrown by Gates, Zuckerberg, and others at public education, they have never risked creating a true Bell Laboratory for education, a gathering space where our profession's most invention-minded educators might come together and dream schooling as never before considered possible. That kind of space – where education's best idea generators, designers, builders, engineers, and makers can collaborate and challenge everything – might be our nation's best investment, – but it would also be our biggest threat to the status quo – the status quo of schooling, and thus the status quo of our sociocultural and economic environments.

Creating a Contagion of Creativity

Our visits to the World Maker Faire and the New York Hall of Science have led us to ask "What is the Futurama of learning?" We wonder, what if the most interesting minds in the world of education came together and were challenged as Bell Labs engineers were one morning in 1951 to imagine that the entire telephone system of the United States had collapsed during the night (Coupland 2014)? We love the story of what those engineers began to do when they were told to build a new system from scratch. And, how those Bell Labs engineers collaborated to imagine communication devices now commonplace in our pockets today (Knowledge@Wharton 2006).

What if we were creating an educational World's Fair? The educational version of the 1951 Bell Labs? Or Lockheed Martin's Advanced Development Projects, also known as the Skunk Works (Lockheed Martin n.d.)? What if we were not just imagining different versions of cells and bells schooling?

Or evolved technologies that still support the dominant teaching wall? What if reform wasn't sitting at desks in rows simultaneously hitting the keyboard to complete screensheets as a substitute for worksheets? What makes the evolution of testing that iterates pencil and paper to online versions any more innovative than a twentieth-century version of efficient administration? And even if big data applications for sorting and selecting kids into groups based on age, reading levels, or grades is more efficient, how is that better for kids now than in 2002?

What if instead of continuous improvement of the same old school models, we chose to create a space that promoted a contagion of educational creativity? Maybe, just maybe, we'd invent as did those who created a new telephone system inside the 1951 Bell Laboratories, or helped engineer NASA's 1961 startup to land a man on the moon within the decade, or the World's Fair Futurama II exhibition of 1963.

We hear all the time that we are teaching kids who will enter jobs that haven't been invented yet. If the schools they attend today are still preparing them for a future that represents the past, what do we do to change that? Where do we look for educational designers, inventors, engineers, and builders? And, how do we accomplish the level of exponential change needed in the context of the educational needs of a few hundred students in a regular elementary school in Iowa or several thousand in a comprehensive school district in Virginia or over 51 million public school learners in America?

We believe educators must do exactly what Bell, GE, Lockheed Martin, and NASA did when they took on the grand challenge to invent something that didn't exist. Look inside the organization and find and protect people who have a creative quotient that is off the scale. Build school laboratories where creative teams know the leaders have their back and they are charged to leverage the resources of the organization to create prototypes that begin in the future, not the present or the past. Think like the best inventors who ever existed because they didn't work to build the next dead reckoning step but to build beyond a horizon that can't be seen. Why not begin building ideas beyond the edges of the universe? Our profession is filled with history's stories of pathfinders and wayfarers who have done just that. Why not educators, too?

Teaching as a Subversive Activity Made Real

The city, New Rochelle, in which Ira lived had an antique alternative school in a nineteenth-century building near the downtown. Political powers, in the wake of a 1961 federal court–ordered desegregation (*Taylor v. Board of Ed. of City Sch. Dist. of New Rochelle*, 195 F. Supp. 231 [S.D.N.Y. 1961]) and a difficult teachers' strike, had handed that alternative school over to a middle school English teacher, Alan Shapiro, and his intellectual partners Neil Postman and Charlie Weingartner, who in 1969 had just published *Teaching as a Subversive Activity*. The three reconceived the alternative school, based in the idea that there'd be a mix of typical "alternative school kids" and other students who simply rejected "regular school" learning.

Nothing was required at Ira's alternative high school, except that students had to take the series of New York State Regents exams required then, and they had a certain number of credits to accumulate. They didn't have to go to class. Ira took one class in his entire time there, and that was called Monday Morning Quarterback, which he claims was a math class because students dealt in statistics and bet on the next week's football games. But some people did take classes. People did group projects or individual projects. The other class he "sort of" dropped into was called Abnormal Psych. The teacher would drop students off at Grand Central Station around 10:00 at night and pick them up at 3:00 in the morning. The whole goal was to interview homeless people living there. That was a class he doesn't remember getting credited on his transcript but that he recalls as one of the most important learning experiences in his life. It is important to understand that Ira's experience was just one possibility. Other students used classes and independent study to graduate in just a year and a half. Still others did most of their learning through internships – in the hospital, in the parks department greenhouse, building a heritage teaching farm in a city park, or working with local businesses.

The whole point was to help students find their learning preferences and their learning environment match. Ira, with teacher Alan Shapiro's support, found a way to get through English at first by bypassing Ira's dyslexia with an internship overseen by the late-night news guy at a little AM radio station. They would ride together from 10:00 p.m. to 2:00 a.m. a couple of nights a week. Ira learned to interview and edit and write verbally. It was an incredible experience, and a year later Ira was editing the weekly student newspaper.

With a friend, Ira spent a couple of afternoons each week for a year going to work in city hall in the development office. He received a civics credit working on downtown redevelopment. That friend is now the world's leading expert on the preservation of ancient stone architecture. Another friend, a classmate in the Monday Morning Quarterback class, has lived her life as a sports statistician for newspapers.

The range of things that people did in this 1970s alternative high school, one of many that emerged in response to the cultural shockwaves of the 1960s, is as remarkable as the diversity of the lives opened by that school experience. Alumni are important lawyers and journalists, architects and top-level programmers, artists and union organizers, professors and teachers. And yet, many could have easily been dropouts.

That school sat within a very large urban high school just north of New York City. Students came with a wide range of risk factors, yet had a 99% graduation rate over 18 years, and a 95% four-year college attendance rate. It was eliminated along with many other innovative high schools in the first George H. W. Bush administration when Diane Ravitch was a conservative educator in the US Department of Education and most of the 1960s–1970s alternative schools didn't meet expectations for public education coming out of the 1989 Governors' Summit that had been held in Charlottesville, Virginia.

What students could do at Ira's high school was strongly supported by their proximity to New York City border. All kids from his community had to do was jump a subway turnstile to get to anything, any resource they needed in the world. But in rural communities of that era no one had a shot at that kind of experiential learning in a built environment with multiple paths to learning.

Today, however, is very different. Now because of the Internet and its connectivity kids can find experts for whatever they need to do, and they can learn to interact with expert resources – museums, agencies, and research sources spanning the globe.

Kids in our schools today initiate projects all the time that demand connectivity with expertise outside our community. For example, eighth-grade girls watched a YouTube video about a high-altitude balloon and decided they wanted to put one up as well. They worked with the teacher and recruited a team of eighth graders who planned and actually pulled off a high-altitude balloon launch. It was a remarkable bit of engineering, math, and science. It was also language arts, geography, and civics. After the launch, the balloon vanished. The transponder stopped working right after the launch. One of our tech integrators who along with a science teacher were the adults supporting the middle schoolers said, "It was great because at least they didn't get depressed." They spent, he said, both in person and then online, the rest of that weekend figuring out what had gone wrong and what they would need to do differently next time. They had launched the balloon on a Saturday and the transponder had been silent all weekend. Then on Tuesday, they got a signal from it. It had landed in a tree on a farm almost exactly where they predicted it would land.

School was over at this point, but for the kids that didn't matter. They were all immediately on their phones working out how to get together and carpool out to the farm to recover the balloon. They climbed the tree and shook down the remains of the balloon. When they played footage recorded by the GoPro camera used to document the balloon's journey, they were over the top with enthusiasm. That's what school doesn't often do: It doesn't excite kids. And when there is no excitement there is no deep learning, no in-depth understanding, and no transfer of knowledge to other realms.

We get frustrated when people think they can't make changes in schooling experiences that would excite and empower kids as learners because of outside constraints. Yet to be empowered and excited about learning is truly the essence of transformation. What do we say to people who feel that change seems impossible? We tell them they have to take risks, or as the Nike commercial says, "Just do it." Explorer educators and learners in schools have to be willing to ride out the initial resistance that comes their way from doing something radical. Leaders have to validate that invention work by teachers isn't just okay but desired. And they must champion radical change. Teachers who push past the boundaries of what's possible often do so because they know the principal has their back. In turn, principals also have to know that central leaders from the superintendent on down have their back when they are creating a culture of change and supporting teachers and students to take risks.

Each learner gets one year to be age 5 or 11 or 18, and the years spent in school actually pass quickly. The imperative to create a contagion of creativity in our system occurs in a very focused way because of children. By creating spaces and times where educators become inventors and innovators, their work becomes the initial and most critical phase of change that leads to strategic, and ultimately operational, work that impacts the organizational culture. That plays out in the voices of young people when they share their own contagion for learning.

For example, when a senior in high school shares his passion for metallurgy and how he's used a YouTube video to guide building his own metal foundry, the learning power he exhibits is remarkable. His own sense of agency comes from opportunities to pursue his own interests, sustained by his own curiosity, and supported by educators who believe in facilitating access to the tools he needs to accomplish his goals.

Our *Futurama*: The Learning Laboratory

If there's one takeaway from our work to envision the impossible into the possible, it is to never be secretive about the changes we are making – and key in that is how to make operational the concept of learner and educator empowerment. We never want the first way for people to hear about a change to be from an angry parent. We have to be transparent and say, "This is what we're doing." Be very public. When people try to do this work under the radar, and then word spreads, the change gets killed. We say to teachers, "When you're doing something inventive in your classroom, send out a message to the parents that says, 'We'll be broadcasting live at ___ time – and you can watch it or watch my tweets about our kids' work.'" Parents may be at work or home but they'll see their kid engaged in challenging work and say, "That's my kid." We want our parents to participate in our invent-and-design work, and that's why we invite them in to join us in learning how to design, make, engineer, and create.

Our summer programs now serve as prototyping laboratories, mini-Bell Labs, and Skunk Works–style spaces – where kids and teachers together make sense of new technologies, teaching practices, and strategies, and then debrief their work together. It's where we can test-bed ideas such as how to help kids learn to enable their own access to complex knowledge they need for project work that otherwise would be inaccessible to them in traditional print forms. It's where both multiage and multigenerational colearning has helped us figure out how parents might participate in creation work along with their children. It's where we are still figuring out how to create contexts of empowerment in which the role of the teacher shifts from being the owner of what work occurs to being a partner alongside learners in cocreating the work. We know this is happening when we walk in and it's difficult to find the teacher in the room but the kids are all active, working with a seriousness and playfulness that reminds us little of school.

When we observe in these prototyping labs, students are just immersed in the learning. They pay little to no attention to adults who may visit or even work in the spaces alongside them. This is perfect. In one such visit, a little guy shared with Pam, "I want to show you what I just did. I'm doing this work with Sonic Pi." Pam had no clue what Sonic Pi was. When she asked him to tell her about it, he looked at her as if she's from outer space and sighed, "Well, you use it to write music."

This young elementary learner was a violinist and had brought his violin book and violin to the summer program. He had just begun coding using Sonic Pi and had figured out how to play back music that he had learned on his violin. His screen was filled with script, and as he demoed his work, the Bach Gavotte in G Minor that he'd programmed played from his PC. His next challenge? He was getting started on Humoresque, his sheet music open in front of him. The room was full of kids who were working on different music projects – and they weren't there because they were assigned to be in the room but because it was where they wanted to work. Their projects were selected by them, not by a teacher for them. They represented diversity of poverty, gender, race, and ethnicity.

Each prototyping laboratory functions with a cadre of master teachers, the learning engineers of our work. Alongside them work teachers who are developing practices such as maker-infused or project learning, how to use cutting edge tech tools, or coteaching in multiage spaces. They work together, observing learners, figuring out how to better utilize space, and innovating learning opportunities with new and old tools.

Equity and access are taken for granted in summer laboratory spaces. Classroom management also is nonexistent because kids work as they never do in the timebound, content-driven schedules of school. We often bandy around the term *engagement*, but what's occurring in our spaces where kids work on entirely different projects is what we now label as *empowerment*.

As we figure out what empowerment can really mean operationally, we note that education structures limit kids' own learning inputs, and that bothers us. Pam's interaction with the young musician using Sonic Pi reminds us of that. Consider, for example, what audio technologies accomplish differently as a sensory experience than the visual inputs that teachers rely upon as the dominant tools of their craft. After all, traditions of print literacy drive instruction in every content area and form the basis for constructing the tests that both teachers make and those that are manufactured by the testing industry to mass measure student's proficiency. This leads us to question of what is being measured by most achievement tests. Is math performance more a function of print literacy or mathematical thinking capability? Is the regurgitation of science content on a test more about a learner's understanding of science concepts or reading level? What about memorizing historical facts and responding to essay questions in print form only? To what degree is learning held in thrall by our obsession with print literacy?

Ira challenged Pam three summers ago (since Pam's a really facile reader and he is not, in terms of print processing) to push herself to "listen read" rather than visually read. He said to her one day when they were visiting schools, "Have you ever really spent much time listening to print?"

Reading print is no longer an exclusive definition of literacy in a time when so many different technologies for information input exist. However, success still gets defined in school through a very traditional literacy lens even though humans begin life as listeners – which is a critical, if not the most critical, input skill for building relationships and learning with others. Yet, children coming to kindergarten in today's public schools spend much of their first few years focused on alphabet soup. That doesn't happen in every culture – for example, in Finland children don't begin to formally learn to read until age seven (Erbentraut 2015). Still, we've chosen in America to define the alphabet as the most important cognitive work kids do early in school – and most of that is decoding phonemes in print as a prerequisite to reading words.

As a result of Ira's challenge to her, Pam decided to mostly just listen to audio inputs all summer. She experienced a real struggle switching to a different sensory input, and that led her to consider the experiences of kids who come to school as auditory learners where everything they are expected to do becomes so print focused that their listening strengths become a deficit in the biased view of some teachers. A key question emerged from her reflections on her listening experiences: *How do the constructs of schooling, such as the Gutenberg "write, print, read, recall" model of learning get challenged if we don't have laboratories where educators can challenge and deconstruct the norm and create new constructs from scratch?*

It was a fascinating experience for Pam after that immersive summer audio experience to realize that she actually became much better at listening as a result of listening. She's also become a supporter of a Universal Design for Learning (UDL) pathway to accessibility tools and resources for all kids. We've redefined UDL as a path available to all learners and not as just a special accommodation – a somewhat negative term that says if you need this then you need extra help that others don't. That's not true. Everyone needs access to a variety of tools, and in this day and age, a print book is no better or worse than an audio book. That's a value judgment educators make, but action research in our learning laboratories helps us challenge those value judgments.

Our learning laboratories help us figure out how to take new ideas from the technological, pedagogical, and neuroscience buckets and blend those to create new ways of connecting learning and learners. Just as the old Bell Labs engineers of the early 1950s were challenged to create new communication systems, we challenge our educators in our laboratories to be learning engineers. They become observers, researchers, inventors, and experimenters and turn what they learn into learning spaces that look nothing like school. And they do this not for just certain demographics of learners or in certain schools or in certain geographic regions. And, when our staff visit other learning laboratories such as the Chicago Children's Museum, the San Francisco Exploratorium, or the New York Hall of Science, they bring back ideas for their own laboratory work, virtual reality studios, vision projects, podcast studios, and more.

When we watch kids in summer learning laboratories, often different versions of makerspaces, we see parents coming in to drop off or pick up children and they sometimes end up observing or even participating with the children. For example, we met a mother who came in last summer with her older child but she also had brought her three-year-old into the laboratory space. He wasn't intimidated by the older kids or what they were doing at all. He just sat on a couch munching on Cheerios and had on his headphones with his own tablet while his brother worked on a Scratch coding project. One of the teachers was working with his older brother, and they were trying to project his code onto a large screen. Another little kid, maybe seven years old, was sitting in front of the projection screen. He was just mesmerized watching this older kid work with the teacher. The mother was taking all of the learning scene in. This multigenerational learning narrative that unfolded there wasn't just an amazing experience. It was nothing like school. The teacher was testing out not just informal strategies for integrating computational thinking across the curricula but also how to support learners in a multiage environment.

Making sense of the complex challenges inherent in changing practices is not easy and not everyone can take on this work. That's the beauty of building a Futurama experience with our educational explorers. We take what some think is impossible to do in public schools and figure out in summer laboratories how to make innovative ideas work before we move them forward into the regular school year.

Challenging the Norm

We see one of the major challenges to envisioning how learning experiences today can be more responsive to a future that is only barely imaginable is that structurally there isn't much in the traditions of schooling that we believe is worth saving. For example, kids are expected to still write a lot in school – but kids don't learn to enjoy or use writing with the power of personal agency.

People don't generally grow up to become writers because of a teacher's interest in five-paragraph essays.

They become writers because something has inspired them, angered them, or they find something they want to change, something they need – there's some reason they need to express themselves. Something happens inside their mind and their hearts, and they recognize that they can get that out on metaphorical paper. Among teens today, maybe they express their voices in a personal blog or another digital platform such as a YouTube channel. Either way, they bring their voices into existence with an audience, and most often that's independent of school writing. And often, their most committed learning happens in the context of what they do outside of school, unless we ritualize those kinds of experiences as being of value.

However, as a result of our work, we see experiential learning all over our district that provides young people with choices, opportunities, and paths to create. Children are driven to create and to share but, sadly, schools drive that out of them pretty quickly unless they land with a teacher who tries to keep creative sparks alive. We want experiential learning grounded in the curiosity and interests of learners to be integral to our systems work, not something that happens randomly in an occasional teacher's class.

"I sat through a meeting about these sixth grade boys who just couldn't 'get' math," the superintendent of a tiny Michigan school district once told us, "but then, driving home, I saw those very boys laying out the foundation for a building on a farm. And I thought, someone is failing, but it is not these boys."

Our work to challenge the norm of schooling has emerged in our own version of a process of idealized design we now see occurring more systematically among educators and students (Gabriel 2011). Consider a tenth grader who, tired of waking up too early to do rural home chores, built an Arduino-controlled hen house in one of our Mechatronics Labs. He had failed the state's algebra test before, but that lack of book math success didn't stop either his physical engineering or his computer engineering. His needs provided the intrinsic motivation that we hope to build in all learners.

"That's the essence of 'maker,'" Chad says.

> The child creates the context – hen house, bear hunt, phone app – it is their world driving their education. It's then our job to put our content into their context. To let them know they are using geometry and algebra and physics when they build that hen house, or words and sentences and paragraphs when they write that story. It is our job to start with their world and build the bridges to our content, to our program.

Scanning those classrooms and the conversations happening within them, you might realize that you can teach in any class, really any content area, and the class can be so radically different – depending on who's teaching the class and the educational experiences they're trying to design within them. You can create – so a teacher can take a government class and inspire a cadre of social change makers, which Chad's government teacher did with him. He didn't know that he was a change maker, but she created experiences in which he was inspired to become one. She could have put Chad in rows and made sure he wrote the paper that he was supposed to write, and had the facts that he was supposed to know. But she didn't. She inspired all learners to think about society and politics and government in the context that mattered to them – to think about ways in which they might be inspired and empowered to make changes when they find problems in government or their community.

Teachers can do that in math. Teachers can do that in English language arts and literature – what a vehicle for empowering learners! They can talk about those ideas that over the course of human history have shaped civilization. They know the power of the pen is mightier than the sword. Yet teachers seldom empower learners to actually utilize those ideas in school because they don't want them to. That's because schools were designed for compliance, not for pushing back at the system.

Making is not a new word. We don't think it's a flash in the pan at all. There are societal changes that now enable educators to leverage making as a tool – or as a philosophy inside compulsory education that we can leverage as a pathway toward a progressive education model. When people say, "Well, we all shouldn't be makers," we ask, "How do you define making?" Should everybody need to know how to use a 3D printer? We don't think so. Should everybody need to know how to come up with their own ideas, and then know how to learn what they need to know about those ideas, and how then to make those ideas real, and introduce them into society in some authentic way, whatever is meaningful to the individual? Then yes, yes. Every learner should learn to do that – and they shouldn't only have their one cool government teacher to do that. We have years of iterative experiences through which we are working to do that. We are pushing back at nurturing the compliance that America's present-day schools are built upon.

How do we change society? How do we change the industrial model for schools? It's really all about politics and philosophy. It's quite simple. There are two forms of education that emerged in the last century. There's one for compliance, and there's one for empowerment. Our current system is designed to make compliant the people we don't want to be empowered. We have rejected that system in our work with colleagues to create spaces for invention and innovation that lead to young people doing work that doesn't look anything like the kind of work specified in the mass standardization movement of the past century.

Despite the continued dominance of the standardization movement well into the first quarter of this century, we believe the answer is "Yes" to the question of whether our nation's model of schooling can change.

We believe it can, but only when the education sector embraces the discomfort of Bell Labs–like learning laboratories in which no tradition, structure, or procedure is held sacred and radical invention is valued as essential to creating a sufficiently transformative trajectory of change. We find that trajectory in our schools today in spaces where teachers take the risk to encourage our young people to do anything that creates a spirit of inquiry – from setting up, maintaining, and studying hives of bees to designing clothes inside a virtual reality environment – even if neither is prescribed in standards or on the state's multiple choice accountability measures.

Your Own Learning

Provocation

"I get frustrated by people who think they can't change. What do you say to people who feel that way? They just see change as impossible. Yet, all you have to do is do it." Ira believes that change is only limited by the capability of people to see possibilities. He has pushed educators outside of their schools to visit and observe in a variety of other settings, from Maker Faires to indoor climbing walls. Because we educators form our perspectives from inside school, it's difficult to get past our confirmation biases. We filter our field of vision so that we don't even see what isn't working because we believe that it is. We reject challenges to our system of thinking about schooling. We can't admit that education needs a radical overhaul, not just tinkering with charters or magnet schools but rather essential, deep changes to transform education into all things future. We struggle to do that because our mental model for schools is ingrained into who we are, what we value and believe, and how we behave as educators. Confirmation bias forces us to reject data and information that challenges our conceptions and to resonate with data and information that reinforces what we already believe, or as Ed Hess describes it:

> Because our minds are fast, efficient seekers and processors of validating and confirming information, we tend to be confirmation-biased learners. Moreover, we have a strong, ego-defense system that defends and protects our existing views of ourselves. As another backup, if we do happen to process information that "disagrees" with our mental models, we are likely to rationalize that information to make it fit with what we already know – a

phenomenon called "cognitive dissonance." That is our "human-ness." (Hess 2014)

Imagine walking into a room in the early morning filled with educators and being told that the system of education in America had failed. You and the team in the room are charged to imme-diately begin building a new system from scratch. You won't be able to leave even if it takes months to do so. You are told that a zero-based process will be used by team members to question, imagine, describe, consider, and challenge all assumptions and biases about learning and to generate design solutions. Zero-based design means you start with nothing that exists today in schools, from bricks and mortar to schedules to staffing to curricula. If you can't build from what you know as school, how do you start?

Consider launching into your Isearch journal (in the cloud or on paper) to write down your thinking about your own potential confirmation biases regarding schools. What do you believe and value about schooling as it has existed in your own life – for you and even for your children? Why?

Structured Inquiry

What do you do when you don't know what to do? That ques-tion is one we ask ourselves routinely when we are faced with the question of what we do to educate children in schools today for an adult life tomorrow. Significant numbers of jobs will be elimi-nated as a result of automation and artificial intelligence. We've seen the emergence of the smartphone, smart cars, smart watches, smart thermostats and so on. The cashiers who once waited on us to check out in our grocery stores are being eliminated. Driver-less taxi vehicles are being tested in Pittsburgh. Articles written by computer algorithms now appear in magazines such as Forbes. Bricklaying robots labor away on buildings in Australia. What does this mean for our homes, communities, and workforces? What will the world be like in 2030? 2050? 2100?

How will children who are in schools today be prepared to live and work in such a world?

In what ways must educational systems change to ensure that children are prepared for a future in which we can't begin to anticipate how the workforce will change?

What competencies will most likely be in demand in the workforces of our children's future?

Reflective Pause

Despite the commonly espoused notion that a key purpose of public schooling is to perpetuate democracy, the model is the least democratic – aside from prison or perhaps the most labor-abusive employers – institution in America today. Schools still represent a hierarchical concentration of power and authoritarianism that is accepted for our nation's children but would be unacceptable – abhorrent – conditions for any adult. According to Chad, "schools were designed for compliance. *Just consider the simple need to go to the bathroom and the rules we have for children to do so.*"

In what ways do we design schools for compliance? How does compliance-based learning impact students? Teachers? What are the short-term and long-term effects of compliance-based schooling?

What impedes us from breaking norms of compliance-driven schooling? How might you begin to break compliance-based norms in your school(s)?

Take Action

According to Yusef Waghad in *Pedagogy Out of Bounds: Untamed Variations of Democratic Education*:

> Democratic education is an educational ideal in which democracy is both a goal and a method of instruction. It brings democratic values to education and can include self-determination within a community of equals, as well as such values as justice, respect and trust. Democratic education is often specifically emancipatory, with the students' voices being equal to the teacher's. (Waghid 2014)

   To question the authority of traditional hierarchies and normative practices means that you must take the time to build a map of the classroom, school, or district and its current operational structures and processes. You can begin to question norms by observing, asking, questions, and engaging in discussions with colleagues and learners at every level of your work.

Four Actions to Break Norms of Public Education

1. Assess your class or school or district rules for learners. Do this by talking to teachers and learners of every age. Ask them to talk about rules that impact them – bathroom rules, classwork rules, test rules, dress code rules, technology use rules, talking rules, hallway rules. Look for other signs of authoritarianism or division of power in your school such as how teachers are addressed (Mr./Mrs. or first name or last name without Mr./Mrs.) and signage across building (No Students Allowed; Teachers Only). Are your walls covered in rules and reminders of compliance and power structures, or are they reflective of an environment that students – current students – are empowered and have control?
2. Collect information about talk among teachers and learners. How much time do you estimate kids talk as compared to teachers in your room, your school, your district? What do kids talk about? To what degree is talk teacher directed? What does "who's talking" tell you about the democratic education in your class, school, school district? How do young people get a message their voices matter to educators?
3. Research the concept of learning agency and dig deep into noncommercial sources to determine what this means philosophically and looks like in action (CORE Education 2014). Find what you consider to be radical examples of this concept. What does it mean to you for young people to have a sense of agency? How do learners begin to develop agency in their own learning? What is the role of the teacher in

setting the stage for children to have a sense of ownership in and power over their learning? How might they get
choices of where to work, what projects they want to work
on, how they show their work to authentic audiences and
to teachers, what they want to make? How do they participate in and lead conferences with teachers and their parents
to share their own perspectives on their work and growth
as learners?

4. Start courageous conversations by taking action to engage
colleagues in questions about compliance-based vs. democratic education. Contrast values that each approach
teaches implicitly and explicitly to children. What values
most align with life readiness for adulthood?

Resources

Alter, Lloyd. 2008. "Disney's New Dream Home: Worse Than We
Dreamed." TreeHugger. 14 February. https://www.treehugger.com/
sustainable-product-design/disneys-new-dream-home-worse-than-
we-dreamed.html.

CORE Education. 2014. "Learner Agency." Accessed 17 September
2017. http://www.core-ed.org/research-and-innovation/ten-trends/
2014/learner-agency.

Coupland, Douglas. 2014. "The Ghost of Invention: A Visit to Bell
Labs." *Wired*. 24 September. https://www.wired.com/2014/09/
coupland-bell-labs/.

Dell'Antonia, KJ. 2014. "Homework's Emotional Toll on Students
and Families." *New York Times*. 12 March. https://parenting.blogs.
nytimes.com/2014/03/12/homeworks-emotional-toll-on-students-
and-families/.

Erbentraut, Joseph. 2015. "Finnish Kids Don't Learn to Read in
Kindergarten. They Turn Out Great Anyway." HuffPost. 5 October.
https://www.huffingtonpost.com/entry/finland-schools-kinder
garten-literacy_us_560ece14e4b0af3706e0a60c.

Gabriel. 2011. "Ackoff's Stages of Idealized Design – a Powerful Tool
for School Designers." School for REAL: A School Design Blog. 15
March.   https://schoolforreal.wordpress.com/2011/03/15/ackoffs-
stages-of-idealized-design-a-powerful-tool-for-school-designers/.

Herman, John. "Welcome to a Journey into the Future." n.d. Phrenicia. Accessed 17 September. http://www.phrenicea.com/futurama_chip .htm.

Hess, Edward. 2014. *Learn or Die: Using Science to Build a Leading-Edge Learning Organization.* New York: Columbia University Press.

Knowledge@Wharton. 2006. "Idealized Design: How Bell Labs Imagined – and Created – the Telephone System of the Future." 9 August. http://knowledge.wharton.upenn.edu/article/idealized-design-how-bell-labs-imagined-and-created-the-telephone-system-of-the-future/.

Lockheed Martin. n.d. "Skunk Works." Accessed 17 September 2017. http://www.lockheedmartin.com/us/aeronautics/skunkworks.html.

New York World's Fair 1964/1965. n.d. "General Motors, Gallery II: *Scenes of Futurama II.*" n.d. Accessed 17 September 2017. http://www.nywf64.com/gm06.shtml.

Postman, Neil, and Charles Weingartner. 1969. *Teaching as a Subversive Activity.* New York: Dell.

Reed, Sally. 1981. "Whatever Happened to Alternative Schools?" *New York Times.* 15 November. http://www.nytimes.com/1981/11/15/education/whatever-happened-to-alternative-schools.html.

Restad, Penne. 1995. *Christmas in America: A History.* New York: Oxford.

Socol, Ira David. 2008. "Insufficiently Transformative." SpeEdchange. 11 December. http://speedchange.blogspot.com/2008/12/insufficiently-transformative.html.

Waghid, Yusef. 2014. *Pedagogy Out of Bounds: Untamed Variations of Democratic Education.* Rotterdam: Sense.

Wallenstein, Joanne. n.d. "The Heathcote School: Progressive Design for Now and Then." Scarsdale10583. Accessed 17 November 2017. http://scarsdale10583.com/about-joomla/local-finds/4742-the-heathcote-school-progressive-design-for-now-and-then.

6

Learning Ready for Today's Real World

IRA: I watched Michigan go through the Third Industrial Revolution. Factories filled with middle-class workers turned into robotic assembly lines. Parts manufacturers crumbled as shipping technology opened the global labor markets. People had built their lives and their assumptions about what preparation for life meant – built over four or five generations – based on the need for humans to weld and stamp, drill and bolt, and then it was just . . . all gone.

PAM: Ira, I think that school leaders must ask themselves when they consider the kind of changes you saw and that are still unfolding, what do those changes mean for the kids we are educating today – for their future as adults? How can we even begin to prepare them? We worry about the forecasts of the loss of millions of jobs as technology automates everything from restaurant services to technical medical work. What will be left for our children and children's children to do?

CHAD: The definition of school as mostly about learning content is obsolete, and kids know it. They know it in deep ways we didn't. We knew we were bored but there was some idea that this was preparation for life. Today's youth question that conventional wisdom. Unlike

many educators – adults in general – their knowledge
and exposure to ideas, for better or worse, expands
beyond the books we may have had in our living rooms,
or inside the heads of family, friends, or neighbors.
Perhaps they are no more curious than we were, but
their access to information, networks, and power has
no boundaries. Their voice can be amplified in ways
we could never have imagined. How might school's
today be reconceptualized to leverage the resources we
have – especially time, networks, relationships, and the
ability to democratize access to tools of creative
production – to develop a healthy sense of self, community, and positive social impact? I see the tension in sustaining our sense of humanity even as smart machines
take over more and more of the bandwidth of work,
community, and home as the fundamental problem at
hand. Control over technology is power. Otherwise, we
are controlled by it.

The Time Before Today

The world is experiencing a rapid shift in the work that machines
can do well, work that once could only be accomplished by
humans. Tasks such as article writing, bricklaying, package delivery, and driving anything now are in striking distance of ubiquitous smart machine takeover. Every day the three of us attend to
news stories that emerge in mainstream and social media about
advances of technology. In sharing these stories with each other,
we've said over and over again, "Wow, this is moving faster than
we ever imagined!"

The skills for the jobs Ira watched disappear over decades in Michigan, the skills for most twentieth-century jobs –
showing up on time for your shift, persistence in boring work,
ability to precisely follow directions – those were important work
skills embedded in Michigan schools, in schools everywhere in
the twentieth century. Those early comprehensive schools themselves once were conceptualized as innovative designs essential

to building the nation's workforce and reinforcing a shift to work norms and skills essential to urbanization and industrialization of communities across America.

But suddenly in the 1990s those work norms and skills didn't matter. There were no shifts to be on time for – you had to design the car with teams in Europe and Japan, across time zones. There were no assembly lines to be bored on – just robots to program, there were very few precise instructions – and if there were, they were on videos or in online manuals. Now there was a demand for problem solving, code writing, global collaboration. And so there were not just fewer jobs for humans to do but the jobs that did remain became out of reach for both workers and graduates as the nation and world turned the calendar page from 1999 to 2000 and the pace of technological automation accelerated (Fitzgerald 2017).

Saying Goodbye to the Twentieth Century

No sector has more responsibility than education to help our nation successfully negotiate a path forward as technological impacts accelerate in this century. However, the school models set up by Stanford University's Ellwood Cubberley in the early 1900s and that politicians double-downed on in later educational reforms have changed little in response to changes outside of schools. Many schools today, in reality, still operate using the Second Industrial Revolution model that Cubberley envisioned to educate young learners for adulthood in 1910 (Callahan 1964). And, even as other sectors, both nonprofit and for profit, recognize the need to educate learners entering today's real world for rapid transitions occurring in the workforce, community life, and home environments, most schools remain a long way away from the schools they must become to serve learners well in this century.

This disconnect between what occurs inside schools and the real world outside schools has become a drumbeat of national conversations about the educational transformation that must occur to ensure young people are learning ready for today's real world. Almost two decades into the twenty-first century, many recognize nothing has become more of an imperative than solving challenges that the rising Smart Machine Age portends as we face catastrophic loss of jobs across all sectors (Rotman 2017).

Our work has been to support school communities to move beyond the horizon of schools of yesterday and become the leading edge of imagining, inventing, and ultimately transforming learning for today's real world. To move schools out of the twentieth century, we've sought to provoke new solutions to educational challenges we could not have conceptualized in schools in 1999. To that end, we keep returning to a question we see as critical to educating children in our schools right now:

How will the children born into this century learn what they need to not just survive but thrive in a world defined by accelerating technologies?

In our ongoing conversations with Ed Hess, UVA Darden School of Management professor and author of *Learn or Die* and many other books, he often says that humans still can outcompete machines right now through our creativity, critical thinking, generation of new ideas and innovations, and emotional intelligence. As to other skills – crunching and analyzing big data, analytical writing, repetitive tasks of all kinds – well, machines are learning at a rapid pace how to do work that, just 10 years ago, the typical person on the street would have never imagined possible.

For example, in 2015 media first reported that Uber had created a 10-year plan to utilize fleets of driverless cars. It didn't take long for the company to roll out the first pilot in Pittsburgh and by 2016 the first selected riders were able to hail driverless Uber cars (Muoio 2016). Driverless 18-wheelers today run the roads from Colorado to Australia extending the capability of commercial drivers to work while they ride in tractor trailers driving essentially on autopilot (Chuang 2017). No matter where we turn, we see evidence of the rise of artificial intelligence from articles written by an algorithm for Forbes and ESPN to medical analytics by IBM's Watson Health Care, a twenty-first-century version of "HAL" that's able to read and process 40 million documents in 15 seconds, leading us into a "new era of cognitive health" (IBM n.d.).

These technological changes have crept up on Americans even as our communities' schools continue to exist mostly unchanged inside the bubble wrap that society creates to protect them as the transmitters of the nation's twentieth-century status quo. In many ways, when we look at the classroom images captured in school in the early 1900s, those images are almost identical in structure and operation to classrooms that still exist today. And, even as personal computing devices herald a new age for the world with clear potential to impact learners and learning, schools continue to replicate models designed and developed at the beginning of the twentieth century.

We believe that schools must quickly move beyond the content-driven curricular recommendations created in 1893 by the Committee of Ten and the school structures built by generations of educators and politicians to realize the goals of that group (Eliot, Hill, and Winship 1894). Those structures – a unification of the curricular scope and sequence of distinct disciplines, a factory-floor bell schedule, and delivery of instruction to students who have learned to wait passively for directions from the teacher – no longer make sense. These structures increasingly isolate our children on islands functioning as schools in an ocean of twenty-first-century changes.

Enter Technological Change

As the First Industrial Revolution morphed into the Second and then the Third, advances in technology and then digital technology created an accelerating economy grounded in the shift of work from tools in hands to machines and assembly lines to computers and global networks. In 1965, Intel's Gordon Moore crafted a perspective on the accelerating pace of computing power that came to be known as Moore's Law, establishing a new norm for the pace of tech development (Bell 2016). Despite the rapid pace of change in computer technologies, few attended to the potential of technology to transform schools and learning.

MIT professor Seymour Papert was one who began to explore beyond the horizon, informed by the great progressive educators of the twentieth century and the rapid pace of technology change. Just 15 years after Gordon Moore first described the exponential nature of technological change, Papert, a student of Jean Piaget, published *Mindstorms: Children, Computers and Powerful Ideas*, marrying the concept of constructivism with constructionism and created a fresh epistemology of transformative learning (Papert 1980).

Through his research and practice, Papert introduced school children to the computer language Logo and to the power of learning outside of the lockstep, teacher-determined methodology of most schools (Blikstein n.d.). Papert believed that the personal computer had the potential to provoke curiosity, unlock learning, and create new pathways for children to think deeply as they constructed knowledge, concepts, and ideas through their exploration of a technological world (Langer 2016). At the same time, he worried about the uses of technology for computer-aided instruction in schools, which he saw as no more than the "making the computer teach the child" (Papert 1980).

In his research and writing, Papert demonstrated a prescience about the impact on learning of educational accountability models established in the late twentieth century. In the nation's classrooms, he found compliance-driven learning environments that stripped curiosity, creativity, engagement, and passion-driven learning from young people as well as from the educators who taught at dominant teaching walls. By 2010, Papert's perspective became the view of many parents and educators experiencing the negative learning after-effects of children passing and failing millions of standardized tests. Foreseen by Papert, the most disastrous result of compliance-driven schooling that began with Cubberley and that was exacerbated by the No Child Left Behind Act has been that children have not thrived as creative and critical thinkers, indeed, as agents of their own learning, inside America's schools (Kaufman 2017).

In 1999, just at the turn of the century, Dan Schwartz interviewed Papert about the impact of computers in learning by children. He extrapolated in his interview notes Papert's belief that "the computer's true power as an educational medium lies – in the ability to facilitate and extend children's awesome natural ability and drive to construct, hypothesize, explore, experiment, evaluate, draw conclusions – in short to learn – all by themselves. It is this very drive, Papert contends, that is squelched by our current educational system" (Choi, Lam, and Irwin 2016).

Beyond recognition for his work as the "father of educational computing," Papert devoted a lifetime to studying what drives learners to engage and thrive, not just for the purpose of doing well in school, but, more importantly, for continuing to pursue their passions, interests, and curiosities for life. When we read Papert, we realize that his questions are our questions and ones to which we have sought answers in our practical work inside public schools to implement a progressive philosophy that harkens much farther back to John Dewey – and to this by Seymour Papert:

> I think what drives me – the deepest question about education is, what drives learning? What drives kids? What drives everybody? And when I look at young kids who haven't yet been to school, they are all driven. They are passionate about what they want to do. They get into it, and they really want to do it. I think that in a lot of people that's strangled as we go through this very traumatic, dangerous experience of school. Those who get through it can open out and find a new opportunity to be creative and free and self-directed like we had before school. So I think the question isn't what drives me, but how is it that you and I and all the people in the world who remain creative and passionate about what they're doing survived the system, that in so many other cases – in the majority of cases – strangles that enormous energy? (Choi, Lam, and Irwin 2016)

By the end of the twentieth century, computer technologies had moved into mainstream America as schools, businesses, and homes connected to the Internet, linking adults and young people to family members, friends, and colleagues while providing instant access to the world's encyclopedic and collective information database. People became 24/7 tech device users as they entered the enterprise, entertainment, and learning environments of Encarta, SimCity, and online banking. Families moved full throttle into consuming more than producing as home shop garages and hands-on hobbies were replaced with satellite television, dial up connectivity, and game controllers. As the world turned to the next century, the Information Age became a force to be reckoned with. And, nothing brought the rapid computerization of the lives of humans to the dinner table as much as the fears surrounding the turn from the twentieth to twenty-first century.

The technology world had merged with the real world.

Who over the age of 40 doesn't remember conversations about the potential Y2K crash of computer networks around the world (Rothman 2014)? As mainstream media put the power of new technologies to impact lives on the radar of lay people, gloom and doom stories of Y2K led to high alert about the predicted collision of the real and virtual world. Why? Because mass failures of the world's computing devices were imminent unless a twenty-first-century, four-digit solution could be found to solve a simple problem caused by a twentieth-century, two-digit calendar year programmed into all mainframe computers and transferred forward to the PC generation.

Technology acceleration became very real and very personal. In the aftermath of Y2K, a deeper look at a critical question emerged in schools, the business sectors, and across communities: How do we educate students for this next century? (Johnston 2001)

Back to the Future

Rather than running around declaring that the sky is falling or burying our heads in sand as some do, we are working to figure out what technological, economic, political, and societal changes mean for education in this century. We know the competencies that are likely to stand young people in good stead in 2050 aren't what we traditionally emphasize in PK–16 school curricula even today. Education reformers have tinkered for decades around the edges of content learning in their efforts to reinvent schooling, and nothing much has changed. Tinkering won't, in our opinion, get us to the education that children need to find success in 2040, 2050, or 2060. We must take more significant action to ensure children are ready for their life's journey, one that we can't imagine or bring into focus with any clarity.

Whenever new technologies appear, they are first used to simply make life-as-it-existed more efficient. This was true when the first water looms wove fabric for traditional clothing, and it was true when American homes embraced microwave ovens and videocassette recorders in the 1980s. But then it became fact that technologies change the use of the technologies, and thus change the world. The power loom changed wealth distribution, living patterns, and thus consumer demand. Henry Ford's Model T changed wealth distribution, the expectations of rural families, and thus spawned a road network that shattered old patterns of society. The personal computer, at first simply a combination adding machine and typewriter, shifted power from centralized offices to any home with a phone line, and in doing that, began to remake the entire economy.

When these secondary – and radical – changes come to homes, communities, and the workforce, educators like us are forced to consider what's essential today to educating contemporary learners well. The initial response of schools to new technologies in the 1980s and 1990s was the expected. Typing classes became keyboarding classes, and filmstrips became PowerPoints. But the appearance of these computers created significant changes in demand. "Once French language learners started reading hockey news in the Quebec City and Montreal newspapers," Ira says, "it opened a world to kids that they simply would not let be put back in the box." Similarly, 15 years later, Pam notes, "with Twitter I could not keep outside influences away from our schools. Ira and Chad – neither working with me yet – were among the many new thinkers chatting with our teachers every night, forcing change."

Those forced changes have altered everything from cognitive authority – how people know something to be true – to the tolerance for mediocre materials to the willingness to engage in passive learning. The Internet-linked computer, and the smartphones that followed, have changed demand, and we must respond.

We believe that educators of this century need to be creators – able to develop and support contextual learning opportunities that connect learners with each other through transdisciplinary experiences. Progressive curricula in this century's world must affirm the importance of *how* to learn more than *what* to learn. Rather than starting with a laundry list of specified standards tied to objectives to be measured with machine tests, we see kids as learning how to find the information and expertise they deem critical, whether on the Internet, from friends, print media, or adults. Being literate in this century is so much more than simply comprehending what one reads, listens to, or sees. Children have to learn how to determine the credibility of those around them and the reliability and trustworthiness of information shared with them. It's not just building a sense of digital, or even traditional, literacy but more importantly, human literacy.

We also find that despite the radical changes wrought by technology across the millennia, the basics of human learning persist today in children. They respond as learners when we use what we understand from today's research into how the brain works and what we understand from our own experiences as parents and educators. Image. Experience. Story. Interaction. Collaboration. Mentorship. Movement. Creation. Design. Making. Apprenticeship. These provide pathways to connect how humans learn to what we learn. How people learn naturally in communities was co-opted hundreds of years ago by those in power who viewed education as a function of their political, religious, social, and economic interests and power.

Those in power sought to control who received an education, what was important to the curricular canon to be taught, and how the structures of education would be constructed from classroom setup to strategies used by the teacher. The Committee of Ten brought the Prussian "way" to America, and it dominated the politicization and corporatization of America's schools all the way to a seminal event, the twentieth century's Presidential and Governors' Summit on Education (1989) held in Charlottesville, Virginia (Klein 2014). This gathering of governors, co-chaired by the youthful Governor Bill Clinton, responded to the "nation at risk" with a Reform Movement that culminated in the No Child Left Behind Federal Act of 2001 (Vinovskis 1999). By 2002, every state under Congressional mandates had developed standardized tests to meet the accountability requirements that those twentieth-century governors had believed would turn around what they perceived as low-quality schools in every state in the nation. Those tests set in motion a tension in America's schools that had not been felt since the days of Cubberley and Dewey (Reese 2011).

Few voices have counteracted Cubberley's drive to treat children as data points to be measured like widget production on assembly lines. One such voice that we still appreciate today is that of John Dewey, who informed a human-centric approach to education in the face of Cubberley's scientific management philosophy. Getting back to the basics of John Dewey's tenets of progressive education paid forward into the twenty-first century provides a fundamentally different frame for learning than that of the standardization movement that has dominated both the work of teachers in the PK–12 classrooms as well as the preparation programs for preservice teachers working their way through higher education to a teaching degree. He writes in an excerpt from his essay *Experience and Education*:

> Traditional education did not have to face this problem; it could systematically dodge this responsibility. The school environment of desks, blackboards, a small schoolyard, was supposed to suffice. There was no demand that the teacher should become intimately acquainted with the conditions of the local community, physical, historical, economic, occupational etc., in order to utilize them

as educational resources. A system of education based upon the necessary connection of education with experience must, on the contrary, if faithful to its principle, take these things constantly into account. This tax upon the educator is another reason why progressive education is more difficult to carry on than was ever the traditional system . . .

One reason the personal commands of the teacher so often played an undue role and a season why the order which existed was so much a matter of sheer obedience to the will of an adult was because the situation almost forced it upon the teacher. The school was not a group or community held together by participation in common activities. Consequently, the normal, proper conditions of control were lacking. Their absence was made up for, and to a considerable extent had to be made up for, by the direct intervention of the teacher, who, as the saying went, "kept order." He kept it because order was in the teacher's keeping, instead of residing in the shared work being done.

The conclusion is that in what are called the new schools, the primary source of social control resides in the very nature of the work done as a social enterprise in which all individuals have an opportunity to contribute and to which all feel a responsibility. (Dewey 1938)

So What Challenge Are We Trying to Solve?

Incremental shifts in practice are not the focus of our work. We are committed to significant transformation of the teaching and learning culture in our schools. We know from our work that for individual teachers and whole faculties to change pedagogies, they themselves must commit to learning how to learn in today's world. This means reflection, inquiry, and study in collaboration with colleagues and mentors. Provocation of thought and processing drives professional growth beyond superficial change of little magnitude to deep change that results in substantively different learning experiences for young people. We have seen this occur when professional learning opportunities shift from the normative top-down, program-driven professional development to experiential learning that gets educators out of the box we call school. When our educators come to embrace and own their own learning in a context of seeing themselves as designers, creators, and makers, it changes the game in how they approach working with learners.

As we have worked with teachers in our district to study and use more progressive approaches such as maker work or problem and project-based learning, we see a different approach to teaching young people emerge – teachers who begin with first the learners and then the learning context in mind. They map required standards of learning to context after, *not before*, they consider what they have noticed and understand about the children in their classroom. They begin with the learner by thinking with children about questions that lead them to big ideas and concepts that are important to learn. They consider how children learn first and what children might learn next. They ask these kinds of questions:

> *What's a problem we could work to solve?*
> *What's something you want to make?*
> *How might we design . . . ?*
> *Who else might be interested in this?*
> *How will you share your learning?*

We also ask teachers one other question all the time: "Rather than just planning for teaching content standards or isolated content skills, what if you designed for transdisciplinary learning where the context you create with students pulls content from multiple disciplines?" We think that when children create, think, make, explore novel ideas, engineer, build, and figure out problems in their world that are worth solving, they make meaning of their own learning and their own preferences for how they like to learn. In doing so, they develop mindfulness about when they need to work together or to work alone. This kind of learning provides a context for life readiness – as family and community members, thoughtful citizens, flexible, competent workforce members, and learners for life.

Too often educational leaders think change begins with con-juring a program to solve a content learning problem, followed by a top-down mandate to replicate it everywhere. Yet, what kills pretty much anything that will substantively transform education, whether it's using iPads or adding maker education into schools, is imposing a program on educators and learners. It is simply not pos-sible to create schools where students lead by removing all agency from principals and teachers. This is why maker work, spaces, even programs, look very different from school to school to school in our system. We have expectations – very high expectations – but we don't expect anyone to follow a specific pattern.

We believe in scaling great ideas, theories, and strategies across our schools rather than trying to scale up programs. Not every-body's going to build a treehouse in the cafeteria as our kids did in one middle school. That was a school-specific desire. A group of middle schoolers in another school decided to build a high-altitude balloon apparatus and send it to the outer edges of the atmosphere. Not every middle school needs to do that. Some kids may decide to do something that seems less ambitious and build a nine-hole Putt-Putt golf course using cardboard. The projects, and the form of the learning environment, need to build on the passions, and build from the experiences, of both students and teachers.

The specifics don't matter. What matters is that when kids do that kind of work, they build on each other's ideas and sus-tain creativity together. They naturally become more in-depth, deeper critical thinkers. They learn to share expertise and how to find expertise.

When Julian from Chapter 4 first got interested in drones, he found his expertise on the Internet – which is the way the world works today – but then he began teaching drone aviation to oth-ers in his high school, and eventually to middle schoolers and even younger children. Currently, we have fifth graders who are running drone pilot miniclasses for peers in their K–5 multiage classroom. Now drone learning in high school feels somewhat passé as teens there have moved on to master Virtual Reality even as their younger peers master drone technologies.

To be ready for today's world, we believe that maker projects and the passion projects that young people individually and collaboratively create all over the district must become truly curricular. It's within these emerging curricula for the Smart Machine Age that students build communication skills, design skills, collaboration skills, expert vocabulary, and complex knowledge of everything from mathematics and physics to civics.

How does this work? When that team of middle school kids decided to create a high-altitude balloon project, they had no idea that their project would take almost an entire year to complete. They learned about communication in a context that they couldn't have envisioned before that. First they had to set the flight up with the FAA weeks ahead of the liftoff. On the Saturday morning according to schedule and plan, two girls who had conceptualized the project and helped build the high-altitude balloon apparatus pulled out a smartphone to talk to the Washington Air Traffic Control, local Charlottesville controllers, and the FAA somewhere in between the two controller stations. A group of astonished parents, educators, and local media gather around them to listen in.

The thrill of the entire student team was palpable as they checked out the GoPro camera loaded in a small Styrofoam ice cooler dangling under the 10-foot-tall balloon. They also had found a tracker app of some sort to keep tabs on the balloon flight. The tracker app tied into their controller on the system they'd engineered so they could figure out the balloon's location – if and when it landed. After trial and error to get the weight of different components balanced accurately with the hydrogen propellant, the balloon finally floated into an overcast sky and almost immediately disappeared off the tracking app. For those kids watching the balloon seek the heavens, that was it – nothing else touched their learning like the balloon project that had lasted a whole year for them.

The high-altitude balloon came down close to where they had computed it would land. When they recovered it four days after the launch, they powered the app off, grabbed the footage recorded at the outer reaches of the atmosphere, and loaded it onto a YouTube to share with the world. Pam still keeps the app with the flight data and GIS location frozen in time on her own phone so she can share it as part of the story of what kids do when context becomes the content learning rather than being a part from it. As one parent commented, "This is learning for a lifetime!"

That's what real learning should be like for all of us in today's world. We get excited when we think about kids getting to experience education in its most meaningful, real context. Learning starts to make sense and kids keep coming back to school because learning matters to them, not because compulsory school law requires it.

Solutions Are Simple and Complex

Willingness to spend time with teachers to change to something you've never worked with before is really scary. Think about the way most schools of education work – people are almost taught to be afraid of students and to control their every movement and word. And that's what classroom management, traditionally, is all about. Educators have to change that paradigm.

To impact paradigms, we invite new librarians to spend time with master teachers at the summer Coder Dojo to build a vision and deep understanding of what we are trying to accomplish and how libraries are accelerators of that vision. That begins with where we started this book, observing the world of children, adolescents, and teens.

We've also learned that when teachers give voice to their fears, then leaders and peers can work with that. But if you never listen to those fears you get nowhere with change.

Ira opens CoderDojo each year by explaining that student-centered, determined, and driven means that the work young people will accomplish begins with them and their interests. He says, "Let's watch our kids. Watch them, and what they can do." As teachers become kidwatchers, they begin to break fears of what kids might do. We say to teachers very often, "What's the worst that can possibly go wrong?" Sometimes, you have to get people to voice the worst to put that in some sort of perspective. Someone might say it would be really bad if the kids set the school on fire. Then, Ira will respond, "But we do have sprinkler systems and fire extinguishers and all sorts of things that help deal with that."

That's really what it came down to with one librarian who just stood in the doorway of her office several years ago and said, "I don't want to do this. I don't want to do this." Her principal's reply? "We're redoing this library. It's going to get done." With high support and high expectations from colleagues and the principal, she ended up tossing out 20% of the books that hadn't been read much in decades. This happened even though she began the change process with resistance to changing anything in the library. Mostly though she had this real fear of what kids would do. She wouldn't let kids climb on a piece of furniture designed for climbing into a reading nook because there were one or two kids who might have a problem with that. She talked through her fears with other librarians and soon started to take risks to change the way she interacted with children, peers, and library technologies.

One of the big changes in the library? She's a librarian who today defines for others what it means to try out new technologies, new schedules, and new instructional strategies in a reimagined learning space.

One Final Note: On Control as a Theme of Schooling

In today's real world, we need adults who can support children in school communities to be empathetic, respectful, and inclusive while also being active, collaborative, and curious. Children need competencies that build their capability to navigate the Internet in search of information, find creative solutions to design challenges, solve problems, communicate using a variety of nonverbal and verbal options, and work well with diverse classmates.

These are the same competencies that forward-thinking futurists believe they will need to be successful in life and the workforce in 2040, 2050, and 2060.

We've found this sweet spot when an educator possesses a philosophical background, worldview, and personality traits that enable him or her to develop trusting relationships. Learning is all about trust. Kids have to trust their teachers more so than, believe it or not, they have to trust the kids around them. And once that happens, it's just magical in a classroom. Or in leadership. And that's applicable across an organization.

We use what we've learned about the need for control to help us break down excuses and even break the rules created to drive compliance deep into school communities. In school districts everywhere, leaders are supposed to recruit and hire people who meet certain requirements. That's true for us, too. We have to ask: Do you have the degree? Do you have that license? Do you have that endorsement? We also figure out often times how to work around that. There might be some merit to those regulations, but we know the regulations don't make the philosophy and practices that children need to be successful at something more than listening and taking and passing tests. And, we've learned to look for teachers who value flexibility and openness to new ideas and strategies, who themselves are life learners, who can share stories that illustrate their sense of efficacy and how they shift power from themselves to learners.

We celebrate our educators' successes in trying out new ways of working with young people. We take people on tours to visit our libraries and have them talk to librarians about the process of changing libraries to learning commons. We also take people to visit teachers who have changed what they're doing, whether it's in a classroom, music studio, or mechatronics lab. We ask teachers who are making changes to mentor other people and to help them with new strategies, whether it's using technology in powerful ways or integrating choice and comfort into the classroom.

This isn't a profession where you can hand out big bonuses, but you can honor people and honor their work, which reinforces their efficacy and sense of why they became an educator in the first place. In doing so you also reassure other people who are thinking of moving that it's safe ground to do that in our schools. That's how we help not just our children but also our educators learn to negotiate the real world outside the doors of our schools.

Your Own Learning

Provocation

While John Dewey was venerated in schools of education in the mid- to late twentieth century, his philosophy fell out of favor when America's schools moved into the reform efforts of the 1990s and into the twenty-first century. Dewey believed in the power of children to make learning choices as they worked together in experiential activities designed for meaningful scaffolding of child-centered context and knowledge building through home and community skillfulness. Dewey's work was amplified through architectural design work and experiential education exemplified by the Crowe Island School near Chicago and in more progressive communities across the United States (Mortice 2015).

Ira attended one such high school in the 1970s, the 3Is founded at New Rochelle High, an iteration of Dewey through the lens of Neil Postman's and Alan Shapiro's philosophical point of view on experiential education, one they framed through the words of David Thoreau:

> Students should not play life, or study it merely while the community supports them at this expensive game, but earnestly live it from beginning to end. How could youths better learn to live than by at once trying the experiment of living? (Thoreau 1893, p. 82)

Postman and Shapiro wrote in proposing a school for the 3Is (Inquiry, Involvement, Independent Study):

> Most school curricula are based on a set of assumptions which the experimental program rejects. For example, most school programs assume (1) that knowledge is best presented and comprehended when organized into "subjects," (2) that there are "major" subjects and "minor" ones, (3) that subjects are things you "take," and

that once you have "had" them, you need not take them again, (4) that most subjects have a specific "content," (5) that the content of these subjects is more or less stable, (6) that a major function of the teacher is to "transmit" this content (7), that the practical place to do this is in a room within a centrally located building, (8) that students learn best in 45-minute periods which are held five times a week, (9) that students are functioning well (i.e., learning) when they are listening to their teacher, reading their texts, doing their assignments, and otherwise "paying attention" to the content being transmitted, and (10) that all of this must go on as a preparation for life.

In other words, we are assuming (1) that learning takes places best not when conceived as a preparation for life but when it occurs in the context of actually living, (2) that each learner ultimately must organize his own learning in his own way, (3) that "problems" and personal interests rather than "subjects" are a more realistic structure by which to organize learning experiences, (4) that students are capable of directly and authentically participating in the intellectual and social life of their community, (5) that they should do so, and (6) that the community badly needs them.

This set of beliefs is sometimes referred to as the "judo" principle of education. Instead of trying to forestall, resist, or neutralize the natural curiosity, intelligence, energy, and idealism of youth, one uses it in a context which permits both them and their community to change. Thus, the experimental program reduces the reliance on classrooms and school buildings; it transforms the relevant problems of the community and the special interests of individual students into the students' "curriculum"; it looks toward the creation of a sense of community in both. (Three I Program n.d.b)

• How would schooling need to change to become the real-world learning environment as Dewey and Postman/Shapiro envisioned? How would it change in terms of the faculty role? The spaces required? The schedule? The expectations about student activities and behavior?

- Consider launching into your Isearch journal (in the cloud or on paper) to write down your thinking, to ask questions about which you are curious, your observations of your own educational landscape, and what it would mean if we embraced experiential education as an alternative to the content-centered schools of the late twentieth and twenty-first century.

Structured Inquiry

- What do you think Postman and Shapiro meant by "Students should not play life, or study it merely while the community supports them at this expensive game, but earnestly live it from beginning to end. How could youths better learn to live than by at once trying the experiment of living?"
- Could schools be more of a place where kids live learning and life? How might you find the schools, such as Big Picture schools, that today exemplify experiential learning? What questions would you have for students and teachers and administrators in those schools?

Reflective Pause

In your opinion, can public schools in general become experiential learning environments? Should they? Why or why not? What would it take to flip your classroom to an experiential learning approach? Your school? Your district?

Take Action

Superficial change is relatively easy. We can put programs, technology, and even furniture into schools that support more experiential approaches to education opportunities for our learners. Deep change – transformation of philosophy, culture, and practices – is far more difficult. Yet, we know it's possible with time, focus, and support for educators to unlearn teaching, testing, and curricular paradigms held over and still in place from prior reform efforts. Ira wrote in this blog post about the experiences of students in the 3Is:

> Most students were rarely there. If you were studying science you were probably at the City's greenhouses or the local hospital or at the heritage farm we created in a City Park. If you were studying journalism you were creating the school's weekly newspaper or maybe, spending nights chasing news with a local radio station's overnight news guy. If you were studying urban design you might be in the planning department at City Hall. Psychology? How about interviewing Grand Central's homeless population after midnight. Great literature? Sitting around a teacher's living room one night a week sharing tea and ideas. There were, of course, classes – but they were different kinds of classes. (Three I Program n.d.a)

Four Actions to Live as an Inquiry Learner

1. John,* a teacher in Michigan, started one morning with Ira in a traditional classroom where kids were disengaged. After thinking together, by the afternoon he had moved desks together and given kids permission to choose whether to and where to sit and stand while they were working. It was a baby step but a step. Every day ask questions of yourself that challenge the normative rules for your classroom, your school, your district. What might change and move the dial so that students engage in more experiential learning opportunities? What can you change in 24 hours? In a month? In a year?

2. Chad looks for every opportunity to resource what teachers need to move the dial. He uses his budget and partnerships to leverage opportunities for more experiential problem and project work. He also reinforces that you don't need much to create a maker environment from household rejects to

---

*A pseudonym.

cardboard and duct tape. Always be on the lookout for resources that you need to support experiences that engage students in inquiry, involvement, and independent work. These can sometimes be funded through crowdsourced funding sites such as Donors Choose, through parent organizations, or from your own throwaways. Remember, if you don't ask, the answer will always be no.

3. Self-educate. Define yourself as a lifelong learner. Don't wait on your district or your school to develop you for you. We've formed our philosophies over time by picking mentors who are regarded by learners and who think all the time about improving the lives of learners in our public schools. We seek out information and expertise all the time from every source possible from social media to print books. We study teachers who constantly are pushing the envelope to take risks and we learn from them. We talk with them. We visit their classes. We engage them in the work we do and we share their work even as they share with us.

4. Stay away from toxic personalities. When educators sometimes say "Yeah, but . . ." or "We already tried that" or "Those kids can't . . .," remember that naysayers are committed to the status quo for the sake of adult convenience. This doesn't mean that people who challenge proposed changes are all naysayers. They aren't. Analytical thinkers who process all the ways that a risk might fail help you see unintended consequences and course correct before a new idea crashes and burns. It's those who refuse to take risks, to consider practices designed to give voice to learners, to engage them in work that builds from their interests, to give up control so that young people can practice exercising control over their own learning – those are the few but the often most vocal who oppose any change in the way it was.

Resources

Bell, Lee. 2016. "What Is Moore's Law? WIRED Explains the Theory That Defined the Tech Industry." *Wired UK*. 28 August. Accessed 16 October 2017. http://www.wired.co.uk/article/wired-explains-moores-law.

Blikstein, Paulo. n.d. "Seymour Papert's Legacy: Thinking About Learning, and Learning About Thinking." Stanford Graduate School of Education, Transformative Learning Technologies Lab. Accessed 16 October 2017. https://tltl.stanford.edu/content/seymour-paperts-legacy-thinking-about-learning-and-learning-about-thinking.

Callahan, Raymond E. 1964. *Education and the Cult of Efficiency: A Study of the Forces That Have Shaped the Administration of Public Schools*. Chicago: University of Chicago Press.

Choi, S. W., D. Mh Lam, and Michael G. Irwin. 2016. "Ghost in the Machine." *Hong Kong Medical Journal = Xianggang Yi Xue Za Zhi / Hong Kong Academy of Medicine* 22 (3): 292–293.

Chuang, Tamara. 2017. "Self-Driving Truck's Beer Run on Colorado's Interstate 25 Gets Guinness World Record." *Denver Post*. 29 June. http://www.denverpost.com/2017/06/29/self-driving-beer-truck-world-record/.

Dewey, John. 1938. *Experience and Education*. New York: Touchstone.

Eliot, Charles W., Frank A. Hill, and A. E. Winship. 1894. "The REPORT of the Committee of Ten." *The Journal of Educational Research* 40 (5): 979. JSTOR: 91–93.

Fitzgerald, Jay. 2017. "Robots and Jobs in the U.S. Labor Market." *NBER Digest*. May. http://www.nber.org/digest/may17/may17.pdf.

IBM. n.d. "IBM Watson Health." Accessed 17 September 2017. https://www.ibm.com/watson/health/.

Johnston, Katherine, ed. 2001. *Educating Teachers of Science, Mathematics, and Technology: New Practices for the New Millennium*. Washington, DC: National Academies Press.

Kaufman, Scott Barry. 2017. "Schools Are Missing What Matters About Learning." *The Atlantic*. 24 July. https://www.theatlantic.com/education/archive/2017/07/the-underrated-gift-of-curiosity/534573/.

Klein, Alyson. 2014. "Historic Summit Fueled Push for K–12 Standards." *Education Week*. 23 September. https://www.edweek.org/ew/articles/2014/09/24/05summit.h34.html.

Langer, Emily. 2016. "Seymour Papert, MIT Scholar Who Connected Children with Computers, Dies at 88." *Washington Post*. 3 August. https://www.washingtonpost.com/national/seymour-papert-mit-professor-who-connected-children-with-computers-dies-at-88/2016/08/03/59009d08–582a-11e6–9aee-8075993d73a2_story.html.

Mortice, Zach. 2015. "Why Don't All Schools Look Like This One?" CityLab. 9 October. https://www.citylab.com/design/2015/10/why-dont-all-schools-look-like-this-one/408886/.

Muoio, Danielle. 2016. "We Rode in Uber's Self-Driving Car—Here's What It Was Like." *Business Insider*. 14 September. http://www. businessinsider.com/uber-driverless-car-in-pittsburgh-review-pho tos-2016–9/.

Papert, Seymour. 1980. *Mindstorms: Children, Computers, and Powerful Ideas*. New York: Basic Books.

Reese, William J. 2011. *America's Public Schools: From the Common School to "No Child Left Behind."* Baltimore: Johns Hopkins University Press.

Rothman, Lily. 2014. "Remember Y2K? Here's How We Prepped for the Non-Disaster." *Time*. 31 December. http://time.com/3645828/ y2k-look-back/.

Rotman, David. 2017. "'The Relentless Pace of Automation.'" *MIT Technology Review*. 13 February. https://www.technologyreview. com/s/603465/the-relentless-pace-of-automation/.

Thoreau, Henry David. 1893. *Walden: Or, Life in the Woods*. Boston: Houghton Mifflin.

Three I Program. n.d.a. "Course Catalog, 1970–1972." Accessed 17 September 2017. http://www.joshkarpf.com/3i/catalog1972.html.

———. n.d.b. "Postman Proposal, 1970." Accessed 17 September 2017. http://foody.org/3i/proposal1969.html.

Vinovskis, Maris. 1999. "The Road to Charlottesville." National Educational Goals Panel. Alexandria, VA: Department of History, Institute for Social Research, and School of Public Policy, University of Michigan.

7

Break Down Walls:
Opening Spaces for Learning

For Gilles Deleuze, "A society is defined by its amal-
gamations, not by its tools . . . tools exist only in rela-
tion to the interminglings they make possible or that
make them possible." The point is that a history of the
observer is not reducible to changing technical and
mechanical practices any more than to the changing
forms of artworks and visual representation.
                                    – Jonathan Crary (1990)

In a high school hallway where lockers have been replaced with
"charging benches," two students sit, or in one case, lie down, and
listen as their laptops read to them. They are studying history, but
they are not in an "instructional environment." They are reading
but they are not decoding. They are engaged but they are not controlled. Downstairs another student renders a historical scene in
virtual reality. She moves with her handheld controls and goggles
as other students watch on large monitors. She is writing sophisticated work, but there is no pen or keyboard. Across town a young
man prepares for the night's performance of the controversial play
he has written about policing and community – a drama built from
the raw emotions of a neo-Nazi riot in this town earlier in the
year. He is teaching, and he is leading, he is writing, he is debat-
ing, he is engaging – this is much more than a course in theater.

IRA: There's a need for new definitions. For almost two centuries now we've confounded purpose and skill, goals and habits, and those cannot remain conjoined. "Reading" isn't deciphering alphabetical symbols, and "learning" is not sitting in classrooms. New technology and new patterns of society have allowed us to split these things apart, and that's a very good thing. The concept of amalgamation plays out in the fusion of learning and learner within an expanded environment that is so much more than traditional schooling allows.

CHAD: We see that adding the full range of tools creates that place where humans gather together to find paths. Kitchens in schools really matter, so do table saws, so do phones and computers, so do laser cutters and 3D printers. Each tool adds possibilities for community members to learn together.

PAM: It is not an "add-on" of tools when Ira comes and says, "We're buying virtual reality systems" or when Chad builds pop-up makerspace kits with everything from hand tools to circular saws to bring to not just secondary but also elementary schools. These are curricular commitments to opening opportunities to every child, to our "all means all" philosophy, to the building of essential knowledge and skills within our children.

The Rhizome Spreads

When we break down walls, figuratively and literally, to let learning flow out of the classroom we construct a new learning process grounded in both Universal Design for Learning (UDL) and a humane view of childhood and adolescence. In many ways as walls break down, learning does become more of a Deleuzian approach, rhizomatic in nature versus hierarchical, allowing for a spread that is more viral and interdependent than what typically occurs in a top-down, siloed schooling model (Kerr 2014). The processes of both breaking down walls and constructing open spaces – both physical and conceptually – is key to real and significant change that allows for the quick spread and connection of ideas, resources, and people. The tools of this century augment and expedite the spread of the rhizome, allowing learning communities to take down the inherent barriers to connectivity that hierarchical leadership models create. The tools are *not* the community, but today's tools do support the "intermingling" of community in ways that global citizens could not have envisioned prior to the 2007 exponential increases in connectivity attributed to Steve Jobs and the iPhone (Molla 2017). In our schools and world, tools that support, connect, and sustain learning and relationships matter.

As the barriers that define our schools drop, relationships among school community members, children and adults, develop. We've noticed that in a flattened hierarchy, one in which top-down leadership is diminished, it's more likely for community members, regardless of age, to move into the role of both teacher and learner. We see this in the teen who helped build a sound studio from scratch and then codeveloped and cotaught an "alt-music" curriculum side by side with a teacher in his school. It's also found in the story of high school performers whose passion for drama led them to serve as drama mentors for elementary English language learners, supporting them along an artistic path to literacy. We find as we observe that a different type of literacy, a literacy for life, emerges in the connectivity of social learning communities in which conversation is valued, curiosity is purposefully supported, ideas are worthy of exploration, and time constraints become less limiting. This is the literacy of the rhizome, a spread of the community's knowledge through words, images, and interactions.

Grounding our work in Deleuze's conceptual framework also allows us to think within the rhizome metaphor and to link understanding of our work to both the qualitative and quantitative nature of multiplicities. We see this in a tension still playing out across our district and the nation between the majority-driven philosophy of learning as quantitative and a minority-driven philosophy of learning as qualitative. The black-and-white nature of education as cast through a multiplicities lens is represented in the school program pendulum that swings back and forth in response to philosophical directions, directions often cast from the political arena. No place is that more evident than in a mathematical reductionist versus poetic holistic perspective on literacy development in formal education settings, or in the hierarchical versus rhizomatic organizational structure of schools.

> The concept of multiplicity reconfigures the ancient dispute between reason and poetry. Quantitative multiplicities can be captured through logical, mathematical, or scientific propositions. Qualitative multiplicities require a broader palette to color in the nuance of each thing, and here, philosophy forms alliances with painters, authors, directors, or sculptors. (Tampio 2010)

While much of the research in education over the past century has focused on making sense of learning through what W. Edwards Deming, the American economist who led reconstruction of Japan after World War II, referred to in the business world as a failure of "management by visible numbers alone," we see a very different model emerging from the qualitative focus we have embedded in our work (Deming 1982). This is a vision in which all learners thrive because the system is less impeded by hierarchy and more supported by the spreading rhizome metaphor.

One rhizomatic path we've watched spread has developed among educators who create a generative literacy that isn't much like any literacy that has existed in formal schooling history. The concept of generative literacy evolves across our schools and is iterative from Paulo Freire's frame on the power of using generative words to help people become active community members in informal processes of building literacy rather than simply being passively taught to read and write as in school (Wingeier 1980). We see breaking down walls and opening spaces as critical to the generative processes essential to literacy, indeed essential as children use devices and tools that lead to a more integrated sense of what it means to be literate in this decade, in this century.

This literacy development moves more rapidly across our district as multiage and co-teaching experiences, both formal and informal, are built out so that children acquire and expand their vocabulary knowledge in a context of social learning communities in which older and younger children play and learn together. In such natural learning communities, children bring language assets to their learning communities from a variety of diverse backgrounds. As natural language expands among children, they scaffold complexity of understanding, deepen knowledge, and build expressive and receptive literacy, drawing from both non-Native speaking experiences as well as from environments that span a wide range of cultures, not just the traditional Anglo culture.

However, for a generative literacy to spread, schools must also create pathways that support young people to learn to communicate using a variety of forms of public media that amplify their voice and influence as learners with agency for their own learning, connected by the rhizome to each other, to those with expertise, and to audiences of self, the local community, and the world. This brings generative literacy from text specific to paper into this century's use of language across a much broader continuum of literacy communication tools.

Generative Literacy as Learning Revolution

In this post-Gutenberg era we believe Paulo Freire's concept of generative literacy lensed through today's contemporary technologies creates a revolution similar to the Gutenberg Parenthesis (Peverill-Conti and Seawell 2016). Current work to redefine and recomprehend what "reading" and "writing" means is essential to learning if we are to give all of our students the opportunities to succeed in all levels of human communication. The world of learning has shifted from "write-print-read-recall" to "search-connect-communicate-make." To thrive in this shift, teachers must abandon traditions of pedagogy and place that circumscribe a narrow point of view of what it means "to learn" and "be literate" and embrace contemporary tools, strategies, discourse, and venues that offer young people authenticity of audience that has never before existed.

"Writing," for example, is too important to allow it to be defined in the terms of the past 500 years – as the creation of fixed print on paper – or to be seen as a communication form in which there are limited ways to establish "truth" and "cognitive authority." Writing is too important because, though forms and structures will differ, writing is the path to power for those born without power. This importance lies not in how to write a "five-paragraph essay" or a "compare and contrast" book review but in the capability to clearly communicate visions both personal and collaborative. Whether the work is a tweet that generates action when that is needed, or a text message to an employer, or the ability to convince others in the political realm, or the expression of one's identity in a form that evokes empathy in those without similar experience, "communicating" "well" is a social leveler of supreme importance.

In both cases, methodology become less important than process. Our students read on paper, or through audio books, or through text-to-speech, or by watching video, or by seeing theater – or by observing their world. They write with pens, keyboards large and small, touchscreens, or by dictating to their phones or computers, or by recording audio, or by making videos, or by writing plays or creating art, or playing music. We do not limit the work by attacking those with disabilities or even inabilities – or even other preferences, because that robs children of both important influences and of their individual voices. Multiplicities are an intention: We build the best collaboration, the deepest learning, when we expand the opportunities for complex vision.

Thus we begin by moving the teaching of writing from the training of a specific skill set toward an interpersonal art form that flows from students and builds communities. Then, through the reimagining of teaching places into "learning spaces," we craft "studios" where all the technologies of school – time, space, tools, pedagogies – liberate and inspire rather than deliver and test. Then, using those recrafted technologies, we allow communication learning to flow.

One Narrative of Change Agency

In our school district, we've opened up the learning process through generative literacy for all students at all levels through a global commitment to UDL – using student passions and student freedom of choice to build engagement and commitment to redefine communication processes, but allowing each classroom to interpret this "opening" in ways that match the specific needs of their students. This process began with bringing historically contextualized views of UDL spaces into the district along with the concept of "Toolbelt Theory" – a student-choice-based technology design (Socol 2008). This is met with a leadership commitment to student-centered democratic education in which innovation arises from student need, not central planning, a development process consistent with many of our educators' long-term experiences with a workshop model. And, finally it's landed with a cohort of teachers who, from first-hand experience, were deeply dissatisfied with the existing model of instruction.

We've spent a lot of time together, and with our colleagues, reflecting on collaborative exploration of an "inside-out and outside-in" series of learning scenes, and exploring the narrative of how we've removed barriers created by classroom and school walls. Like the *Beholding Eye* of D. W. Meinig, we all experience change agency differently because we have different points of view shaped by our own backgrounds, beliefs, and points of view on education (Meinig 1979). We see the beginnings within our district that have led to open spaces for learning differently within and across schools because we each entered this work at different times. However, we share in common a commitment to progressive education with equity of access to rich, experiential learning for all children, and that's what unites our voices with those of educators in and outside our district with whom we collaborate as we create a different narrative for what learners' user experiences can become.

One such narrative of change began on the day after Ira's first day of work in the district when he presented on the topic of "Implications of Post-Colonial Impacts Still in Today's Schools" at an annual district conference, Making Connections. This district conference model was originally created in 2004 with the purpose of cross-pollinating progressive ideas and practices emerging inside and outside our district's boundaries.

The workshop presentation that Ira shared on that first day was fine, one of those one-size-fits-all professional development sessions that school districts offer from time to time. However, it was his more authentic school-based work that week walking with teachers, librarians, and principals, often provoking staff to consider a very different way of thinking about school, that really provided an inflection point in our S-curve learning beginning in 2010. The day after the conference, we almost drove past a school that had chosen to dig in on literacy and technology integration, a school that had just signed on for the district's first one-to-one laptop pilot with sixth graders. The laptops had been there less than a week. Pam remembers making a spontaneous comment: "Ira, let's stop by and see what they're doing."

The teacher we stopped to visit that day has continued to play a key role over time in the narrative that led us to understand the importance of educators with the spirit to take risks and the heart to stick with making radical educational shifts, in this case from pencil to device, even when such shifts feel like an insurmountable challenge to integrate new tools into the lexicon of learning culture. Lyn* had also just attended Making Connections where she had heard another district teacher in a workshop at the conference share her use of an (at the time) new app, Edmodo. Lyn was one of four teachers piloting a grade level 1:1 rollout. Two days after the district conference, she jumped right in and said "Boom! I'm going to do this Edmodo thing with my kids."

She was courageous, an educational explorer willing to take the risk to try out a new application or, in this case, new tech devices, a new app, and new strategies by adopting and adapting UDL experiences for all learners in her classroom.

---

*A pseudonym.

When Pam and Ira dropped by, her class was working in this brand-new Edmodo application, and the only thing the kids wanted to do was make their own avatars. Lyn was trying to get them to write a paragraph about Romeo and Juliet and she said something like "And, the paragraph should look like this." Then she projected on her smartscreen a paragraph for the kids to basically replicate in their own writing. They were paying no attention to her because they were so excited about their new computers – plus half the kids couldn't figure out how to get in the application anyway. On this day, Lyn wouldn't let them help each other even though they were volunteering to do so. This wonderful teacher was moving so fast, working so hard. It was so painful to watch as she attempted to move from the dominant teaching wall and work with every child on each computer to help them get into the system and start using it.

We realized this wasn't a good implementation of 1:1 tech at all. But what was good was this totally brave teacher who was willing to go after stuff. And she did. By the next time we visited, she was working on a project in which the kids were writing scripts for silent movies they decided to make. She was energized. They were energized. The focus had moved from doing the same work children had always done using new devices to a focus on changing culture, community, and processes of learning through new tools that opened literacy doors for all that had been closed for some for centuries.

Within a year of that day she had changed the culture and space of her classroom, not just the use of new tools. The space became one of the first DIY classrooms in the district. By the end of the year, she had shifted at least half of the chairs out of the room and replaced them with comfortable seating and set up the concept of choice in how and where learners worked on and off their devices. She had that first group of sixth graders bring their own comfort in her room, so she had one wall where kids stacked up all their pillows and stuffed toys to use as they worked in writers' workshop.

In the years that have passed since Lyn participated in that sixth grade 1:1 pilot, she's tried two new grade levels, first a

coteaching seventh grade space and now an eighth grade classroom coupled with leading the Language Arts team. However,
visitors will still find kids sitting, standing, or lying on the floor
with their laptops as they write, read, or work on projects. And,
they will certainly notice that she moves with a deliberate pace
as she circulates to work with students – it is often hard at first
glance to distinguish her from the students with whom she is
working. Lyn's classroom is a different learning space today, one
in which kids have significant choice in how and when they
sit, stand, or recline to write, read, or work on projects with or
without their 1:1 devices. They have a sense of autonomy over
the projects they work on, who they work with, and how they
show their learning. Her kids show their capabilities to communicate well in a variety of platforms from inauthentic state tests
to more authentic portfolio exemplars. She has moved into a
teacher leader role and is an influencer in her school and across
the district.

The shift of this teacher to include a continuum of choices for
children represents the best of how UDL philosophically defines
who gets access to and equity in opportunities to learn. It's not
about just the special education children or the at-risk learners
using UDL strategies and tools but rather about accessibility for all
the learners in her classroom. That Romeo and Juliet assignment
morphed from being a replication of a paper-pencil activity into
silent movies, global read-alouds via Google Hangouts, projects
involving Zombies, and dance. Her children built from what
they already knew or had experienced along a generative literacy
pathway that allowed them to scaffold their own diverse interests
and common experiences so that they expanded their learning as
a community, not just as individuals (ETEC 511 n.d.).

Opening Space for Learning
Through a Support Philosophy

We've learned that teachers go through stages as they shift to
more learner-centered practices and tools. When supporters are

in place to think with teachers, ask questions, provide resources, and connect them with other educators also focused on change in response to learners' needs, the teachers almost always take themselves and learners to the next stage. This support happens best side by side with peer teachers in small professional learning communities that include, in our district, instructional coaches and digital learning integrators. This support can also come for teachers who don't have that support level in their school communities through connected relationships built in social media platforms such as Twitter. Socially cohesive learning communities build from different experiences but all have one common theme: educators who believe in and value that what children have to say matters lead children to build a sense of learning agency as they collaborate together. Children in such supportive communities develop knowledge and skillfulness by connecting with a variety of sources of expertise including aspirational peers, adult mentors, virtual networks, and the teacher.

Change does not often happen by chance but because of purposeful focus and support. While we appreciated Lyn's willingness to take the risk to implement a shift from computer carts to 1:1 devices, we realized in that first observation that a plan to support that shift didn't seem to be in place. We sat down before we left the school and talked with the principal about the disconnect in our internal understanding of what it would take to implement a 1:1 rollout and the reality. No matter how much we had studied the research, we just didn't have the staff or structures to really help at the most personal level of shifting the practices that needed to change in her classroom – and those of the other three teachers.

We made arrangements for Ira to spend time in some follow-up work with teachers in the school both virtually and face to face. He began to correspond and connect with the teacher we'd observed as well as with other staff. Later in the year, when we visited again, we were amazed at the transformation in the classroom, the teacher's pedagogy, and the learning work the kids were doing.

This happened because the teacher was so open to learning but also because we provided some support for her to think differently about space and lesson design with Ira, other teachers, and even in Twitter. Later that spring, Pam keynoted a state conference and ended up using a black-and-white silent movie about middle school relationships that the kids in Lyn's class had written, filmed, edited, and then published using their new classroom devices. The audience couldn't believe it was made by kids or that it had been uploaded to YouTube to share with the world. Our experiences learning with Lyn was a turning point for us all to understand that breaking down walls can lead to learning with authenticity and realizing this kind of deep change happens one person at a time.

As the projects that Lyn's students accomplish have changed and become more complex, their work has taken her with it to a very different world in which open spaces for learning transcend simply sharing her work, and that of her students inside the school community, for it's also been shared authentically with other schools in our community, at conferences, as well as globally. Opening up space rhizomatically while taking down barriers allowed her students to spread a contagion of creativity across the class and school as they learned to use any media format available to them to communicate about books they read, their personal narratives, and knowledge they acquired. And, Lyn has also influenced other teachers across the district and in her own school as she's continued to share and refine her work.

Teachers all over our district now work from a UDL philosophy to redefine literacy from text-based paper and pencil to communication in any form that a child dreams to learn and use. There are examples everywhere from a middle school language arts teacher whose kids 3D print or make artifacts prior to a writing workshop to the high school teacher who encourages kids to write their prose as rap lyrics, or the elementary teacher whose kids create the Jamestown story in Minecraft. Even though we know we still have a lot to do to support this kind of work becoming fully rhizomatic, it's almost possible to see it spreading week by week from class to class and across the district.

There Are No Simple Recipes Really

It's a huge challenge in education from a superintendent's or a principal's perspective to support a district, a school, or an individual to change practices. Change ultimately and always begins with the individual. Often, the most challenging struggle occurs when people are looking for the easy answer of how to get there – to make the changes progressive educators would like to see. There's no one path. There's no list of eight things to do to get there or a recipe list of what you need to buy. That's one of the really hard things for us to articulate because it would be so much easier if we could just write the "how to" book and say, here's how you do it. There is no recipe even after all we have experienced, documented, and shared. Chad references the question we most often get asked: "How did you make these changes happen?" Our answer is that we didn't. **The educators with whom we work make changes happen.** We simply opened paths for them to experience, observe, and connect with others who wanted more for kids than simply getting a proficient rating on state tests. If there's any secret sauce, it's in the support we provide for teachers to search, design, create, test, engineer, make, and reflect together.

Educators who visit the district to see any of a number of priorities we've implemented rarely really ask us much about the specific priority they've come to study. Instead, they ask us about change leadership. If we're on a conference panel, the topic might be Maker Ed, but the questions are always on how to drive change in a school district. Making just provides the context. Replace the topic word with anything you want to see change. How to get makerspaces across the district becomes how to get "fill in the blank" across the district. It's the same darn question whether we are asked about making, project-based learning, space redesign, connectivity, or UDL. So, we've learned that figuring out how to realize the change process is really what challenges educators from all over.

What's different and unique about our work is that we are trying to convert a public school system, as Pam's articulated so beautifully over the years, that wasn't designed to build from the experience of the child or to empower the child. We constantly work against the mainstream. We're breaking the rules and rejecting the excuses that work against changing an institution that fundamentally works against conversion to a progressive model of education, one that is grounded in a more qualitative multiplicity, that leads to rhizomatic learning that's generative in user experience versus decontextualized through standards.

Shifting away from compliance schooling feels next to impossible because even those who become teachers for all the right reasons don't come with a knowledge of how to support children as learners in a progressive space. Most educators have never experienced this kind of learning themselves with the exception of a very few who've been educated in alternative settings. However, we've found that with the right support, teachers will start challenging the status quo because they value children and want them to experience a deeper learning than can be shown on standardized tests. Some people get inspired because something they created as a scenario in a classroom or something they changed with a child was so positive that it took them from point A to point B.

We've seen this happen exponentially in informal settings with adults, too. For example, when teachers are on a train ride to the World Maker Faire held annually at the New York Hall of Science, they tend on the way up to chat mostly about their daily work, families, and so on. On the way back, however, the energy and intensity of the conversations ratchet off the dial. They're into what they want to try, to change, to do differently, and who else they know who might be interested. They're connected with thoughts about what it means to learn that never were there before. They go back to school, try out their ideas, and invariably begin to make the work go viral with others. This also occurs when teachers gather after school at a coffee shop to discuss what they are learning about empowering children's agency through student-led parent conferences. Or, when a librarian builds a mystery Skype relationship between a class in her school and one in a distant state and that relationship leads to face-to-face visits and expanded opportunities for children to share their diverse communities with each other. We've noticed over and over again that teachers who connect and inspire each other take that inspiration back into their class communities where it develops into a contagious creativity to construct new learning paths for themselves *and* the students they serve.

Compliance-based education will never get to these kinds of exhilarating experiences for children or educators who are caught in the lock-step march of teaching to standards for the purpose of passing tests. If teachers impose compliance-based education on a group of human beings for 180 days, it's the rare exception when some kids get inspired and do something brilliant. The conditions just aren't there. However, if you convince a teacher or the school to try something that connects kids to a sense of personal autonomy in pursuing learning interests and passions, almost inevitably, something will come from that.

The Role of Leaders as Students of Past, Present, and Future

Leaders have to seize that moment, and make sure that stories of progressive change agency don't get lost. Often times, teachers are so conditioned to only see success in the traditionally measured way, the quantitative multiplicity of logic and data, that a school leader or peer has to point out to them, "Wow, Johnny told me he couldn't wait to come back to school tomorrow. Can you imagine him saying that a year ago?" The teacher may not have recognized what a powerful thing inspired learning is until it's pointed out. So, a lot of our work is constantly – constantly! – working with whatever scenario exists, and looking for the opportunities within those scenarios to support teachers to see beyond the normative culture, imagine what's possible, and take the risk to change something. We haven't discovered a specific recipe for that. Leaders just have to look for and know when they see kids excited and inspired as learners and immediately share feedback about what they notice with teachers – and the kids.

Educators must constantly consider and reflect upon the philosophical foundation from which they operate. There are times when as an administrator who fundamentally believes in teacher autonomy and organic change, in schools as community, and in your role as one of support, you may observe some egregious behavior that negatively impacts or even harms learners. That's when mission-driven leaders pull moral authority from their toolbelts to make sure decisions and behaviors of adults in the community are in the best interests of kids.

Leading to break down walls and open up space for learning is not rooted in Utopia. Beliefs and values matter in the process of shaping structures in which educators operate. If educators believe in constructing spaces that build learning grounded in experiential design, then the adults are going to fundamentally operate from that philosophy. Pam thinks about that and the idea of getting to yes. She talks a lot about it, and we all do because you have to get yourself to yes. You have to be willing to accept the risk of kids and adults learning through experience, not from words on a blackboard, whiteboard, or PowerPoint.

There's inherent risk in experiential learning. You don't know where such learning will take the community of learners or individual students, but when kids explore their interests through projects that are important to them, their passion quotient grows exponentially. We've seen real rewards from this shift, whether it is watching teens graduate who otherwise would likely have dropped out or students who begin to see themselves as designers, inventors, and even as entrepreneurs because the process of creating *becomes* the learning. Or, as Yong Zhao writes:

> Thus the entrepreneurial model of PBL or product-oriented learning makes the creation and marketing of products the center of the learning experience. It is about creating works that matter – matter to the students and to potential customers, not necessarily to the prescribed standards or curriculum. The works do not have to be one end product, like a piece of art, a book, or a video. They can also be a service or program. For example, students could offer

tutoring services, online or face-to-face, or a service to help others improve their math or writing. (Zhao 2012)

When students find themselves creating from an entrepreneurial mindset, it's often because they are engaging in a classroom in which a teacher is doing the same. This kind of entrepreneurial mindset is not one that only leads to starting a company or marketing a product (Zhao 2012) but rather one that's embedded with educators who see the potential of learning well beyond expectations of the past. It's not about how many books a student has read but whether the student can write and publish a book. It's not about memorizing history facts for a test but where the student can build a virtual reality story from history and share it with others. It's not about whether a student studies ancient architecture but rather can that learner work with a team to design, build, and sell a tiny house? An entrepreneurial mindset allows adults and young people to learn to assess and take calculated learning risks in which the reward is greater than not taking it. The reward becomes worth taking the risk, and then to make something exist that didn't exist before, and maybe that solves a problem in the classroom, the school, the community, or ultimately even a grand challenge of the world.

We have framed our work to create a context for learning through the tool theories of Alcott, Freire, Illich, Zhao, and Socol. The beholding eye of D. W. Meinig (Meinig 1979) provides multiple lenses of perspective upon learning scenes, as does the theory of cultural vision expressed by Jonathan Crary (Crary 1990). Our collaboration as leaders has integrated our own different lenses on why we believe what we do about learning, and the needed shifts in pedagogy, tool use, space, and community that are essential to implementing progressive learning philosophy in today's schools.

For example, the leadership perspective crafted through Chad's efforts to break with the supposed "efficiencies" of the Cubberly-inspired industrialized education model has created authentic spaces in which all children can design, make, and launch projects in our schools. We've also learned to accomplish research and use data differently through historical school and tool analysis and learning space perspective gained from Ira's use of the Grounded Theory approach, a rejection of traditional hypothesis and control groups in favor of deep-mapping observation techniques and continuous improvement of practice. And, Pam's early life and environmental experiences inform our understanding and collaboration as she uses her background in ecology to process how concepts from the natural world apply to the edu-ecosystem we label as schools.

In taking on this grand challenge, we explore every day with our colleagues how to create a system that doesn't subtract joy, empowerment, agency, enthusiasm, and passion from learning while also building one that ensures children are literate, able to think and work in mathematical languages, and have the knowledge and tool belt competencies they need to understand the world in which they live – *and* – to live a healthy lifestyle and be good family and community members – *and* – to gain workforce readiness skills.

That's a challenge worth solving, right?

Your Own Learning

Provocation

UDL usually has been assigned to the domain of strategies and assistive technologies needed for disabled students to access learning and the world around them. We have defined that differently. We believe that when we equip all learners with multiple tools – a personal toolbelt – they will be more resilient, capable learners today and tomorrow. This challenges the thinking of some educators. Is it reading if a middle school girl listens to an audio recording of a novel she can't otherwise read visually? What if a high school student needs a talking calculator to support their mastery of algebra? If an elementary student who stands up while being read a story is able to sustain attention, is that okay? What if a group of students wants to create a website to share a project with the world rather than presenting it to the class?

What does UDL mean to you as an educator? In what ways do you as an adult learner use UDL strategies and tools in your own life?

Consider launching into your Isearch journal (in the cloud or on paper) to write down your thinking, to ask questions about which you are curious, your observations of your own class, school, or district's philosophy about universal design. What can you change that would give you an opportunity to extend choice and comfort in your environment to others? Seating? Work choices? Tools? Where can you go to find about more about UDL? Google it or search on YouTube. Begin an anthology of resources on equity and access.

Structured Inquiry

Getting to a mindset of UDL doesn't start with tools or strategies or behaviors. It begins with knowing, understanding, and empathy. UDL ultimately begins by considering the user experiences you would like to create for learners. Ira writes in a great post on user experience:

> How much more effective might we be if our user interface design was intentional, and intentionally designed to support children?
>
> *What do kids see? What do they feel? What do they smell? What do they hear? What is their experience as they move through your school?*
>
> One of the things that is clear is that every single thing kids see, hear, feel, smell, taste, sends a message about your school. Every single thing. And many of the messages schools send are as awful as they are unintentional. (Socol 2016)

After reading Ira's post, observe your school for what young people see, feel, smell, hear, and experience as they move around inside and out. What do you notice? Walk the school with a learner and get them to chat about what they notice. Where can they go? Not go? Talk with teachers about their philosophies on the user experience they want for learners. What rules create good user experience and which ones disenfranchise students from success and positive culture? How do you know? What will you do next?

Reflective Pause

Chad has spoken publicly and privately to the importance of equity and access for all children to the best work educators can offer. This philosophy is one of UDL, and Chad lives that every day in his work to create environments that represent the experiential nature of progressive education. He knows that the factory school model of the twentieth century is best known for sorting and selecting learners into those who get access because of their economic class and their access to the knowledge that is reinforced in school. He points out routinely that without a light shining on equity and access for all learners, we tend to default back to what we know, and that is the cells-and-bells model of the past century. In an interview on Deeper Learning posted at the Alliance for Excellent Education, here's what Chad had to say:

ALLIANCE: How does a district ensure that Making is for all kids, no matter their socioeconomic or racial status?

RATLIFF: We've had a tradition in American education of reserving the most interesting and intellectually challenging work for some children but not providing access to all. Our Makerspaces and Maker culture support all children to have an equity of learning and in access to rich experiences. We don't want either project-based learning or Maker-infused learning to be seen as what the "top" or "gifted" kids get to do while other kids get something less challenging and more compliance-driven. We find that the more the full range of kids get access to Maker work, the more engaged they become, the more they see their voice as mattering, and the more they become agents of their own learning who have influence in their classes, school, and community. We need to keep focused on working to do the

right thing for kids and that means ensuring that all
means all when it comes to a full range of active-
learning experiences. Making to learn does that.

(Reid 2016)

What structures need to shift in your class, school, or district
to ensure that all children get access to "rich experiences? How
might you begin making changes in practice that led away from
compliance-based work and to active-learning experiences for all
children? What do you envision as the impact? What would you
do first to move in this direction?

Take Action

When Paulo Freire wrote *Pedagogy of the Oppressed* to describe
how adults in poverty in Brazil learned to read and write, he most
likely had no idea that his work would be read by countless students of education all over the world. He developed banking as
education metaphor to describe how learners as objects are held
in thrall to their oppressors by the reinforcement of passivity. He
offers a contrasting potential for learning to be something very
different when approached through a "problem-posing" educational model (Freire [1970] 2005):

> It is not surprising that the banking concept of education regards
> men as adaptable, manageable beings. The more students work at
> storing the deposits entrusted to them, the less they develop the
> critical consciousness which would result from their intervention
> in the world as transformers of that world. The more completely
> they accept the passive role imposed on them, the more they tend
> simply to adapt to the world as it is and to the fragmented view of
> reality deposited in them. (p. 22)
>
> Whereas banking education anesthetizes and inhibits crea-
> tive power, problem-posing education involves a constant unveil-
> ing of reality. The former attempts to maintain the submersion of
> consciousness; the latter strives for the emergence of conscious-
> ness and critical intervention in reality. (p. 28)

We don't intend to bring all the voices of influence in our professional learning to our stories, but we do find the connection of Freire to Ivan Illich's *Deschooling Society* as having a relationship to Deleuze's rhizomatic metaphor. We encourage as you self-educate through our narrative that you take time to not just read quotes we've included but to dig into historians, philosophers, and practitioners who offer a variety of perspectives on progressive education.

> Once we have learned to need school, all our activities tend to take the shape of client relationships to other specialized institutions . . . In school we are taught that valuable learning is the result of attendance; that the value of learning increases with the amount of input; and, finally, that this value can be measured and documented by grades and certificates.
>
> In fact, learning is the human activity which least needs manipulation by others. Most learning is not the result of instruction. It is rather the result of unhampered participation in a meaningful setting. Most people learn best by being "with it," yet school makes them identify their personal, cognitive growth with elaborate planning and manipulation. (Illich 1973)

Four Actions to Break Down Walls and Construct Open Spaces

1. Lean in to what universal design does for you personally. Map all the ways you use tools to assist you to access the world. Do you wear glasses or contacts? Need to adjust your car seat when you drive? Use curb cuts when you exit a store with a cart? Apply what you learn to mapping your school to improve accessibility and equity for learners in all the spaces of your school. Write down what needs to change. Check your school website for accessibility that complies with federal standards and law. Challenge assumptions of adults about all kids getting access to a variety of tools and choice in using them to construct learning. Be courageous in the face of criticism about UDL.

2. Rearrange your room to provide learners with standing desk options. Add some soft, comfortable seating or active seating and encourage different kids to try it out. Ask them for feedback.

3. Invite kids for lunch to talk with you about what they find helpful and challenging as learners. Talk with them about homework challenges. Ask them if they were given choices of how to show you what they've learned how would they like to do that.

4. Write down what you believe or don't believe about choice, comfort, accessibility, equity, tech tools, and so on. Be honest with yourself. We all have biases about what we believe the rules to be. If you think kids all need to read a book to call it reading, write that down. Then ask yourself: What if you are wrong about it? What if a kid who gets access to listening to a book is able to show you they understand the book? Then what?

Resources

Crary, Jonathan. 1990. *Techniques of the Observer: On Vision and Modernity in the Nineteenth Century*. Cambridge, MA: MIT Press.

Deming, William Edwards. 1982. *Out of the Crisis*. Cambridge, MA: MIT Press.

ETEC 511 DLG 10 – Ecology of Educational Technology. n.d. "Zhao and Frank." Accessed 29 October 2017. http://dlg10.weebly.com/zhao-and-frank.html.

Freire, Paulo. (1970) 2005. *Pedagogy of the Oppressed*. New York: Continuum International.

Illich, Ivan. 1973. *Deschooling Society*. Harmondsworth: Penguin.

Kerr, Stacy. 2014. "Three Minute Theory: What Is the Rhizome?" https://www.youtube.com/watch?v=gnteiRO-XfU.

Meinig, D.W. 1979. "The Beholding Eye: Ten Versions of the Same Scene." In *The Interpretation of Ordinary Landscapes: Geographical Essays*, edited by D.W. Meinig and John B. Jackson, 1–8. New York: Oxford University Press.

Molla, Rani. 2017. "How Apple's iPhone Changed the World: 10 Years in 10 Charts." Recode. 26 June. https://www.recode.net/2017/6/26/15821652/iphone-apple-10-year-anniversary-launch-mobile-stats-smart-phone-steve-jobs.

Peverill-Conti, Greg, and Brad Seawell. 2016. "The Gutenberg Parenthesis: Oral Tradition and Digital Technologies." Communications Forum at the Massachusetts Institute of Technology. 31 August. https://commforum.mit.edu/the-gutenberg-parenthesis-oral-tradition-and-digital-technologies-29e1a4fde271.

Reid, Donique. 2016. "Making an Impact: One District's Approach to Deeper Learning." Deeper Learning. 21 June. http://deeperlearn ing4all.org/making-an-impact-one-districts-approach-to-deeper-learning/.

Socol, Ira David. 2008. "Toolbelt Theory for Everyone." SpeEdChange. 23 May. http://speedchange.blogspot.com/2008/05/toolbelt-theory-for-everyone.html.

———. 2016. "Your School's UX. What Is It? And Where to Start. – Student Voices." Medium. 7 May. https://medium.com/@irasocol/your-schools-ux-what-is-it-and-where-to-start-c9922768b01d.

Tampio, Nicholas. 2010. "Multiplicity." In *Encyclopedia of Political Theory*, edited by Mark Bevir. Los Angeles, CA: Sage.

Wingeier, Douglas E. 1980. "Generative Words in Six Cultures." *Religious Education* 75 (5): 563–576.

Zhao, Yong. 2012. *World Class Learners: Educating Creative and Entrepreneurial Students.* Thousand Oaks, CA: Corwin.

8

Timeless

IRA: I think the essential book about education is Peter Høeg's *Borderliners*. Yes, it is a novel, but that's another of our myths, that nonfiction is always more truthful than fiction. Anyway, the driving concept of *Borderliners* is that formal education is entirely a construct of time. His preteen narrator makes it all clear: "At Biehl's you had to sit down for five to six hours every day – not including the study period – five days a week plus Sunday for the boarders, more than forty weeks a year, for ten years. While constantly having to strive to be precise and accurate, in order to improve. I believe that this went against the nature of children" (Høeg 1994, 254).

PAM: You've called time the first technology of school.

IRA: It's the first, the most abusive, and the hardest for educators to really understand.

CHAD: It's [Raymond] Callahan's *Cult of Efficiency* (Callahan 1964). So ingrained that it's impossible to see. How schools use time is less about learning and more about fitting the functions of schooling into a daily structure. School schedules were developed to teach compliance, something students would need in order to work on the factory floors of industrial America.

IRA: Especially in the United States. The idea of work ethic,
       which is about devoting time rather than accomplish-
       ing a goal, and that of efficiency, the shortest path as
       the best one, are mythic underpinnings of white cul-
       ture, of the culture of power. Battling a society's core
       myths is hard.

Timebound to Timeless

Time is a learning trap. The system sends that message to kids
at home and in school: "If you finish faster, you get free time at
the end of class" or "Finish your homework, then you can watch
Netflix." That message has piled more and more school expectations onto our kids and filled every moment of their day, primarily to meet demands for coverage of learning standards. In doing
so, schools have sacrificed opportunities to slow down and allow
learners to explore their world, instead rewarding kids' efficiency
while asking for more of their time. By occupying schools with
industrial work, organized by bells neatly into time-clock inter-
vals and extended into the home via reams of printed homework,
educators have stolen the power of time and the gift of natural
learning from children.

Yet, human learning is timeless and continuous. Kids learn
best when they are free from the constraints of time, lost in
the magnificent freedom of discovery: jumping in a puddle and
observing the splash; persevering through a hard level in a game;
reading, writing, drawing, or building. Discovery-based learning
is an endless space in which adults forget to eat and kids even
forget they need to use the bathroom.

We are figuring out how to unlearn the industry of school
time and to reconnect with what learning can be when unbound
from the classroom's dominant teaching wall, overstuffed curricular standards, and bell schedules. Schools can change what,
when, how, and with whom young people learn. If our purpose
as educators and parents is to guide students toward life success
and not test success, then we must dig into changing structures
that, by design, limit learning. For example, when Ira works with
educators, he often refers to the endless IEP meetings he has

attended (individualized education plan conferences for special education students):

> I'll hear someone say something like, "He can pay attention forever to something he's interested in." Well, duh. Of course he can. I can, you can . . . we are all wired this way. But the traditional premise of school is that this is seen as atypical. The expectation is that students will immediately engage in any random topic placed before them: phonemes for 12 minutes, subtraction of apples from apples . . . time's up, on to the study of Ancient Mali! The idea is completely mad and yet, generally unquestioned.

When children construct their own world, no matter how fleeting that seems in adult time, they discover a personal power that carries them forward in pursuit of curiosity and interests. This is the intrinsic motivation of learning agency we most want our children to harness. It extends control over their own lives and futures. And, it is the exact opposite of the extrinsic rewards system created by the existing grammar of schooling, a rewards system created to entice students to comply with adult control of when, what, where, and how to learn.

Time is that "first technology" because there is absolutely no escaping it. You can run outside but there is still *the learning day* (school time) and *the nonlearning day* (out of school time). What's more, the school can use homework to extend its control of time into the child's home, separating that out-of-school time into good and bad. As Chad even notes about his own children, "You only get to do the fun stuff after you finish the boring stuff; every kid knows this."

Learning is, of course, timeless. It exists in its own temporal zone, unique to each individual, and different for each thing learned. But school is all about the clock. In Høeg's novel, the main character, Peter, creates total panic among a school's adults simply by messing with the bell schedule. So trained to the clock are the faculty that, by creating an extra 10 minutes at one point in the day, Peter destroys the school's operation. "It's more than a great story; it makes perfect sense," Ira says. "If you take away the clock, and thus start times and end times, the 15-minute time limit on recess, the literacy block, and that moment in the week when we get to do art, well, will the adults in school know what to do?" (Socol 2012).

Learning becomes timeless when we trust in childhood and relinquish control to children. If we let them lead, they explore, widely and wildly. Their curiosities take them places that most adults no longer can envision in the random clutter of curriculum, designed to be taught and tested in isolation of the child as full participant in rather than just a recipient of learning. Given the opportunity to construct learning, young people use technologies of all sorts to manipulate the world, not only traditional tools such as pencils, art brushes, saws, and drills, but also modern tools such as mobile devices. Children can control their use of space and environment, and they learn much more than the curriculum chosen for them when educators support that.

When we create spaces in which children can choose to extend their learning, their investigations, for as long as they desire, we breed empowerment and ownership. By providing a variety of accessible learning pathways, kids develop a remarkable breadth of capabilities. If we trust in childhood and believe that we can help them learn from mistakes, they take off. Kids who have given up on school become leaders; kids who have felt invisible develop a sense of voice. When we choose trust, we grow hearts and minds. Setting aside *our* controls and filters gives students space to develop *their own*. They begin to seize opportunities to personalize their own learning in response to their own questions about how they learn best. As adults we can learn about the intersection of personalization of time, comfort, and choice as we watch children engage in the process of making learning decisions. How do children choose to place themselves in space to work? Are they naturally inclined to sit, to stand, to lounge on the floor? Do they choose to work around an open table flooded with natural light, beneath the table in a quiet nook, or outside under a tree? How do kids use time differently when organizing it for themselves?

Time as a Tool of Engagement

Most people can describe something in which they've engaged that meets the definition of learning flow as defined by David Shernoff and Mihaly Csikszentmihalyi: intense concentration and absorption in an activity with no psychic energy leftover for distractions, a merging of awareness with action, a feeling of control, loss of self-consciousness, and a contraction of the normal sense of time (i.e., time seems to fly) (Shernoff and Csikszentmihalyi 2009). Shernoff and Csikszentmihalyi researched engagement in high schools and found that young people seldom experience learning flow inside schools. In fact, most work assigned by teachers seemed to result in loss of motivation, attentiveness, and curiosity, all key to learner self-efficacy.

As we have worked with teachers who create authentic learning opportunities for young people, we've observed that when flow occurs in a class space, engagement heightens active and focused intensity among students. Teachers who understand this concept of flow optimize engagement, leading to intense concentration among learners so that time feels as if it does indeed fly. What makes flow learning different is that it isn't driven by extrinsic compliance to finish tasks but rather reflects an internal urge to keep going, to not disengage, to keep coming back to accomplish even more.

When learning becomes timeless, it becomes authentically human, owned by learners. It is then that educators set the stage for kids to grow into successful adults, prepared to enter a future none of us can really predict. No place is that any more important than in the middle grades.

Students who function on the margins can benefit from systems that recognize their value and potential and that accommodate their needs. A school community's perspective on time dictates whether students can use available time to actively pursue learning.

Ira describes what the absence of learning flow meant to him as a disenfranchised learner in almost all classes – except one:

> School was boring and stupid to me, so I interrupted every chance
> I got, until even that didn't work. Then I'd work on getting

thrown out. And I could do that all day, until I got to shop class. A few years ago, I was talking with someone from the class about how great it was that we learned to arc weld, and he mentioned that the rest of the class learned to use acetylene torches. I had no memory of that, and then when he said, "They weren't going to let you walk around with a torch," it hit me. The teacher's control was so soft, and I was so engrossed in the welding, that I didn't even notice that I was being steered in a particular direction. And that meant I had no need to fight against it.

Years later, he can still describe every motion he made to build a steel and glass table in middle school.

Ira's shop teacher let students pursue what they were interested in making. They didn't have to worry about language arts or math standards in there. They could come back at lunch or stay late to work. Time became the variable and, thanks to flexing both curriculum and schedule, success the constant. He often wonders what his school experience would have been like if authentic learning had been a goal for him in other classes. Could middle school teachers have leveraged his love of stories, writing, maps, architecture, and design to engage him as a learner despite the challenges of dyslexia? Would he have spent less time in the principal's office or suspended out of school?

Formal education doesn't attract young people to learning by countering their natural instincts to be curious, ask questions, interact, and test out their ideas. That's one concern in middle schools today, where teachers are beset with fitting in broad swaths of mandated content in an effort to make sure students pass state tests. How can schools stretch opportunities when time is so controlled and limited? What should the focus of time be, particularly in the middle school transition from childhood to adolescence? Changing the way we use time doesn't happen by chance, as Thomas Armstrong writes in *The Best Schools: How Human Development Research Should Inform Educational Practice*:

Middle schools, or something very much like them, are needed to provide students in early adolescence with an environment that can help them negotiate the impact of puberty on their intellectual, social, and emotional lives. Educators need to understand the developmental needs of young adolescents, and in particular their neurological, social, emotional, and metacognitive growth. Some of these developmental needs are ignored or subverted by inappropriate educational practices such as fragmented curricula, large impersonal schools, and lesson plans that lack vitality. Practices at the best schools honor the developmental uniqueness of young adolescents, including the provision of a safe school environment, student-initiated learning, student roles in decision-making, and strong adult role models. (Armstrong 2006)

After all, what is the goal in adolescence? Developmentally, it's a time to separate from adults and build peer group relationships, to experiment with things, to figure out who you are. That has nothing to do with our school subject matter or our school day. In fact, it's completely counter to what educators do with time in school. If you ask kids what they like about school, they will answer, "seeing my friends", "lunch," or "recess." So, it's no surprise that when you give kids freedom, control over time, and opportunity to engage with friends, learning becomes a very different reality than what currently exists in most schools.

When we've observed students in school creatively using a variety of technologies, designing and making, and working together on projects that challenge them to consider the needs of others as well as solve community problems, we notice that the social and academic curricula begin to merge and time fades as a construct of the schedule. Kids take work home and connect with peers outside of school to keep going on projects. They come in early, stay late, or use available time during the day to keep working. It's why we've supported maker education, problem- and project-based learning, comfort and choice, and technologies as interactive and connected tools of learning rather than as passive tools of teaching. If empowered agency is a goal for learners so they will thrive not just survive in their adult future, this kind of work must happen purposefully, not by chance.

The physical, social-emotional, and cognitive development of the human body and brain demands a different way of thinking about learning at every age. Educators recognize this and yet the momentum of the machine of school allows them to continue to run public schools exactly as they have been run for over a century. To change this will take a disassembling of what's been assembled into school as we know it. Unless that occurs, the structures and schedules that drive schooling will remain so firmly attached to teacher belief that real change is impossible. Critical questions in seeing new possibilities for schools, possibilities that demand we become less time bound in building each day of learning, include:

How do educators break themselves from the system?
How do the faces of children become more important than years or decades of training? and
How do educators become more intuitive, empathetic, and authentic in their work with young people?

Professional Learning Reimagined

Answering these questions begins by challenging status quo educational beliefs and behaviors. It is only when deep dissonance is created that most educators begin to seriously question curriculum taught in isolation rather than in interdisciplinary contexts, age-based grade levels versus multiage settings, and individual rather than collective teacher efficacy. To shift beliefs about school structures and schedules, there must be strategies in place to make learning timeless for adults, too: strategies that reconnect them to their innate curiosity as humans, strategies that allow and encourage their own learning and stretch out time, strategies that immerse them in experiential learning outside of school, and strategies that build professional opportunities to reimagine the use of time in learning. When professional learning is built with these strategies, rather than based in 45-minute sessions or two-hour conference workshops, educators begin to reflect on real experiences and begin to advocate for similar ones in their own classrooms and schools.

Each September, Chad and Ira take a new group of teachers to New York City for the World Maker Faire. Together, they ride the train from Virginia to the key subway hubs in Brooklyn. They attend the Faire, but also explore informal learning spaces, from the Irish Hunger Memorial to the World Trade Center, the High Line Park to the Brooklyn Bridge. It's a nonstop four-day experience.

"I like sending educators into 'noneducational' experiences," Chad reflects.

> When we first started taking people to Maker Faire in New York, I said, "What is it about this that works?" The dissonance struck me when people would come back and say, "Wow, this was the best professional development I've had." We didn't do anything to make it professional development. It wasn't a conference or a workshop or a class. It was simply informal learning that wasn't time bound or controlled. It was what I now call *micro-immersion*. A mixed group of people with a shared interest, some with similar experiences, some without, boarding a train to New York.

Chad and Ira lead the groups at the World Maker Faire, observing what happens when teachers spend informal time together, talking about who-knows-what, some related to work, some not. When the group arrives at the New York Hall of Science, teachers figure out where they are going first. They look to Chad and Ira for guidance. Instead of directions, they are met with "Figure stuff out. Think about how you want to appreciate this experience. How does it matter to you?" And the teachers go do just that.

During the trip, the teachers connect over meals, on the subway, ambling down the streets of New York. They are immersed in learning, yet the experience looks nothing like traditional professional development. On the train ride home to Virginia, the connections intensify, the conversation flies, the ideation flourishes. And, magic happens. When teachers return to their schools – bam and then bam! – transfer is inevitably executed. It just never fails. What is fascinating is that no reading assignment was dictated, no unit plan product stamped with a due date. Instead, teachers form a true community of practitioners, develop ideas, and implement them in their schools. Over and over again, the teachers come back from the trip and begin to work with their students in a much more open way, and to engage with them without the typical structural boundaries of time.

This kind of micro-immersion experience triggers learning transfer, a key goal of professional learning. We work in a public sector where educators' work is constantly under scrutiny. We know funds must be spent wisely and effectively. To that end, nothing is more important than setting up professional development that motivates teachers to transfer new learning into practice. The research of Joyce and Showers on transfer is as relevant today as it was decades ago. They found, in the early 1980s, that simply attending courses, workshops, and conferences – traditional professional development alone – doesn't end up making much difference in changing classroom practice (Showers, Joyce, and Bennett 1987).

We have found that enticing teachers out of professional development that mostly mirrors the traditional classroom and into immersive experiences such as the Maker Faire trip does, indeed, make a difference. Curiosity is renewed, conversations that seldom occur inside the school are stimulated, and educators explore efficacy as a collective endeavor rather than an individual act. Through conversation, they begin a collective transfer process on the trip. Upon return, the conversations continue, both face-to-face and via social media, as they experiment with the implementation of ideas. The trips have made clear the importance of creating open, flexible experiences with unstructured time, allowing teachers to explore, share, reflect, and engage.

In reflecting on why transfer occurs after this immersive learning, Chad has noticed that some teachers focus on the trip as a philosophical experience, others make sense pragmatically:

They will get their notepad crammed with notes and because the teachers have become "all kind of cool with each other," they'll open up and talk about what they are doing and what they are thinking about changing. Some teachers automatically observe what they could do differently in the classroom. They walk the Maker Faire, see a piece of technology, and think, "How might I put that in my classroom to better support what kids are already doing?" These teachers often begin by looking to enhance their current teaching experience but at some point during the trip take the next step of actually changing it. Others deliberately notice the exhibits that attract kids. They'll go to each of those and start talking to kids, talking to the people running the maker booths, and making notes. From their observations, they figure out that making can generate from what a learner wants to do and still support curricular goals.

Almost two years after one Maker Faire trip, Ira and Chad visited a middle school teacher who had participated. As they watched the teacher work with students, the long-lasting impact of the micro-immersion experience hit home. In a mechatronics lab, the teacher introduced a challenge to students. With little constraint on what the students would produce, the teacher simply said, "I'd like you to make a game." Rather than providing more instructions, he provided tools – simple classroom tools, woodworking tools, 3D printers, a laser cutter. The kids went to work, and the result was what Baby Boomers refer to as the "instant magic" of a Kodak moment (Jacobs 2012). We later discussed the benefit of other educators seeing how kids ran with that simple direction from their teacher. The students' approaches were unique but they all demonstrated intense engagement, exemplifying learning flow. None of their games were similar. Some built mechanical solutions into their projects; others cut pieces with laser cutters or made them from odd pieces of wood or cardboard left over from other projects. The students considered how to make their games challenging, even tricky, for potential players. The teacher didn't talk about grades, objectives, or an endpoint for the work. Instead, the teacher asked questions, redirected student inquiries to peers with tool skills, and facilitated the flow of making.

Micro-immersion experiences work for teachers because of two reasons: (1) stepping away from the routine creates dissonance and pushes thinking out of the ordinary, and (2) micro-immersion creates opportunities for learning flow in adults. As a result of our work with micro-immersion professional learning, we've sought to look at different ways to create flow experiences for teachers that intensify their concentration and focus on timeless learning opportunities for kids.

Reimagining how to use professional learning time differently has become a key focus in our work together as well as with others in the district team. We've developed the micro-immersion model to include multiday peer-to-peer site visits to schools, museums, and public libraries outside our community. We've transitioned summer programs that once had a primary purpose of serving learners into a platform for professional learning. Master teachers are paired with teachers who want to learn how to implement maker learning, PBL, computational thinking, interdisciplinary units, multiage settings, choice and comfort, and so much more during the school year. Together the paired teachers work with learners in the low-stakes summer learning environment to develop pedagogical, tech tool, and kidwatching expertise. This immersive professional learning drives boots on the ground transfer into practice and connects participating teachers to beliefs and actions essential to making immediate, even pivotal, changes in learning space and pedagogical redesign when they return to restart a new school year.

Over time, we've found that making sense of what changes in professional learning need to occur to meet contemporary learners' needs begins with an understanding of the challenges faced by learners and the teachers who work with them. Watching kids and teachers work, play and learn in settings where they find flow has taught us that for learning time to change, pedagogy must change, too.

Looking in Classrooms

Educators have long tried to make kids fit into school schedules and structures. But, shadowing students going through a day of classrooms has led us to notice what kids are expected to do to be successful typically doesn't reflect engaged flow as an end in mind for their learning. We quickly realized that pedagogy needs to change. Even compliant learners don't get what they need in schools as they exist today. This really is not the fault of teachers. Teachers have been trained by their own schooling and higher education to do exactly what they do. They have little time of their own to explore as individuals and as members of communities. To figure out what to do differently, educators need extended time to observe, reflect, and notice how their craft actually impacts learners.

For decades, educators, parents, and administrators thought they knew what learning looked like: 20 to 30 kids in rows, eyes fixed on a teacher stationed in front of the dominant classroom wall. If students are compliant with teacher directions and appear to be listening, administrators will observe, "Most of the kids are engaged." But on local to national surveys of students, many say they're bored to death. There was an interesting Twitter flurry among teens a few years ago, "I'm so f-ing bored at school." You could watch #boredatschool spread across the map every morning, coast to coast. Whether an anecdote such as the Twitter story or through the annual Gallup Student Survey of over one million learners, young people tell us their level of engagement, sense of hope, and experiences of interest and fun in school drop significantly over the years they spent in school (Gallup 2016).

During a classroom walkthrough, Ira says,

> I videotape kids' feet. That's what I always look at. Kids keep their upper bodies compliant. Their feet tell you what they're doing,

whether they're asleep, or just totally panicking. If you look at their feet, you get this whole different perspective on how they are doing in class. Principals walk and when they do observations, they look at the teachers mostly. That's completely wrong.

Educators know that time stands as a key variable in learning. They've played around for a long time with changing school structures to use time more effectively to accomplish learning work. However, to a great extent discussions about the use of time often center on maximizing time on tasks essential to passing tests, whether standardized or teacher made.

Today, Pam uses a different approach to thinking about how learners' time is used when she visits schools: "Every time I walk into a school, I ask myself, what do I want to see more or less of? What kind of work will be internally motivating to learners and their teachers? How do we make work more timeless for our children?"

Progressive educators play continuously with these kinds of questions. Dewey played around with these ideas. The Italian Reggio Emilia Schools constructed a different approach to time (Gribble n.d.). So do Big Picture Learning schools (Big Picture Learning n.d.). Most progressive educators have had to take school offline into a totally different environment to be able to really make deep change work. Redefining approaches to time so that learners engage in authentic learning experiences usually means becoming a lab school, a magnet school, a charter school, or a private school. Going back to the concept of equity and access, if you abandon the comprehensive schools and say this work can't happen here, then most children in America will never get progressive education opportunities. The maker pathway has been a key focus area for transforming learning in our district and reimagining the use of time has been key to bringing engagement practices such as maker education into the school day.

Pam remembers years ago, when she, Chad, and Maker Faire founder Dale Dougherty discussed whether maker education could ever work inside a public school setting. Dale was convinced that making would never happen in the context of the school day because of the external constraints on schools, testing being the most significant one. When they connect today, Pam likes to remind Dale, father of the maker movement, that neither of them expected the idea of maker education during the school day to go viral. Neither would have bet that educators and students would be invited to the White House under the Obama administration to share their work because maker education had become significant to those with an eye toward our nation's future, or that schools in Pam's district were to be featured in a cover story in *Newsweek*, "Maker Movement Reinvents Education" (Stewart 2014).

Space-Time

As Chad and Ira supported innovative creation of informal learning environments such as music construction studios, those environments have spawned other innovations across the school district network. Makerspaces have become part of an ecosystem of spaces where people are doing work that engages all kids and promotes the flexible use of time. As Chad puts it:

> The essential thing about Makerspaces is that they really cannot be "spaces," at least not the way schools understand spaces. I mean, yes, there's a space with specialized tools, or spaces with different specialized tools, from welding to music construction, but these spaces are jumping off points for kids. They are the place you run to when suddenly your poetry needs to become a song, or your study of electricity needs to become a real motor, or your study of the Middle Ages needs to really understand armor. Just as the "classroom" should become a place where you run when you need calculus to build a better airplane wing, or algebra to make your three-legged stool stand up correctly. These learning labs must exist outside of any bell schedule, if they are going to really respond to kids' learning patterns. Of course we're not totally there yet, but we know our goal.

Work to destructure time isn't limited to elementary and middle schools. One of the best examples of prototyping different uses of time emerges in district high schools through a team-based, interdisciplinary approach, interpreting STEM and humanities through their connections with, not their isolation from, each other. In this model, teachers integrate curricula, walking away from the constraint of required seat time, and working together to team-teach in half-day blocks not governed by a traditional bell schedule. Most importantly, as walls have literally been taken down in team-based learning spaces, high school teachers who collaborate and share space describe it as a professional learning opportunity to observe each other every day. They notice that teens in their classes stay engaged with project work that stretches through class time and even into lunch or before and after school. The students talk about the difference that experiential learning in makerspaces, music construction and media studios, the teams' labs, and the library makes to their commitment to staying in school. They engage in work that leaves them with a sense of accomplishment as they design, invent, discuss, make, connect, and share their learning collaboratively and individually.

In fact, they report a very different story of school than students nationally report in the Gallup survey. As Devon,* one member of a team of high school students who built a tiny house together shared, "Last year I would get my parents to pick me up early from school any chance I could. I hated coming to school. This year, I come every day because of this project. My team needs me to be here to work during and after school so I need to be here. And, this work matters to me." The quality of Devon's work became known through local media coverage of the project, and she ended up working as a project management summer intern in a local company. When young people such as Devon get the chance to explore their interests and passions in a context that matters rather than being held prisoner to arbitrary schedules and curriculum, they come alive as learners, seeing themselves as

---

*A pseudonym.

connected, confident, and committed learners. This doesn't happen by chance or through a one-size-fits-all program but rather when teachers willingly provide young people with the opportunity to cocreate learning that matters to them.

Radical change is neither easy nor sustainable if people are isolated from each other. No recipe or program formula exists for work to change that. Brilliant educators are hidden in schools across the United States. They are the designers and inventors of amazing creative work, and they bring to the table all the capability we need to change practices and structures in schools today. Changing how learning becomes timeless for young people starts when teachers experience flow in their own learning. When that happens, professional learning becomes an optimal experience, just as psychologist Mihaly Csikszentmihalyi described in *Flow: The Psychology of Optimal Experience*: When time slows, concentration increases, and the result is "joy, creativity, the process of total involvement with life" (Csikszentmihalyi 1990).

Designing to maximize flow has impacted our work to modernize district facilities. It's essential to moving teachers away from the dominant teaching wall that defines American-built schools. We see flow happening in a newly built multiage elementary space designed as a home of opportunity for 120 K–5 learners and six teachers. Time flows differently when children work together, the older becoming aspirational peers for younger children, no bells demanding that they stop what they are doing to move in short blocks of time from math to reading to science to history in a repetitive daily cycle. Instead, they work on projects that engage them in experiences across content areas and extend time as they see the need. They use a multitude of tools, from cutting-edge tech devices used to connect, build, and create Minecraft worlds to a full kitchen where they cook meals for their entire community.

When we visit community members at work in this flexible space, the low hum of busy children resonates across the six classrooms. It's difficult to spot teachers, who may be kneeling by an individual child, circulating the room, or engaging with a small group. They count on the children to help each other. During a recent visit, a boy and girl were figuring out how to better control a drone in one area of the learning space. They shared how much fun it was to watch a drone-capture video of friends playing soccer at recess. If students want to keep going on projects, they need to know their teachers encourage it. The entire community values the freedom to extend learning beyond the defined state standards, as well as the responsibility that comes with it. In this multiage space, it's hard to tell where "instructional" time begins and ends. What is even more intriguing is that multiage work and space redesign has spread across the entire school. More walls are coming down, more collaborative opportunities for children are being created, and the fixed nature of learning time is shifting.

Our observations of educators and young people who experience timeless learning confirm that authentic, meaningful learning is less controlled by adults and more reflective of learners who develop agency. We also have seen how shared professional experiences that move educators out of environments traditionally defined as teaching places create dissonance. That dissonance results in a redefinition of teaching places as learning spaces. In learning spaces, educating young people for the purposes of school shifts to educating them for life, both in the present and in the future.

When we consider exemplars of how time can be flexed in and out of school, we come back to the same question that we have long discussed: How do we create learning experiences that are timeless for adults and young learners in today's schools? We've come to the conclusion that it's really a question of will. Our values and beliefs are reflected in how we choose to structure the use of time. Educators can create spaces for learning that challenge learners to pursue interests so that the end of the school day becomes neither a boundary for learning nor the next stage in the cycle of endless compliance work. We see this happening in schools in our own community and even in some across the nation. However, the will to change means taking the risk to be provoked and to inquire, reflect, and take action.

The work of the late, progressive educator Ted Sizer frames our own current work to "radically innovate" the way we consider the use of time, to move toward changes that build from natural learning processes that represent uncharted territory in this century given the focus on management by schedule and standards.

Ted Sizer, teacher, author of *Horace's Compromise* and dean of the Harvard Graduate School of Education from 1964 to 1972, proposed significant changes in the operations of high schools in the 1970s and 1980s (Sizer 1984). While perhaps not what Clayton Christensen (Christensen, Raynor, and McDonald 2015) would define as true disruptive innovation, his ideas about changing the culture of schooling provoked thought about the purpose of education and eventually led to private and even some public shifts in the way we organized time, curricula, and personnel inside high schools. His design principles challenged every norm we still accept today in high schools, from selected-response testing and grading practices to teaching courses in isolation to assigning transcript credits based on seat time. These norms are the legacy of the Committee of Ten whose early 1900s efforts sought to create schools that educated few for college and middle-class work, consigning most to a future in blue-collar factories and service (Eliot, Hill, and Winship 1894).

Perhaps this factory approach worked in 1910, although we have doubts about that. We believe, like Sizer (who has provoked our own thinking), that young people need learning opportunities substantively different from those of cells and bells schools to be well-educated in this century (Sizer 2009). We also believe that the competencies of learning that matter most are timeless, indeed, represent the best of any-century learning. Here's what Sizer said in a 1984 interview in, of all media, *People*, about needing something more than "reform by cooker cutter":

> The structure absolutely conspires against serious work for all children. A kid bounces off seven adults a day, from Physics to Phys. Ed to French to English to Social Studies, less than 60 minutes

each, in groups of 20 or more. What you should do is dramatically simplify the time each student has with one teacher. A practical example would be to cluster the curriculum into four areas: inquiry and expression, mathematics and science, literature and the arts, philosophy and history. Instead of seven teachers, each student would have four. If there's an aphorism running through my book, it is that less is more. Slow everything down. Make sure there is real mastery . . . It would mean two periods a day. Some schools have already experimented with these "curriculum blocks" with excellent results. It would mean, more importantly, that a small number of teachers would follow the way a student's mind develops . . . Teachers must have the leeway to say, "That kid needs two years on this subject and this kid needs six months." The solution is not to hammer people into a mold – reform by cookie cutter – but to adapt to the particular strengths of the kid. Right now the system makes no individual adaptations. (Keller 1984)

Developing lifelong learning competencies and proficiency in their use takes time. When young people are afforded the time they need to engage individually and together within social learning communities, they grow cognitively and emotionally from experiences in which they formatively think, empathize, design, acquire new information, build, communicate, collaborate, problem solve, create, and iterate. Humans, with these competencies writ large, have advanced civilization across generations as a result of the inventiveness and ideation of their thinking. And, even when writ small, such competencies help people develop a greater potential for a high quality of life in homes, communities, and as citizens in our democracy (CERI 2010).

This is why we have worked hard together to strip away what Callahan labeled as the Cult of Efficiency approach, which resulted in stripped down learning forged in the crucibles of the Second Industrial Revolution. We believe that our work supplants that efficiency philosophy with a progressive approach in which time does not hold children hostage. While there is still much work to accomplish, we know we must abandon educational methodologies that at best sort children and at worst fails them. That's the path we are on to make learning timeless. We do that by asking ourselves questions, ones that challenge us to consider how people learn, what's important to learn, and why what we do in school matters to young people.

When do learners get the opportunity to learn different communication skills and show audiences what they can do formatively over time?

How do they become active users the global communication network?

How does every learning opportunity in school become a real experience in developing knowledge and competencies for life, not just for a class or course?

How do we build contemporary curricula, assessment, and learning opportunities that learners actually want and need?

What was true in the world of 1910 isn't true in the world of today. That's why the questions we, and others, ask are valuable to defining how learning must evolve in response to the world in which we live today and the future of tomorrow.

Times change, but learning remains timeless.

Your Own Learning

Provocation

Sizer articulated a philosophy of progressive education and operationalized these common principles (Coalition of Essential Schools n.d.b) and philosophy into the Coalition of Essential Schools (Coalition of Essential Schools n.d.a):

1. Learning to use one's mind well
2. Less is more: depth over breadth of coverage
3. Goals apply to all students
4. Personalization
5. Student-as-worker, teacher-as-coach
6. Demonstration of mastery

7. A tone of decency and trust
8. Commitment to the entire school
9. Resources dedicated to teaching and learning
10. Democracy and equity

When we converse about what schools should be like today, is Sizer's work still relevant, still of value? What's missing from his work? How might you provoke colleagues to consider structures, values, and behaviors inside your own school or classes that impede the kind of timeless learning that we propose?

Consider launching into your Isearch journal (in the cloud or on paper) to write down your thinking about Sizer's common principles, time, and learning. Research contemporary schools that use time differently to create learning that exemplifies Sizer's common principles.

Structured Inquiry

In any conversation we have with educators about what limits teachers and learners from creating spaces where they both can learn with maximal opportunity, connectivity, experience, and agency, the limitation of time almost always is the first item on the list. This quote by Ira speaks to learning in what once existed as one of the few spaces in his middle school where kids and teachers had the luxury of time to explore and extend learning without the imposition of standardized testing and standards – the shop class.

> I remember this guy building a rowboat across the whole seventh grade year. I mean he built this magnificent wooden boat that he worked on every day. He didn't do anything else. He didn't do any of the projects. *It was just all about the boat.*

What values are represented in this small mental "clip" about learning? What sparks questions in your own thinking about the image of a boy spending a year building a boat?

What would need to change in your class, school, or district to create opportunities for learners to pursue learning without time limits? Where does that happen now? If not, why not? How might you lead a discussion about making changes more consistent with Sizer's common principles? What barriers would you need to overcome to get agreement to try out a change in schedule, curricula, or assessment? What confirmation biases about what school is supposed to be would you need to challenge to consider making a change?

Reflective Pause
Consider that an authentic measure of anyone's learning is not what we do when we complete a test, whether an essay, multiple choice, or even a project produced as part of assigned learning. The measure of learning at its most authentic represents what people do when they don't know what to do, indeed what they choose to pursue when given the opportunity, or when no one is watching.

How might teachers make such learning accessible to young people? What beliefs would be essential to give up the concept of decontextualized learning?

How might young people be given generous opportunities to show us not just *what* they are learning but equally, if not more importantly, *how* they are learning?

When you walk a school, what do you want to see more or less of? What kind of work builds the highest level of internal motivation within learners and their teachers? How might we make work more timeless for our children?

Take Action
Schools have mostly tinkered with time in school. This has happened with block scheduling, extended learning time, year-round schools, and so on. Few radical shifts have occurred in how we consider time as a variable even in schools that have rejected traditions of time and schedule. Recent adaptation comes from educators trying to find more time for remediation so that learners get extra help to pass state or common core tests. That leads us to ask what timeless education really looks like and for what purpose should we consider using time differently? How do educators

begin to see outside the filters of what we think we know about the barriers of time and what's important to learning for life? Where does homework fit, or not?

Four Actions to Create Timeless Learning for Educators and Young Learners

1. Get out of schools. Really. Figure out where you can take educators to think differently about time without being in a school. It could be a business such as a bank, a hotel, a vineyard, or a local tech company. Almost always when we ask about bringing educators to use a conference or meeting space, they say yes.

2. Ask yourself if you were to release controls over time, what would be possible that's impossible now? What could change? How might curricula, class schedule, resources, and staff align so that teachers and learners have more control over time? Write your ideas down and create a pitch you can make to teachers, a principal, the superintendent or a school board to do something different. What's your compelling narrative? Your why?

3. Interview kids. How would they use time differently? See if they will go on the record about their perspectives on how they use time. How much time do they see as wasted time in their learning lives? Why? Video them with permission. Set them up on a panel to talk about time use with a faculty. Bring them to a school board meeting to discuss the best uses of their time in school and out as learners.

4. Talk to parents. What do they value about learning time? At school? At home? How do they see time use for learning from their parent perspective? What are the value drivers for them? Write down perspectives from parents, learners, and educators and contrast with your own. Document what you have learned and consider how to engage a team, leverage resources, and prototype a change in how time is used in school – not for remediation but for child-driven learning.

Resources

Armstrong, Thomas. 2006. *The Best Schools: How Human Development Research Should Inform Educational Practice*. Alexandria, VA: ASCD.

Big Picture Learning. n.d. "10 Expectations." Accessed 9 December 2017. http://www.bigpicture.org/apps/pages/index.jsp?uREC_ID=389378&type=d&pREC_ID=902773.

Callahan, Raymond E. 1964. *Education and the Cult of Efficiency: A Study of the Forces That Have Shaped the Administration of Public Schools*. Chicago: University of Chicago Press.

Centre for Educational Research and Innovation (CERI). 2010. *Improving Health and Social Cohesion through Education*. Paris: OECD. http://www.oecd.org/edu/ceri/improvinghealthandsocial-cohesionthrougheducation.htm.

Christensen, Clayton M., Michael E. Raynor, and Rory McDonald. 2015. "What Is Disruptive Innovation?" *Harvard Business Review*. 1 December. https://hbr.org/2015/12/what-is-disruptive-innovation.

Coalition of Essential Schools. n.d.a. "About CES." Accessed 9 December 2017. http://essentialschools.org/about-ces/.

Coalition of Essential Schools. n.d.b. "Common Principles." Accessed 9 December 2017. http://essentialschools.org/common-principles/.

Csikszentmihalyi, Mihaly. 1990. *Flow: The Psychology of Optimal Experience*. New York: Harper Collins.

Eliot, Charles W., Frank A. Hill, and A. E. Winship. 1894. "The REPORT of the Committee of Ten." *Journal of Educational Research* 40 (5): 979. JSTOR: 91–93.

Gallup. 2016. "2016 National Gallup Student Profile Scorecard." http://www.gallupstudentpoll.com/197492/2016-national-scorecard.aspx.

Gribble, Kate. n.d. "What Is the Reggio Emilia Approach?" An Everyday Story. Accessed 9 December 2017. http://www.aneverydaystory.com/beginners-guide-to-reggio-emilia/main-principles/.

Høeg, Peter. 1994. *Borderliners*. New York: Macmillan.

Jacobs, Deborah L. 2012. "What Will Become of the Kodak Moment?" *Forbes*. 19 January. https://www.forbes.com/sites/deborahljacobs/2012/01/19/what-will-become-of-the-kodak-moment/.

Keller, Jon. 1984. "Theodore Sizer Wants to Stamp Out Cookie-Cutter Education by Making High School Voluntary." *People*. 5 March. http://people.com/archive/theodore-sizer-wants-to-stamp-out-cookie-cutter-education-by-making-high-school-voluntary-vol-21-no-9/.

Shernoff, David J., and Mihaly Csikszentmihalyi. 2009. *Handbook of Positive Psychology in Schools*. Edited by Michael J. Furlong, Richard Gilman, and E. Scott Huebner. New York: Routledge.

Showers, Beverly., Bruce Joyce, and Barrie Bennett. 1987. "Synthesis of Research on Staff Development: A Framework for Future Study and a State-of-the-Art Analysis." *Educational Leadership: Journal of the Department of Supervision and Curriculum Development, N.E.A* 45 (3): 77–87.

Sizer, Theodore. 1984. *Horace's Compromise: The Dilemma of the American High School*. New York: Houghton-Mifflin.

———. 2009. "Ted Sizer's Opening Remarks, Fall Forum 2000, Providence, Rhode Island." *Horace* 25. Coalition of Essential Schools. Oakland, CA. http://www.essentialschools.org, http://files.eric.ed.gov/fulltext/EJ868296.pdf.

Socol, IraDavid. 2012. "ChangingGears2012:UndoingAcademicTime." 26 January. http://speedchange.blogspot.com/2012/01/changing-gears-2012-undoing-academic.html.

Stewart, Louise. 2014. "Maker Movement Reinvents Education." *Newsweek*. 8 September. http://www.newsweek.com/2014/09/19/maker-movement-reinvents-education-268739.html.

9

Where Design Begins

Design and thinking is . . . [the] idea of making creative leaps to come up with a solution . . . [It] allows people to not just be problem solvers with explicit, but also tacit knowledge . . . They are learning by doing . . . coming up with solutions by making things.
– Bill Moggridge in *Design and Thinking* (Tsai 2014)

Our own design journey began in 2002 when educators in our schools were challenged to propose innovative instructional units that would be multidisciplinary in scope and inclusive of new learning technologies. The superintendent at that time had experienced the challenge and fun of creating a video movie at a conference. When he returned to the district, he directed the central office team to enable every child to experience the exhilaration of making their own movie, too. From that moment forward the concept of design for learning projects developed with an end in mind of engaging our learners in interdisciplinary project work using technology to create their own entry points into learning through both thinking and doing.

PAM: Design begins with ideas . . . ideas that come when we have to find solutions to very big or sometimes very small challenges. Anyone can think about design. Anyone can be a designer. Anyone who looks at something and thinks "I could make that better for the people who use it" becomes a design thinker. In our district, we see our young learners and our workforce as offering us the best of what designers do – creating pathways to that which is possible so that we can better meet others' needs as well as our own.

CHAD: If somebody says to me, "Well, how did you execute that? Or, how did you pull that off? Why didn't you ask permission to do that?" I'm able to say internally to others, well, it meets criteria for what we are trying to accomplish. We've created this progressive learning model that is design driven from what we want our kids to accomplish to how we believe transforming learning can occur along multiple pathways. It's right in the language of the strategic plan.

IRA: And, here's something to consider if you want to support people to be creative as designers and makers. Don't have more rules than you need. One of our belief systems that's really helped with this, and it's one that's controversial among educators, is that a school or a classroom doesn't belong to this principal or that teacher. Technology doesn't belong to a school. We believe all our resources belong to the kids of the school division and we use resources as we need them. We're fortunate here to have a culture where there's no real problem with that.

The Design Journey

The journey of a thousand miles begins with one step.
— Lao Tzu, *Tao Te Ching*

Why did we pursue design as a process? After the former superintendent issued his challenge, the Design 2004 Project was created with an intention to stimulate transformational learning innovations at a time when school districts in Virginia and across the nation were consumed with standardization of curricula, multiple-choice high-stakes testing, and programmed instruction driven by the federal No Child Left Behind Act (NCLB). We believed as a team that Design 2004 would provide opportunities for teachers to imagine learning that would engage young people in interesting, thoughtful work. And, yes, we did want our young people to have fun. In 2002, teachers from all levels came together in design teams to propose instructional units in response to what came to be known as the Design 2004 Project.

Our first design projects were funded with local "seed" grants to support professional development, technology and other resource acquisition, and team activities. In the summer of 2003, teachers gathered in their design teams to debrief the impact of the units. As they reflected upon the stages of their yearlong journey, teachers were emphatic that Design 2004 could not stop with their work in those initial projects. They had seen firsthand the enthusiasm quotient of students involved in the projects just skyrocket as they worked together in what educators today refer to as the four Cs – collaboration, critical thinking, creative thinking, and communication.

At the time, we didn't realize that we were on the same flight path as the Partnership for Twenty-First Century Skills, today often referred to as P21 (P21 n.d.). As we began to find more resources on the web, we realized that the business sector, educators, technology companies, and nonprofits were all exploring the edges of a horizon that would take us to new frontiers of learning, pushed there by changes occurring in the workforce as well as learning opportunities developing inside schools as a result of technological advances.

We aligned in 2007 with an offshoot of P21, a state-level initiative, by joining with other districts educators who believed that learning in the twenty-first century could not be held in thrall by NCLB. That group, EdLeader21, began to drive toward district-level initiation of the 4Cs. From insights gathered from Design 2004 innovation teams a key driver emerged for redesign of curricula, assessment, and instruction in the district. The critical impact of Design 2004? The development of 12 Lifelong

Learning Competencies, which today are the expected competencies for graduates of our high schools, are perfectly aligned with what is now referred to across the nation as the 4Cs (Albemarle County Public Schools n.d.b).

In the Classroom: Kid Designers

> Think left and think right and think low and think
> high. Oh, the thinks you can think up if only you try.
> — Dr. Seuss (1975)

Nowhere does imagination and curiosity run more wild than in the bodies and minds of children. When given the opportunity to explore and discover, young people generate more new ways of solving problems, figuring out solutions, and creating new ideas and products per capita than in any other sector, public or private. The thinking and doing of design come naturally to young people everywhere. Yet, they enter school settings set up for compliance-driven learning rather than sustaining and developing their capabilities to create, think critically, collaborate, and communicate.

On our journey we have explored how design applies to the work we've done to research and develop concept-centered curricula, performance-driven assessment, and contemporary pedagogy (Albemarle County Public Schools 2004). We've discovered that design is elemental to the work of young people to solve problems, construct and complete high-interest projects, engage in "make to learn and learn to make," and determine solutions to grand challenges that help to improve the lives of community members locally and globally – from creating in school community makerspaces to programming classroom 3D printers to designing and building underwater ROVs (Craddock 2014). As young people are given the opportunity to systematically design and make through a process of exploration, ideation, experimentation, and evolution, they become active learners who find voice, agency, and influence in the learning work they pursue (Design Thinking for Educators n.d.).

Young people are coding designers, space designers, service learning designers. They design, choreograph, and construct as artists. They use high- and low-tech tools to design and make products that no one would ever have believed possible before we embarked on this journey. They design by themselves and with each other. One high school student designed an app that would alert a deaf peer to loud noises, a safety consideration. Another designed an app for his school (mpcraddock 2013). One elementary faculty engaged its entire school in a design charrette to figure out ways to improve the school climate. Children suggested round tables in the cafeteria, multiage recess, art in the hallways, and a LEGO wall. They worked together all day in the gym generating ideas and recording them on video as well as butcher paper. When they finished their ideation, the staff began to turn children's ideas into reality. As one child said to a visitor observing in the school that day, "We design everything in this school."

Together, faculty and children redesigned the school. Over time, the cafeteria was transformed with café-style seating, and outside picnic tables were added to encourage dining out in the natural world. The library was developed as a space of choice and comfort with a variety of seating options and a makerspace. Hallways became messy exhibition spaces where kids could work on a LEGO wall, collaborate on projects, and show off completed work, museum style. Today it isn't unusual to see children setting up culminating project work that represents multiage connectivity. For example, kindergartners in a French immersion program partnered with high school French students to plan a French market where children could shop for everything from fresh fruit to small bakery treats. Children designed the market and made everything from the signage to items for sale. While these kinds of activities are not unusual in our schools and certainly represent the best kind of engaged learning, we have found that design thinking demands competencies that maximize learner engagement in a process approach to learning. To accomplish design work embedded in the curricula demands time for teachers to plan, process, reflect, and iterate their own work by design. That does not happen by chance but because of a commitment to structures that support this very different kind of work that is less about the structures of passing tests such as pacing guides and more about the opportunity to design project ideas with peers.

In the School: Teacher Designers

> It's not when you press the shutter, but why you press the shutter.
> – Mary Ellen Mark, photographer, in Gilbert (2015)

Teachers are by nature and necessity great designers and makers. The problem is even when they've had opportunities to think about improving the user experience of young people, they've had little time to act upon inventive thoughts. Teachers have worked for decades in assembly line teaching environments while doing their jobs in egg-crate schools governed by manufacturing-driven bells and schedules. Yet, teachers enter the profession with a high degree of efficacy and a great deal of empathy for the "end users" of schools, the learners. This sets them up to become design thinkers in their own work. We've made that a priority, and we see design focus spreading across classrooms and schools, ever moving our maker work to a new level of consciousness while connecting us to maker education community members across the country (Stewart 2014).

When given the opportunity to learn to use design thinking in their own collaborative work as professionals as well as with students, teachers share their own high levels of creativity, curiosity, and imagination as they explore, generate ideas, prototype, experiment, and improve processes and products of teaching and learning. Whether it's the librarian who brought in a sewing machine and taught lessons on how to sew or the elementary teacher who set the stage for empathy-driven maker projects by asking children to interview family members or friends about something they need, teachers who purposefully plan design thinking into instructional activities empower learners through deep learning experiences. We saw this in action when we observed male teens designing and sewing their own unique bow ties for high school prom night. It also emerged in a child's invention of a cell phone holder that would attach to her grandmother's cane so that she had her phone with her at all times.

In our district's journey, Design 2004 morphed over the years to incorporate professional learning communities and networks, instructional coaching, project-based learning, twenty-first-century learning skills, connected and digital learning, and learning space redesign – all the products of design processes. Ongoing work has reflected an end in mind through periodic addition of resources to create S-curve inflection points of steep innovation toward lifelong learning readiness (Johnson and Mendez-Garcia 2012). In a recent iteration, Design 2015, educator teams created 26 prototypes for transformative learning and spaces in libraries, classrooms, gyms, cafeterias, hallways, arts spaces, and outdoor areas (Albemarle County Public Schools n.d.a). The intended outcome? To create pathways that would make contemporary learning work go viral beyond the explorers and the pioneers in our schools to educators who need more time to implement use of new technologies, pedagogies, and assessments that deepen progressive approaches to learning.

From Design 2015 came new ways of thinking about the work learners do routinely, the tools they use, the spaces available for learning, the accessibility of curricula, and the use of time and environment. In the projects, commonalities emerged across seven pathways identified as essential to the process of transforming the learning ethos of schools. The Seven Pathways to Transform Learning became design principles for how we approach professional development, strategic focus, and goal-setting processes (Albemarle County Public Schools n.d.c). Design thinking has opened these pathways for teachers in our district to consider not learning reform but rather learning *transformation*. Each pathway by itself is unremarkable in terms of full-scale change, but together they multiply the possibilities of learning for all young people. And now that we've moved past Design 2015, iterating that process in our schools has led to numerous examples of design thinking applied across the curriculum. One school has even set a goal of formally and informally integrating design thinking into every area of a child's school day, and the dream of becoming an East Coast elementary version of the Stanford D-School.

In the District: Community Designers

Everyone likes creativity because everyone believes they are, or were, or can be creative. And they are right. The truth is that the best scientists, entrepreneurs, engineers, soldiers, CEOs, sports coaches, hockey players, and World of Warcraft players are all creative. That scaffolding of Design Thinking, that collection of behaviors is the heart and soul of creativity. It includes being attuned to the people and culture you are immersed in and having the experience, wisdom, and knowledge to frame the real problem and – most important of all perhaps – the ability to create and enact solutions.

– Bruce Nussbaum (2011)

We talk about the idea that design thinking lets us work on getting essential changes right. We know that whole scale attempts to "scale up" innovation, often interpreted in the education world as programs, just don't often work. Each of our 26 schools is unique in its own terroir, evolving as the adults and children within the community change over time. Instead of mass producing change, we've chosen another path – one that promotes young people, teachers, and school communities to design up using their unique talents and the diversity of community members to create different pathways to transform learning ("The Meaning of Terroir – Introduction" n.d.).

Commonalities emerge as school community members cross-pollinate both face-to-face and virtually. When the Lifelong Learning Competencies and the Seven Pathways became frames for our work, they didn't come from the top-down but rather from the bottom-up work of educators doing the daily experimentation and adaptations of ideas that they found made sense when working with learners in their classrooms and schools.

Today, we use the *Walk Out Walk On* (Wheatley and Frieze 2011) approach of scaling across – not up – as a strategy for developing our work (Gooding and Lipley 2004). Schools make different choices about where they want to focus their creative energy. They build ideas differently – a more organic rather than lock-step model of design thinking. The real problem of how to engage children who struggle in school may be similar across communities but educators must explore differently how to make sense out of where to start on the path to make learning accessible. Contextually, different demographics, different teachers' expertise, size and location of a school, parent community support – the elements that create diversity – are all critical considerations in design process. Noticing all those elements helps teachers figure out the problems they need to solve as a community and when noticing happens, mindfulness follows.

We've found time is key for children as designers – which is why we our teachers provide time for learners to explore and experiment as they ideate and make (Roscorla 2017). It's why teachers embrace flexible spaces that allow for a continuum of learning situations that don't preclude direct teaching with classes but also support one of the Seven Pathways, choice and comfort, as a dominant narrative of students working together and finding connections to personal interests that compel them to engage. It's the essence of why we provide teachers with choices in time, schedules, and opportunities as they work collaboratively to create, design, invent, construct, build, engineer, and produce in their own learning work. As an educator said to us once, "We all have the same amount of time – it's what we choose to do with it that determines how our life will go."

Formal language also drives our work at every level of the organization from goal setting as individuals to strategic focus at the district level. The Lifelong Learner Competencies that have been embedded as core to key formative and summative outcomes for learners of all ages through graduation from our high schools exemplify a long-term commitment to consistent focus on progressive education. The Seven Pathways weren't totally solid, and in fact were still being developed, when we started up the first pop-up makerspace. However, making had also become an important learning pathway, especially when it came to equity and access, so the opportunity to create a culture of making as learning in a barrio community resonated with us, particularly because it allowed staff to connect culture, community, and connectivity in the children's home environment, not school.

As the Lifelong Learning Competencies and the Seven Pathways became part of our own pedagogical culture, they also became levers for our work and used to frame community design discussions about making the vision for active and empowered learning a part of our invention, innovation, strategic, and operational areas of focus. We began to practice a process we've labeled as YELP, borrowing the acronym from the popular check-in site that helps people navigate to places they desire to go.

In our YELP model, we work as leaders to go through a process that begins with affirming educators' suggestions or ideas for innovative approaches with a response of **Yes**. Even if an idea has to be shaped so that it fits within a budget, policy, or even legal code, we try to figure out how to get to "yes" (Moran 2016).

Second, we believe that little change occurs when people work in isolation, so we work with our idea generators to identify who also should be part of a team to develop and try out a new idea such as the creation of virtual reality labs in our schools or removing lockers from high schools.

Engaging teams has turned out to be one of the most important tasks of leaders in our schools in accomplishing invention or innovation work because the skills of collaboration and reflection are so important to increasing the likelihood of success, just as being willing to take a risk and fail helps a team keep going in the face of missteps.

Leveraging resources from available funds may be a significant challenge, but we have learned to look for funds from every source possible including donations, grants, and redirected from funds available in our own budget. That means sometimes we need to stop doing something to innovate. For example, when custodians asked why we continued to fund locker replacements, a huge expense in secondary schools, and principals asked to replace lockers with charging bars and bench seats, we redirected capital funds to create what has become a favorite innovation in our high school hallways.

When we are creating innovation and invention work to test out ideas that we believe will benefit our learners, we've also learned that **Prototyping** is critical to ensuring that our philosophy of "Aim small, miss small" means that our investments are protected by taking minimal risks. So, when we first pulled lockers out of a high school and replaced them with spaces where learners could gather for small group learning, heads-down headphone work, or personal down time at lunch, we observed and talked with teens using the spaces to determine what worked and what improvements were needed before we expanded the project. As a result, we changed some things from the original projects such as bench height, adding white boards, and putting more charging outlets into the areas.

By engaging community in design, we are able to invent and innovate, and from assessment of work in those areas, we then can determine what moves forward as strategic focus areas.

Pivot: Making Can Happen Anywhere

A few years ago one of our colleagues, Gloria, indicated to Chad and Ira that she wanted to do a summer project in this massive trailer park – a barrio really – and that a church was willing to lend her a double-wide trailer if she could figure out how to make the project happen. They drove over and found the trailer had nothing in it. It seemed like a such good idea to do something for kids who lived in the trailer park even though this was two weeks before school was over. There was just no way to pull off a startup maker project. However, as Ira and Chad sketched out ideas on a whiteboard and spent time learning more about the community, they began to figure out how to leverage resources into the project. A week after school ended, despite the challenges, a makerspace was up and running in the trailer.

As a project not everything works that fast, but educators should be able to work that fast when the opportunity presents itself. Chad and Ira realized they could reach kids for the summer who otherwise would not make it to summer programs at school, even though they're probably not even a mile from there.

From the first moment Ira and Chad began to talk about this project, they knew it was the right thing to do. They said, "We can make a summer anchor academy out of this in two weeks." And they did. They designed up fast and the process worked.

What's interesting about the narrative of the pop-up makerspace is it links perfectly to the concept of effectuation – and it's a perfect example of leveraging resources to support inventive change (Society for Effectual Action n.d.). Chad and Ira are always looking for new spaces to identify an opportunity and then begin the invention development processes. Instead of sitting down and doing project mapping, what they usually do, and did in this case, was to look around and ask, "What do we have? And what can we make out of it?" In this case, the district had a very talented guy just wrapping up his administrative leadership program, and he needed to complete an internship. So, they identified him as a talented person who was ready to take on a different challenge. They had energy in a number of educators around making to learn. They had access to a trailer in a barrio. They had access through Gloria to a community that the district hadn't been able to penetrate. And, a high school was just a mile away. They knew the school had furniture. The assets to the project were all the right stuff.

The team called the high school principal closest to the barrio and said, "We need a whole bunch of tables and chairs and – also a couple of carts of computers." He pointed to some new flexible furniture we'd purchased for his school and asked, "Why don't you take this stuff? It's cool and flexible and little kids would like it, why don't you take this?" Then he said, "I'll have our custodians load it up for you. Out on the loading dock. Just come get it." That's an attitude that works here.

Pam was visiting the pop-up space a few days after the maker academy and realized that the little kids were all trying to watch the World Cup on a laptop screen. They were gathered around this one laptop (we'd actually gotten a wireless hub in the trailer) and they were all animated, arguing about their favorite teams. This barrio is a melting pot of Hispanic Latinos from South America, central America, and Mexico and you can imagine the diversity of opinion about soccer teams. Pam just watched; a 3D printer was running in the background while the kids were building some kind of cardboard house with Arduinos and hot glue guns. Everyone was engaged and working together. No one missed a beat. It wasn't long before she sent a text message to Ira indicating that the kids could use a large monitor screen.

Ira was developing a sense of how to leverage resources at his disposal at the time, and upon receiving the text asked himself, "How am I going to most easily do this?" From Pam's text he knew the kids were using technology collaboratively in the space to do things such as build Scratch code and watch the World Cup. He knew that to go through purchasing to order a monitor from an online company wasn't going to work because that would take weeks and the academy would be over before it arrived. He knew he had to work on this differently, so he drove up to Target, bought the largest TV monitor he could for $300 and drove back out to the trailer park, turning the receipt into the bookkeeper of course! We handed the monitor to the intern running the pop-up makerspace. He got it connected, and the kids not only were watching the World Cup together in a few minutes literally after Pam sent that text but also were able to watch each other building code over the course of the academy.

An organization has to be set up philosophically so that educators can move quickly in response to inventive ideas or needs that kids or adults have. The pivot to open the pop-up maker space and secure a tool that was needed for kids didn't wait for the hierarchy to make decisions. That comes when progressive philosophy drives decisions that respond to the community. Connectivity is a key pathway, and if people are isolated from each other, they don't talk. If they don't talk, the synergy of acting on ideas never gets built. This kind of work may happen serendipitously but it happens by design.

That's also how our local career and technical education center acquired a school bus that teens at the center are turning into a mobile food bus, a food truck on steroids. Pam heard the director talking about an interest in creating a food bus for use by the culinary arts students. That conversation led to a quick e-mail from Pam to the director of transportation, who immediately wrote back and said "We can provide a bus that can be retrofitted into a kitchen." From there, business partners were solicited for donations and funds acquired that would allow students in construction, automotive, information technology, and culinary arts to work collaboratively to create the bus. That's how staff in our district take an idea and design up – and that "can do" design approach innovates work in all kinds of ways, and that seldom surprises us.

We didn't get bogged down with the barrio pop-up makerspace project, and that comes out of the culture we've fostered to make it okay to move fast. We knew this project could address equity and access for kids who might not get to other formal summer school activities or have parents who could pay for enrichment opportunities in the summer. It also provided a space for us to explore the question of how cultural responsiveness really plays into some of this work we're trying to accomplish – another example of a learning laboratory created in a very different environment than a school.

When we created that makerspace we knew that trying to have some sort of a rigid schedule for the kids was likely not going to work for their families or for them. It almost became a "whoever shows up at whatever time they show up" and enters the trailer becomes a designer and maker. It was a community space. It was not like school.

As we were getting ready for another summer learning laboratory, in this case a Coder Dojo, we realized we needed at least 40 or 50 iPads (CoderDojo n.d.). We start thinking. What schools have those? We realized that we were in this weird moment because we're switching gears and we have our computer services technicians who are trying to shift with us. One of the techies said that one of the larger elementary schools, some distance away and in an entirely different feeder pattern from where we were running the Coder Dojo, had the iPads we need. He called and spoke to a secretary, asking her, "Do you have carts of iPads we could borrow for our Coder Dojo? And she said, "Oh, yeah. We have at least two of those." Ira sent one of the tech team out there. He tracked them down and borrowed a truck and moved them to the high school. We let the principal know officially by tweeting him a picture of his iPad cart in the back of the truck so he would know where they were going.

Schools are some of the most bureaucratic places found in any sector; Ira worked for the New York City Police, so that's saying something. In other places, administrators tend to think that good stewardship of public funds means people hold tight to resources, but resources lose value unless they're in use all the time. There has to be a strong understanding of that in order to make a system work functionally across every dimension of what it takes for a school or district to provide equity and access in learning to push past the discriminatory practices that create barriers to progressive learning.

Design for learning is about time. It's about cultural responsiveness. It's about tuning in and noticing. It's about empathy (Brown 2011). And, it's about the art of listening to all the nuances of children learning so that we become designers of the most delightful user experiences we can provide. Designing opportunities, flexing spaces, and finding the resources are essential to educators who create paths for children to see themselves as capable of designing, creating, making, building, and engineering their curiosities, imagination, questions, and ideas. They spend less time considering how to get kids to replicate the same work and projects that represent past lesson plans and more time noticing and listening to the children around them to discover how might children find voice, agency, and influence through experiences that allow for differences, interests, passions, and questions.

It's hard for that to happen during the school year when so many competing interests from passing state tests to covering curriculum are on the minds of teachers. That's why we've used summer activities to help us test-bed design thinking and maker activities. Test-bedding ideas in the summer allows us to bring in teachers to cofacilitate activities and in doing so to learn along with the children. Teachers have time to stop, process, and reflect on how they can take back and use what they learn during the school year. We want to break generations of traditional practices that are grounded in compliance-driven learning work. To do so, we have to create very different learning experiences for teachers and students together. Design and maker experiences let us experiment. The Maker Ed and Make organizations have both supported our work, providing resources and engaging our staff with other design and make educators in the United States (Maker Ed n.d.).

It doesn't matter which school community has a need; our goal is to help design a way into meeting that need. As we expanded and shifted old shop classes in middle schools into mechatronics labs or maker spaces that blended old and new tools and technologies, we realized that we needed to move the curriculum up into high schools. Where and how to make this happen was a challenge until we explored possibilities. We realized that a space existed in a high school that had once been the shop class but, sadly, the expensive equipment that once was available to learners in that space had been stripped out and lost – band saws and other construction tools – when shop classes were disbanded years ago. Chad had been working to equip this discovered space into a significant maker area, but the expense of outfitting it was prohibitive. When he found duplicates of equipment in another high school, Ira and he appropriated those and moved the resources to supply the new makerspace.

From a Twitter connect, we found an engineering teacher with a maker mindset who was entrepreneurial in his former

workshop school. The one thing he wanted in the newly constructed lab was a CNC router to add design opportunities to
the space. We opened that space for business over the summer,
figuring out how to purchase the CNC router so he could take on
projects with students that otherwise they would not have envisioned doing. Today that space bustles with the energy of teens,
male and female alike, who come in to work on formal and informal projects. The work going on in the high school mechatronics
labs led to a grant to innovate high school credit options through
a summer laboratory that would support our young makers to
come in and work with an innovation team in a project called
Design, Build, Launch (DBL).

In DBL, students have designed projects of personal interest
ranging from swinging desks for classrooms to a unique grip wrap for
baseball bats. They have spoken with entrepreneurs and presented
their startup work to get feedback and next steps support. Some of
their projects are strictly focused on areas of interest to them personally. Others are directed toward social good. They can receive
high school credits for math or electives as they work. This has led
to us thinking differently about what high school might become if
we began to focus on project work more than content work.

We find out a lot from observing and talking with kids as they
work to design. They learn a lot from each other as they elicit
feedback from peers and try out their ideas on others. When we
put together what we learn from design-oriented workshopping
with learners and teachers in our prototyping laboratories, it tells
us what ideas are ready to scale across schools, which ones may
only be "lines of best fit" in certain schools, which ones need to
still be in design process, and which ones simply don't work at all.
Kids teach us. We learn.

Your Own Learning

Provocation

Dale Dougherty, father of Make, provided a perspective in an
ISTE interview that has informed our vision for design and make

opportunities and how to do that without expending so much time on planning that opportunities pass us by:

> Making is very playful. It's something you can make a mistake at and it's part of the process. You didn't get a wrong answer; you tried something and it didn't go the way you expected. If adults are honest about the world, we don't have all the answers. We try a number of things and go down a lot of paths, some of which turn out to be productive and some of which don't . . . It's about developing an experimental mindset. Makers are a community of experimenters who try things. Some don't work, but they keep going. (Krueger 2014)

What's a project that you'd like to see happen quickly and without going through a traditional planning model? What challenge are you attempting to solve? How might you accomplish that? What might impede you moving forward or get in your way? What assets will help you move quickly? What might you learn from the experience?

Consider launching into your Isearch journal (in the cloud or on paper) to write down your thinking, to ask questions about which you are curious, and document your takeaways from Dale's beliefs about making and learning – and ours, too. You also might want to explore *Freedom to Make: How the Maker Movement Is Changing Our Schools, Our Jobs, and Our Minds* (Dougherty and Conrad 2016).

Structured Inquiry

Some people use the power of constraints to build a tension of creative problem solving. Others simply freeze in the face of taking the risk to get a project started because of rules – even unwritten ones. When Ira commented, "Here's something to consider if you want to support people to be creative as designers and makers. Don't have more rules than you need." That statement strikes at the core of what organizations do best: make rules.

What makes rules essential from your perspective? How might a school community design for learning with as few rules as possible that impede change?

Reflective Pause

In our district, we've taken risks going back to 2002 when we created the Design 2004 request for proposals. Everyone at the time was fearful of the impact of NCLB, and based on what we know now, that fear was justified. Yet, we didn't let that fear stop us. Because we didn't, we've moved beyond the horizon of twentieth-century schooling and shifted to a progressive education approach that represents the best of what we know about how children learn.

How do you push yourself to take a risk and get past the fear that you might fail? What would you need to do that?

Take Action

History is an endless story of invention pivot points, whether it's 1848, 1908, 1945, 1968. Or today. The railroad and telegraph. Airplanes and automobiles. The unleashing of atomic energy in World War II. The microprocessor.

Imagine traveling back to even relatively recent times in which structures and systems of the world fundamentally transformed. Imagine teachers in turning points in history. Envision the needs of children coming into school in one point and going out in another.

What's the intersection of contemporary needs and mindsets of the world changing around children in school and the nature of school as status quo transmitter of what has been than what will be? What do educators think about when those changes around them impact families, jobs, politics, and ultimately civilization? What happens when the curricula we are attempting to transmit becomes less relevant? What are we here for?

Moving quickly is just not done in education. Too often, we've heard keynote speakers refer to educators as creating and implementing plans that are reminiscent of the Soviet-style five-year plans of years ago: Make a plan knowing that, by the time you get to the end of it, no one will remember why you needed the plan anyway. Strategic work represents an organizational commitment to deep change that demands focused research, study, planning, and action. Invention work, on the other hand, often happens serendipitously. While it also needs to be planned well to execute with risk mitigation and a high chance of success, leaders who are rule-driven micromanagers struggle when staff want to move quickly. I hear from teachers and principals across the country who are willing to take risks that often it's the upper management staff, especially superintendents, who are quick to say no to trying new ideas out. As Chad says, "These competencies and pathways are what I consider to be levers. So, if somebody says to me, 'Well, how did you execute that? Or, how did you pull that off? Why didn't you ask permission to do that?' I'm able to say internally to others, well, it meets criteria for what we are trying to accomplish."

Four Actions to Build Pivot Power

1. Begin to take risks. Every day ask yourself: What am I going to change today that will make experiences for learners better? This might involve using technology tools in different ways to create more interactive and connected experiences with peers inside and outside the classroom. Or, it could be as simple as inviting students to share with you what they are curious about beyond the standard objectives of the day. Use what you learn from watching and listening to students to do something different with kids the next day. Make it a practice to challenge your own behavior norms, whether it's how you begin a faculty meeting or time with young people.
2. Make something. Anything. Make yourself vulnerable. Make something from cardboard. Create something to share with colleagues and students. Something useful. Something whimsical. Something in response to a need that another

person has. Making is a path to learning. If you take the risk to make something – even badly – it's easier to support others to become makers of ideas, designers of experiences, builders of moments that encourage creativity, boundless energy, and enthusiastic learning.

3. Research design strategies. Google design stuff you have questions about. Watch videos about designers – architects – artists – engineers, makers. Visit skyscrapers, museums, coffee shops, community makerspaces, parks and gardens. Notice how people use spaces to interact and find solitude. How is design an expression of human learning? What do you think about when you study design? How do people interface with the built world, the natural environment, each other? Share what you are learning in social media and around the table with friends and colleagues.

4. If you haven't studied entrepreneurial thinking, it's time. You don't have to, and likely if you are in education you won't become a money-making entrepreneur. However, change doesn't happen in education without thinking like an entrepreneur. A good place to start is with the research of Saras Sarasvathy, who studied the difference between causal and effectual thinkers – the difference as she notes between being a "general and an explorer." Sarasvathy writes:

Expert entrepreneurs are not usually in the ball counting business or the gaming business. Instead they are actually in the business of creating the future, which entails having to work together with a wide variety of people over long periods of time. Sturdy urns of the future are filled with enduring human relationships that outlive failures and create successes over time. (Sarasvathy 2008)

Start with Sarasvathy's work. Then find out if there are startup weekends planned near you and attend one. Take an education idea you want to pitch and develop it. Ask colleagues who they know that is doing something different with kids. Seek out educational innovators on Twitter and in your home community. Hang out with them and seek them for their energy, ideas, and support. Read a story or two about entrepreneurs who are engaged in social good projects. Think about how you are like them or could be like them as you develop, design, make new paths for your own learning.

Now pivot.

Resources

Albemarle County Public Schools. 2004. "Framework for Quality Learning." https://www2.k12albemarle.org/acps/division/fql/Pages/Curriculum.aspx.

———. n.d.a. "Design 2015 Projects." Accessed 8 October 2017. https://www2.k12albemarle.org/dept/instruction/design-2015/Pages/Projects.aspx.

———. n.d.b. "Lifelong-Learner Competencies." Accessed 8 October 2017. https://www2.k12albemarle.org/acps/division/Pages/Lifelong-Learner-Competencies.aspx.

———. n.d.c. "Seven Pathways to Lifelong-Learner Competencies." https://www2.k12albemarle.org/dept/dart/edtech/digital-learning/Pages/Seven-Pathways.aspx#&panel1-1.

Brown, Brené. 2011. "The Power of Vulnerability." https://www.ted.com/talks/brene_brown_on_vulnerability.

CoderDojo. n.d. Accessed 8 October 2017. https://coderdojo.com/.

Craddock, Michael. 2014. "La Academia | Makerspace @ Southwood—Under Water ROV Testing." https://www.youtube.com/watch?v=UhtCUmatn-U.

Design Thinking for Educators. n.d. "What Is Design Thinking?" Accessed 8 October 8, 2017. https://designthinkingforeducators.com/design-thinking/.

Dougherty, Dale, and Ariane Conrad. 2016. *Free to Make: How the Maker Movement Is Changing Our Schools, Our Jobs, and Our Minds.* Berkeley, CA: North Atlantic Books.

Dr. Seuss. 1975. *Oh, the Thinks You Can Think!* New York: Random House Children's Books.

Gilbert, Sarah. 2015. "Mary Ellen Mark's Legendary Photographs – in Pictures." *The Guardian,* 26 May. http://www.theguardian.com/culture/gallery/2015/may/26/mary-ellen-mark-legendary-photographs-in-pictures.

Gooding, Lucy, and Nick Lipley. 2004. "Walk-in Centre Roll-out Proposed." *Emergency Nurse: The Journal of the RCN Accident and Emergency Nursing Association* 12 (4): 2.

Johnson, Whitney, and J.C. Mendez-Garcia. 2012. "Throw Your Life a Curve." *Harvard Business Review.* 3 September. https://hbr.org/2012/09/throw-your-life-a-curve.

Krueger, Nicole. 2014. "To Make Is to Learn: A Q&A with Dale Dougherty." ISTE. 19 August. Accessed 8 October 2017. https://www.iste.org/explore/articleDetail?articleid=132.

Maker Ed. n.d. Accessed 21 November 2017. http://makered.org/.

Moran, Pam. 2016. "Hacking Schools: Getting Ourselves to Yes." https://www.youtube.com/watch?v=_2MtUegl7YI.

mpcraddock. 2013. "Design 2015 in Action." Where the Tracks End . . . 13 October. http://mpcraddock.tumblr.com/post/63916724873/design-2015-in-action.

Nussbaum, Bruce. 2011. "Design Thinking Is a Failed Experiment. So What's Next?" Co.Design. 5 April. https://www.fastcodesign.com/1663558/design-thinking-is-a-failed-experiment-so-whats-next.

P21. n.d. "Our History." Accessed 5 November 2017. http://www.p21.org/about-us/our-history.

Roscorla, Tanya. 2017. "Why the 'Maker Movement' Is Popular in Schools." 26 November. http://www.centerdigitaled.com/news/Maker-Movement-Popular-Schools.html.

Sarasvathy, Saras. 2008. "What Makes Entrepreneurs Entrepreneurial?" Society for Effectual Action. http://www.effectuation.org/?research-papers=what-makes-entrepreneurs-entrepreneurial.

Society for Effectual Action. n.d. "Effectuation." Accessed 8 October 2017. http://www.effectuation.org/.

Stewart, Louise. 2014. "Maker Movement Reinvents Education." *Newsweek.* 8 September. http://www.newsweek.com/2014/09/19/maker-movement-reinvents-education-268739.html.

"The Meaning of *Terroir* – Introduction." n.d. Accessed 11 March, 2018. http://www.musingsonthevine.com/tips_ter1.shtml.

Tsai, Mu Ming. 2014. *Design & Thinking.* https://www.youtube.com/watch?v=Z_YwyMssN0Y.

Wheatley, Margaret J., and Deborah Frieze. 2011. *Walk Out Walk On: A Learning Journey into Communities Daring to Live the Future Now.* San Francisco: Berrett-Koehler.

10

Zero-Based Design: Engineering Biodiversity of Learning

> It is reckless to suppose that biodiversity can be diminished indefinitely without threatening humanity itself.
> – E.O. Wilson Biodiversity Foundation (n.d.)

It doesn't take long to figure out when observing the natural world that biodiversity creates pathways for organisms to not just survive, but also to thrive within ecosystems. Unlike the cornfields of Michigan where row after row of hybrid plants are identical to every other one, nature seems to appreciate differences among species. It's a way of foolproofing longevity that stretches back generations across millennia, and the variety within and among species tends to support an entire ecosystem to sustain balance and thrive. In the scientific world, geneticists worry about our dependence upon crops that have been standardized genetically. The hybrid tomatoes keep longer in the grocery store, but the scientists know they are subject to potential blights that can wipe out the entire crop in a short period of time. It's happened before – with corn, potatoes, and citrus crops. It's why plant geneticists recommend never becoming reliant upon a single hybrid. It's why ecologists know that biodiversity matters in an ecosystem. It's the opposite of what we are doing inside the human ecology of our schools.

PAM: The supermoon we had the other night – think of every question a child might ask. Think of every connection that might make. You get to every content area, every standard, and you can do it without any experience of "school," just through kids' curiosities burning brightly.

CHAD: When my kids see the world, they wonder, and when they wonder, they inspire themselves to learn. I see this every day before school, after school, on weekends, in the summer. Where I don't see it is in school – especially in middle school.

IRA: William Alcott – and we're talking early 1830s and he was, more or less, creating schools from almost nothing – talked about how the garden was essential, how a collection of distracting wonders was essential, how a covered porch – allowing learning to stay outdoors in any weather – was essential . . . At that very start the idea was to bring childhood wonder into the building that would become our schools. He argued for movement, for play. People think school-as-we-know-it is some natural inevitability, but that is untrue. A place for childhood was perverted into something else, and we need to begin by understanding that.

Zero-Based Design

"Zero-based design." What might it look like if we'd never seen a school, but needed to bring our children from age 4 to age 18, or age 22? What would we do? What would we ask? What should the childhood experience be? What should the adolescent experience be? What do we want our students to understand as they grow?

Should every child jump in puddles? Climb a tower? Look underwater in a tidal pool? See Macbeth? Cook an egg? Change a spark plug? Read a book by an Indian author? Watch films from the Library of Congress collection? Compare the *New York Times* and the *Guardian*? Twist on a swing? Dance on a stage? Laugh at a Dr. Seuss book?

What are the things you want for your child?

In 1832 William Alcott wrote, "We too often consult our own convenience, rather than the comfort, welfare, or accommodation of our children" (Alcott 1832). So, how do we fully consult childhood when we design our educational ecosystem?

Let's begin here: There is no average child. There is no way to describe the average of Pam, Ira, and Chad. There is no way to describe the "average" of the first five kids who walk into your classroom. And we should not want to. Monocultures are not healthy ecosystems; they are not sustainable ecosystems.

The Freedom to Be Different

When we've walked the schools across Ireland and visited schools across the United States, it's evident that wide diversity exists in our schools. Everyone knows that. The children who live in the wide-open expanses of Iowa with miles between their homes represent significant differences from their peers attending public or private schools, whether rich or poor, in or near New York City. While great ideas might scale across their diverse ecosystems, standardization of what children need to learn, how to learn it, and how to demonstrate learning treats two schools a thousand miles apart as if they are factories run by the same company in two different states.

While the procedures of creating widgets might be standardized in two different factories, the needs and interests of children in two different school communities are not the same. We believe standardization of their educational experience – curriculum, assessment, and instruction – disregards their differences but also represents "hybridization" of learning to create the same expected outcomes for every child in every school in every community in America. It's been called No Child Left Behind (NCLB) and now it's called Common Core. Soon states will have all filed their next generation mass standardization plans with the US Department of Education in response to the federal Every Student Succeeds Act of 2015 (Aldeman, Marchitello, and Pennington 2017). The intention of all these movements to set standards might have been done with good intentions by some, but the outcome could be as disastrous for our schools as the fungal disease that attacked America's hybridized corn crop was in the 1970s (Tatum 1971).

We have seen how standards limit the interests and passions of both children and educators to explore and extend their learning. Instead, teachers feel compelled to keep pace with covering content so kids will be ready for the never-ending stream of standardized tests that have brutalized our schools for almost two decades. Field trips and other enrichment experiences have been stripped from schools, creating greater opportunity gaps between the middle class and those living in or near poverty. Students in many schools move lockstep through programmed materials that have been teacher-proofed, whether out of a box, a text, or online. Yet, despite all the efforts to test our young people into success, we continue to bemoan their lack of success and intensify efforts that filter P-based learning (passion, projects, and problems) from our classrooms. Some tout corporate takeover of American education, but the data are in and charter management and virtual companies do no better, and often worse, than the schools they are designed to replace (Woodworth, Raymond, and Van Donge 2015).

We believe that the mass standardization movement has always been wrong for schools. Schools are different. Children are different. Communities are different. Variety is good for the ecosystem, and we believe it's good for schools, too. Creativity emerges from different needs in Iowa than in New York City. Problems demanding critical thought are different in Dublin than out in the Ring of Kerry. Collaborative opportunities are different in rural Virginia than in suburban Oregon. Communication occurs differently in urban Vermont than in inner-city Philadelphia. We wonder how development of the cognitive and social competencies essential to living and working in an increasingly global world can be derived from the variety of community ecosystems in which young people work and play. If we can't figure this out, then we fail our learners by defaulting to prescribed standards that deliberately produce one-size-fits-all curriculum, assessment, and instruction, creating the same hybridizing model for our schools that geneticists warn against in the natural world.

We need variety and biodiversity in schools, too. The walls of schools are a contrived barrier that keeps kids and teachers apart within the system. The walls of schools keep new practices, tools, and strategies out and traditions in. When we think about creating a biodiversity of learning, we turn to new ways of thinking about how systems change. That doesn't happen without removing barriers that wall off the potential for change. We have found that breaking walls is best interpreted through the ecological lens as defined by the work of Yong Zhao and Ken Frank, who framed the problem of introduction of a new species in Lake Michigan as having similarity to introducing a new practice, tool, or strategy into a school (ETEC 511 n.d.).

We also believe in the concept of terroir, used so beautifully as a metaphor by Margaret Wheatley and Deborah Frieze in *Walk Out Walk On* – that the soil and climate of two different continents produce variations in crops even when the seeds planted are the same (Wheatley and Frieze 2011). Schools are like that, too. Two schools may be situated in different terroir even though children work and play similarly no matter where we visit. However, those children grow up in different cultural contexts that shape what they bring with them into school. Educators do the same. Because of that, each school represents a unique identity, one shaped locally, not by the federal government. While school communities certainly benefit from cross-pollinating of ideas and resources, allowing them to localize their identity makes a lot of sense when it comes to figuring out what children need to thrive as learners.

Together the concepts of biodiversity and terroir combine to support the idea that schools in different localities need the freedom to be different. It doesn't mean that neurology research shouldn't drive educators' understanding of how children learn and the pedagogies they need to use in response to that understanding. It doesn't mean a curricula free-for-all instead of a coherent focus developed locally. It doesn't mean there shouldn't be any sense of standards at all for what's important to learn in and across disciplines. It does mean that broad parameters should allow children who need to learn about simple machines to do far more than simply memorize them for a test. It means that if a child or class is obsessed with simple machines, they don't need to stop immediately to begin studying phases of the moon. When learning is allowed to be project, problem, and passion driven, then children learn because of their terroir, not disengage in spite of it. When we recognize biodiversity in our schools as healthy, then we increase the likelihood that our ecosystems will thrive.

Maximize Creativity by Minimizing Constraints

To achieve change in schools, leading in this century must be as a much of a subversive activity as Postman and Weingartner defined in 1971 (Postman and Weingartner 1969). To accomplish change, educational leaders have to subvert the policies that have been imposed from outside our system and subvert the grammar of schooling that says to do something a certain way because that's the way it's always been done.

To do that, you have to use a community organizing strategy. You have to rally the leaders in the buildings, teachers particularly, students even, and get them thinking – give them permission to take risks, permission to take chances. When teachers say "This is what I want to try, this is what I want to do," they are more likely to try out new strategies or resources, because we have embedded and integrated "yes" into our organization's language.

We ask ourselves questions all the time. For example, if broadening maker opportunities makes sense across schools, then how do we make it systemic without replicating it through contrived constraints and formalized into a curriculum? How do we sustain a "not top-down" approach? It's truly about the constant cultivation of an environment from a leadership perspective that isn't about standard operating procedures or hard definitions of what school staff are expected to do. Sometimes the ambiguity actually makes it quite challenging, but at the same time the ambiguity is what makes it work.

People need some constraints for creativity, but constraints that function only in ways that will get them to an end in mind. Our end in mind is grounded in the Seven Pathways and our Lifelong Learning Competencies (Albemarle County Public Schools n.d.b, n.d.c). The leadership practices and tactics we use are similar to those we believe make sense when used by teachers and students. We believe that when you place more constraints on a school by policy or procedure, you'll see less creativity and risk taking. And the more constraints a teacher adds to the project, the more it becomes the teacher's project.

However, when you constrain as little as possible, it maximizes creativity. For example, think about students with access to an LED, copper tape, and a battery. If the teacher constrains those three materials very little, kids will come up with divergent solutions in using them. Who the heck knows what's going to emerge from kids when we don't give them the worksheet recipe or the kit directions to follow? A teacher can teach basic electricity through those materials. But if she chooses to define how materials are used or specify what it will light up, the more the project becomes the teacher's idea and her definition of a successful project. Yet, when a project begins with students' context and interests, it's more likely to lead to a school or classroom culture that supports learners to pursue problem-, project-, and passion-based learning. Teachers who allow context into a project constrain that project minimally. They know if they constrain as lightly as possible, learners are going to land where they need to be with content while also experiencing a sense of control and agency in their own learning.

We constrain similarly from a leadership perspective because we've identified formal language for outcomes that actually reflect many of the tenets of progressive education. Our lifelong learning competencies are life skill measurements, life experience measurements, life capability measurements (Albemarle

County Public Schools n.d.b). They describe learning how to learn, and are key because as leaders these ideas have become our constraints. We don't count units of knowledge and lock ourselves into that. We don't count compliance rituals and constrain our views that way. These lifelong learning competencies reflect principles of progressive education. We say enact them any way that you see fit.

Enact what fits your school, your culture, your students. Seek to find context at the student level, context at the teacher classroom level, context at the district level. Support your school communities to evolve differently, based on *their* terroir, so that the languages spoken, the demographics that represent more or less diversity, or the interests of the neighborhood represent strengths that may be untapped. A school dealing with rural poverty should look quite different from one dealing with urban poverty – in how curriculum is made real and learning opportunities are made available that serve young people differently. Build schools as part of the community, not apart from the community. The resultant social cohesion and collective efficacy will change not just the school but the entire community.

Educating people in only one specific way robs communities and cultures of the context of their own lives that they need to bring to learning. Students are at risk in different ways. Children from our most affluent areas can also be at risk. Even though they have all the material possessions that we could dream possible, they still may have unmet emotional needs. They certainly can be constrained in any sort of creative endeavor because their lives are carved out for them. Teen suicide rates are higher across the country in the upper-middle-class demographic. When we began working together, Ira told Pam that one of his struggles was finding "empathy for rich kids." But we work to overcome those biases and know that, while resources may help equality and equity for populations that have historically been underserved, the better solution to offer true equity to every child is make the system responsive to the needs of the child.

The highest goal is not finding a middle, it's finding the best answer for every kid. It's meeting children's needs through access to cognitively and emotionally safe learning spaces. No one path can be the only path to meeting needs of students in our schools.

Behaving in Resourceful Ways

Each of our stories represents differences among our schools, and no two school stories are the same. All our stories add up to a narrative in which each school community's environment supports people to see themselves as able to create and through that creative process to see themselves as leaders. This sense that people don't have to replicate school as it occurs in other communities starts to catalyze the belief that anybody's thinking can exert learning direction and influence in the community.

For example, last summer Chad picked up some sewing machines for a summer maker laboratory in a middle school's mechatronics space. They'd arrived before the end of the school year, and there were both girls and boys in the space when Pam visited one day. The kids had unboxed one of the sewing machines. And when Pam walked in, some of the girls were sitting in front of it staring at the machine with a look of "What do we do with this?" They had no idea what to do to use it. The teacher came over and said, "I don't know what to do with it." So, everyone sat there.

Pam wondered, "What are these girls going to do?" She decided to just wait. The first thing they did was start looking at the manual, but they couldn't figure out from the directions how to thread the needle. The kids were really working on deciphering the diagrams and the tiny print. Then one said, "I bet you can find how to do this on YouTube." They pulled up a video on a phone, and there was someone showing how to thread the needle. As they watched, one of the girls finally started to figure it out even as they struggled to get the winding correct. They looked at Pam at one point as if she might have some information to help. She laughed, "Don't ask me. I refused to do this with my mother when I was your age."

One of the kids said, "I bet Mrs. Smith knows." Mrs. Smith was the school secretary. They found her (she's not too far from retirement age and more of a grandmother than mom figure to the kids). She came and looked at the machine, "Oh, yes, I can help you do this." She helped them get the needle threaded and then started to show them how to begin laying down stitches.

When Pam went back to the middle school maker laboratory later in the summer, the girls were making clothes that they were going to share in a maker exhibit at the end of summer. They were planning to have a fashion show. They had moved from staring at a sewing machine to designing, drawing, and cutting fabric. They had figured out that, interestingly, the mother of one of the boys in the lab space had taught him how to sew using a similar sewing machine. They recruited him into the group and away from his woodworking project to teach them how to sew. It was fascinating to watch this diverse group share their ideas, their expertise, and their projects with each other as they learned together rather than in isolation from each other.

This is what happens in a social learning community. People don't wait for a leader to tell them what to do. They just start doing it.

If you need expertise, you figure it out – you become resourceful. However, becoming resourceful does not happen for children in one lesson or one unit. Educators know that the longer young people stay in school, the less they will trust in their own curiosity and autonomy as learners. The very nature of schooling today reduces the opportunities for young people to make choices, reflect metacognitively, and work for the sake of learning itself versus against it, often because of grading practices. As we have subtracted experiential learning, creative outlets including play, arts, career-technical ed, and hands-on opportunities from the repertoire of practices once valued in more progressive times, our students have become to a great extent dependent and reward driven, constrained as critical thinkers and creative individuals.

No place does this show up to a greater degree than in comparative research examining creativity assessment data from prior to and after implementation of NCLB (Gray 2012). Teachers express frustration with dependent learners, who by the time they enter high school often are focused on what they need to do as "high performers" to get an "A" or simply as "average or low" performers to avoid failing a class. They've learned that asking off-curriculum questions, pursuing personal learning interests – both examples of curious learners – often leads to rebuffs at best or discipline at worst. But teachers who are committed to supporting learners to own their own learning can change practices to build a different culture of resourceful learners.

One example of a purposeful strategy to build resourcefulness lies in the quality of feedback teachers give students. As Matt Haas, a colleague leader writes, feedback can be scary to students when used in highly ineffective ways. Instead, as he notes: "feedback of all kinds is such a lifeline for the growing mind that negative or counterproductive feedback for student work has the same horrifying impact on learning as a haunted house has on its visitors. I believe that ineffective feedback slows students down at best and causes them to quit at its worst." He notes that when learners have the opportunity to metacognitively reflect, be participatory in feedback oriented to their own learning goals, and build autonomy in learning, they become resilient, indeed, independent in their own pursuit of learning (Haas 2014).

If curiosity is missing in schools today, it's not because children lacked it when they arrived but rather because educators have been programmed by mass standardization to discourage it tacitly and explicitly (Kaufman 2017). Moving young people to positions of personal resourcefulness, and in doing so, to rediscover their curiosities, creativity, and independent learning motivation means abandoning practices that oppose all of that and putting time into coaching and learning practices that empower and engage learners in developing agency by design. Teachers who slow down the pace and take the time to build capacity among diverse learners to follow different pathways to learning also find that the culture of the classroom shifts as they implement specific strategies designed to support choice, independence, comfort, and collaborative community. This does not happen by chance, and it's one reason we build independence foundationally through the Responsive Classroom approach in elementary schools (Delisio 2011) and are in transition to our high schools becoming much more focused on personal learning independence and having fewer programmatic constraints (Albemarle County Public Schools n.d.a).

Ultimately, resourcefulness is what humans have always done to take on grand challenges, whether settling the world or going to the moon and back. They had to be resourceful. *Resourceful* means being able to create, to think, to be able to find what you need, to be able to interact and engage with other people who have expertise and to share your own expertise, to realize when you start to work in a maker environment that what you think you know about a person is not what you know at all. You may find the person who does not feel they're very literate actually is quite literate if you tap into something they know how to make and you don't.

No Two Schools Are the Same

Zero-based learning design is a kind of resourceful design that begins with a clean slate and applies a fresh look at what schools can become when learners become the client and the learning designer seeks out what they value in their learning experience by noticing them, talking with them, and observing the interface of space and opportunities valued by learners and not created for the convenience of the adult in the room. Zero-based design captures timeless moments of flow; the designer removes structures and procedures that impede learning flow. Creation of learners' delight and joy in learning is the end in mind. And, when designers inquire, empathize, respond, and create opportunities in response to learners, they build open ecosystems that recognize the value of diversity and personalized pathways – not tech personalization alone, but personalization of curriculum, assessment, and pedagogy that evolves as learners' interests, questions, and curiosities emerge. Heterogeneity is valued as an asset in the environment.

Replication and homogeneity are recognized as structural design elements of Frederick Taylor's efficiency and effectiveness model that led to standardization of factories and factory schools in the 20th century (Modern History Sourcebook n.d.).

While factories might have benefitted from this compliance-driven model in the twentieth century, children have always been disadvantaged by one-size-fits-all, cookie cutter approaches that diminish the strength and asset of their diversity and differences in the school ecosystem. The application of scientific management theory set up a model that created schools that didn't just operate like factories but also applied the science of hybridization to scaled standardization within our schools.

Scaling up fails because it imagines, in the language of *New York Times* columnist Tom Friedman, that "the world is flat" (Friedman 2005). To imagine that 520 years after the voyage of Columbus we'd love the phrase "flat world" is both highly amusing and deeply saddening, but it represents the desperation for sameness that has long characterized British and American imperial thought. This idea would have never come out of French culture, or even German culture, where notions of difference are embedded. Hamburg, Berlin, and Munich have very little in common. Saigon, Algiers, and Martinique (to name three French colonial capitals) in no way operated along the same lines.

This is a conceptual difference with vast implications. And it may begin with the word *terroir*, a word we've known for a long time but which was reimagined by the brilliant book *Walk Out Walk On* (Wheatley and Frieze 2011). *Terroir* in French means something like "a sense of the place," and is used most often to describe why the same grape vine will produce different wine depending on where it is planted. Terroir is not simply a "natural" phenomenon. French viticulture understands that it isn't just the weather, the unflat world slope, or the soil that causes variation, but the way that the farmers themselves function, how they care for the vines, how they pick the grapes. So, it is presumed in France that every wine, from every year, from every different place, will be different. This is quite a different concept from the T-test that lies behind both Anglo-style brewing and American education.

The world, apparently, is as flat as we choose to see it.

A few years ago Ira sat in a session at a comparative education conference and heard people working with a highly successful tech firm's education division describe their intention of doing the exact same thing in every school, whether that school was in San Jose, California, or rural India. After the session he asked one of the presenters if he really thought that there were no differences across the planet. "Well, sure," he replied, "but for the sake of this project we've chosen to ignore that" (Socol 2010).

Which describes the "flat world" cultural concept perfectly, and makes "scaling up" possible. If the world is all the same, we can find the model·that works in Oklahoma City and replicate it exactly in Lagos. If this is how math is taught in Beijing, we will teach it this way in Newark.

Yet, no two children are the same. No two teachers are the same. No two communities are the same. No two ecosystems are the same. But these facts dispute the rationalism and science of the last 300 years of "Western" thought. The entire goal of statistics is to create "norming," so that, for example, one looks at the North Atlantic and the South Pacific and calls both "ocean." In educational terms, we've had a series of U.S. secretaries of education who look at any two children who are six years old and says, "first grade." It makes life so much easier if we can imagine the world this way. You barely have to look to be sure you know. Which is why Arne Duncan, former secretary of education (Brown 2017) and now in the private education sector, and David Brooks at the *New York Times* (Brooks 2011) think they know what makes for a failing school and that it always comes back to a question of whether kids passed a test and, if not, who is to blame? Matt Landahl, former principal, responded to that perspective:

What David Brooks fails to realize is that for a school leader to swim up the fast flowing stream of "not teaching to the test," it takes an incredible amount of support, collective courage, and belief in children to accomplish doing things the right way. Most people in education right now, because they are in schools that don't face these issues or they simply refuse to face the issues themselves, don't really have an idea of how tough it is. (Landahl 2011)

If you believe in that rational, flat world, everything can be scaled up. You define a "best practice" or a "successful design" and you just repeat and repeat. But if you don't see humans that way, you need a different path. That different path accepts that the surfaces tell us a lot less than we think, and that no matter how much the global economic engine tries, whether that's Benjamin Disraeli/William Gladstone or JPMorgan Chase/Apple Corporation, the world will always be a stubbornly diverse place. So instead of modeling, scaling up, building replicas, in our district we seed and watch ideas take root in many soils and grow in many ways. This, according to the authors of *Walk Out Walk On*, is "scaling across" (Steiner 2013).

Scaling across doesn't result in the same outcomes as the scientific management system implemented in education, the one that governs what children are all expected to learn, when and where they learn it, how the teacher will "deliver" instruction for learning it, and the measurements for testing whether it was learned. As Chris Lehmann of Science Leadership Academy fame often says in keynotes, "We deliver pizza, we should not deliver instruction" (Reich 2012). The scientific management approach to education doesn't account for the unique nature of communities or children. Educators use time, resources, and personnel as standardization tools to create and sustain a mechanistic model to replicate the processes of teaching and learning, regardless of what we understand today about the neuroscience of learning, the sociology of diverse communities, and cultural change processes. We stand behind an assumption that standardization fails to deliver learning that makes sense in the context of individual learners' development, their diverse communities, or a school's cultural assets. Moving from the current scientific management system demands a different kind of approach to change that is not iterative but rather zero-based in design.

Such radical change begins with dissonance that opens windows and doors to the world through our questions, our values, and our dialogue. It acknowledges that learning today extends beyond the walls of schools and boundaries of districts, offering teachers and learners connectivity with expertise, experts, and audiences around the globe. To accomplish this kind of deep change, educators must receive the support they need to take risks to try out new paths to engage learners in work that helps them makes sense of their learning. Voices of educators must bring laser focus to equity and access, the elephant in the room of every challenge we face to ensure that all children are afforded agency, voice, and influence, not as an option or privilege but as a right. This cannot happen without significant transformation of every dimension of school as we have known it in our own childhoods, professions, and as parents.

Imagine Learning Built from Scratch

Imagine contemporary learning spaces that challenge every convention of the places we built as schools in the twentieth century. Imagine gathering spaces that encourage young people to work and play together in natural learning communities supported by teachers who create pathways that guide them towards adulthood. Imagine a merger of transparent natural and built environments that allow learners the delight of multisensory inputs through access to natural light, fresh air, and green space. Imagine a continuum of flexible spaces designed to create an atmosphere of choice and comfort as students pursue their interests and passions through transdisciplinary learning that fosters collaboration, critical thinking, creativity, and communication.

Now imagine unleashing the potential to learn in spaces where the literal and figurative walls of school have come down between learners and teachers who serve them. In such spaces, the dominant teaching wall, desks in rows, print texts, and digital worksheets have disappeared, replaced by thriving, active communities of learners who use a variety of tools to produce more and consume less. Rather than content, the context of experiences drives learning.

The important imaginative work of educators and young people needs to occur in an inventive, creative space in which constraints are minimized, interaction within community is maximized, and the process of learning shifts from time bound to timeless. Here, we dream, attempt, describe, converse. We pass along concepts, not plans. We share observations, not blueprints. We accept that whether it is a child or a school, we cannot evaluate anything with a checklist or a score, but only with very human description. That's a less rational world that requires more humane effort, and it contains troubling mountains and deep valleys because it is not flat. But it is the world in which we actually live. It is the one in which we challenge you to invent learning anew. It does not happen by chance.

Invention: How We Hack School

As noted before, we employ a model that we believe is simple enough to follow but that challenges the philosophy of many in the education sector. It's what people do who move inventions to innovations, a creative process that reflects what a mentor once said to Pam when as a young administrator she questioned whether to approve a teacher taking a different approach to use novels rather than basal readers with middle school at-risk learners. He said, "If you say no to her, not only will she not come back with another idea. She'll tell 10 others and they won't come either." The model we've developed is simple to remember, four steps that make sense in navigating to successful exploration of new ideas, strategies, and actions that are a part of creating and designing experiences that engage, delight, and challenge learners. It isn't always easy to implement given the values and beliefs of the bureaucracies of schooling.

Invention: The Model

Step 1: Get to Yes

This is a different version than the *Getting to Yes* of Fisher and Ury, even though it also occasionally demands negotiation to find a path that both teacher and administrator or teacher and student can mutually support when creative ideas are brought forward (Fisher, Ury, and Patton 2011). However, some of the most creative, indeed inventive, work that occurs in schools has occurred because an administrator has said yes to a teacher or even a student.

There's no better example than the one we often share with educators outside of our school district, and that's the story we shared in Chapter 1 of how one of our middle school cafeterias became home to not one but two student-constructed, rolling tree houses. Pam's story of getting to yes represents the ingenuity of what middle schoolers are capable of creating when turned loose by their administrators and teachers to engage in zero-based design – and the challenges of the value for yes in a national climate of standardization – and litigation (Moran 2016).

Working in education has trained leaders to say "No" far more than we say "Yes" regardless of whether our rationale to deny originates in law, policy, funding, or simply past practice.

Getting to yes is a lifetime challenge in education, whether we are a teacher, a principal, or superintendent. Our urge is *not* to say "What if?" Instead we are quick to go to "Yeah, but let me think about it," or "It's not a good time for this project" and then the conversation ends there. Getting to yes is one of many important leadership altering lessons that comes from both experience and taking the time to find and listen to mentors of all ages

Looking back at the tree house project, it was obvious their work mattered to the young people in the cafeteria. Their conscientious approach to the work was similar to adults on a construction job, whether articulated by a boy prompting two others about being sure they finished nailing in a board correctly or a girl who shared that she knew how to use a drill because her dad had taught her how. Another student commented that his dad was coming in after school to work on the project with the students since they needed some extra hands. As their teacher said, the students were applying the language of math while measuring with care even as they didn't even process they were using math in their work.

Why can't every day be more like the tree house project for kids in every school in America – not learning to pass a test but learning because it makes sense to do so?

While saying yes to the tree house project in the first place was step one, three other steps are critical when educators or kids want to hack something about school. The next three steps take more effort, a combination of leadership and management, than just saying yes.

Step 2: Engagement of Team

In our version of navigating change, bottom-up ideation and top-down support are prerequisites in the first stage of moving invention to innovation. Team engagement does not happen by chance. It demands asking critical questions: "Who else might want to join you to make this happen? Who can we recruit? How do we add diversity?" Team is key. When a team designs together, you see their ideas diversify and get tighter. Teams amplify creativity. They explore blind spots. They consider user experience and explore empathy differently. They can ask each other the essential question of "How might we reduce constraints on what kids can do here versus increasing constraints?"

The tree house project was realized because of an adult team's willingness to challenge the norm of a learning culture created through mass standardization and a team of middle schoolers who decided to build something that the adults would never have envisioned in a cafeteria. As Yong Zhao so eloquently describes it, "It is precisely the lack of explicit objectives determined by external parties that fascinates children" (Zhao et al. 2015).

The work of teams to see themselves as inventors, designers, and builders has played out in every school in our district, transforming learning in significant ways. We've had high school principals who radically shifted the way that kids who have lived in remediation throughout their school lives are served, resulting in a cotaught, project-based, rich interdisciplinary curriculum, a "four teachers in two rooms" model of learning. Elementary school faculty have successfully scaled a design and maker, team-taught, multiage learning environment, moving away from age-based grade levels. We've seen learning commons go viral in libraries across the district because one elementary librarian took the risk to move to high school and realized that almost no kids were voluntarily entering the library or checking out resources. Her ideas turned into sketches in an online tool and became reality as she together planned and created a series of environments including a hackerspace, music construction studio, makerspace, poets' cafe, student help desk, gaming center linked by high and low sitting areas, study areas, and a large group gathering space.

It doesn't matter where we go, in and outside of our built and natural environments – when teachers are unleashed to see themselves as creators, designers, inventors, builders, and engineers of contemporary learner-centric education, we see progressive education spreading virally across our schools. This happens not because of us but through supporting the agency of educators who influence their own communities and others around the globe as they connect virtually and face-to-face.

Step 3: Leveraging Resources
Leveraging resources is critical if we are to move beyond the educational maxim "If you keep doing the same things you've always done, you'll get what you always got." Education is not inexpensive and, unlike what some say, money does matter. Most school districts in our nation lost significant funding ground as a result of the Great Recession. In most cases, even with some recent increases, district budgets have not kept up with inflation or growth, and new initiatives are rare without redirecting or leveraging resources differently. We have experienced that, too. That's why we see leveraging resources differently as essential to

advancing invention and innovation work. In some cases, that has involved redirected funding as we have shifted from paper resources to digital resources, including universal design for learning tools that allow students curricular access that never before was possible. Leveraging resources can occur at the level of a classroom teacher, a department, grade level, school, or district-wide.

For example, rather than using capital funds to replace hallway lockers on an annual basis, our discovery that only a handful of high school students were using lockers led us to redirect funds to remove lockers and replace them with charging bars, whiteboards, and bench seating to create informal learning space in hallways. It's not unusual to see small groups of students, individual students, or teachers hanging out in halls, usually with earbuds on working on their laptops. We've used funds to get teachers out of schools and supplement traditional education conference events by taking our staff into totally different environments that create dissonance about what's possible. Sending educators to the Chicago Children's Museum to visit the Tinkerlab led to some of our earliest commitments to infusing maker work into our classrooms, particularly when teachers saw five- and six-year-olds using construction tools such as hammers and drills that often would be banned from schools.

We've repurposed professional development funding, technology funds, instructional resource funds, and capital improvement funds as we've focused on project-based learning, maker work, and interactive and connected technology applications, all building pathways that increase learner engagement and agency through use of funds to achieve equity, access, and parity. Repurposed funds have allowed us to work with classroom teachers, librarians, physical education instructors, STEM educators, visual and performing arts teachers, career and tech education teachers, and principals to imagine and design comfortable and flexible learning spaces. As we transfer the focus of learning away from the one-dimensional dominant teaching wall of the past into multidimensional learning opportunities in which young people work together or independently, they learn to select the tools they need to accomplish the work they do. They make decisions about locating themselves in space: sitting, standing, curled up on a couch, or lying on a rug. We've learned that life readiness is about what children do as five-year-olds and what they do as teens to build and continuously hone competencies of how to learn more so than what to learn. Making this shift happens when resources are leveraged so that we can get to yes whether it's a group of teachers who want to develop a summer rock and rap academy or a student who wants to start up a drone club.

Step 4: Prototyping Change

Prototyping allows educators to move ideas into reality while taking risks that will not have a major impact on all district staff. We have watched as districts have taken on major changes in practices, rolled out 1:1 devices by the thousands, or mandated professional training to implement program after program only to see failures create turmoil at best or massive system failures at worst. We've learned from our own examples that when new ideas come forward to aim small so that, if failure happens, it won't impact the whole system. When we hack libraries, schedules, learning spaces, curricula, and pedagogies, we are trying out ideas in test beds to figure out how to support contemporary learners. Prototyping helps us get that right.

When we first began transformative work in libraries, we started in a middle school. We learned in working with the librarian that she needed to feel safe to take risks. We learned when we moved the transformative process to a high school that collaborative ideation allowed creative ideas to emerge and morph into a hackerspace, a music construction studio, a student help desk, a poets' cafe, a design and make lab, and a variety of spaces where students could gather to study quietly or work in small groups. Circulation increased. More students and classes visited the library. And in 2013, the library won an NSBA Magna Award for its innovative shift to a learning commons (National School Boards Association 2015). When we were in a design process for a new addition to an elementary school, we were intrigued with multiage learning and ended up creating a 120-student, flexible learning, multiage space grounded in team-taught zones that support project-based, interdisciplinary learning. Since then we have rolled out two more multiage spaces and have one more in planning phases.

Supporting Transformation Through Design

Supporting transformation that's significant happens when we work through process steps for creating a substrate that grows change virally. Our role centrally is to create the conditions to support deep change. This begins with getting to yes, helping team members find each other, leveraging resources that will increase the likelihood of a successful startup, and building the prototype to test-bed ideas. If data – yes, data, qualitative and quantitative – suggest the prototype has legs to make a difference in building more pathways for kids to successfully develop life-long learning competencies, then we will share and support others to scale prototype ideas across the district. We don't expect replication as with a program but rather adaptation of approaches that make sense to plant in other school community terroirs.

That's our process of valuing inventive approaches so they might grow into innovations that if successful may become strategic priorities and ultimately operational strategies. The calculus of an organization can look much like an S-curve graph or it can be more of a flat-lined state of no progress. We've built a cycle of growth in our district so that when we have reached a plateau, we look for ways to create an inflection point to advance a new phase of growth. At the inflection point, we resource the spread of ideas while we test innovations in more and more locations. When an innovation spreads, we often see exponential change occurring at inflection points along our organizational S-curve. It's simple. When we look to move change at a faster rate, we look for fresh ideas to support, we build teams around the idea, we leverage resources, we prototype. Then we evaluate and make decisions about moving the work into our strategic work.

In a nutshell, that's how we hack school.

Your Own Learning

Provocation

What challenges your thinking about what the purpose of schooling would become if we were to take away prescribed curriculum, standards, and testing? What would you need to learn to work in an educational setting in the absence of direction about what to teach and when and how to assess? What would a school community grapple with if they were charged with creating child-determined, context-centric learning?

Consider launching into your Isearch journal (in the cloud or on paper) to write down your thinking. What makes sense about that – or not – to you?

Structured Inquiry

Public schools can be spaces where progressive education thrives, but this will only happen with rejection of the philosophy that we can't teach and children can't learn what they need to learn without significant constraints on what, when, and how content is taught to children at specific chronological ages. By reducing constraints to as few as possible and focusing on graduate outcomes aligned with lifelong learning competencies, we can unleash the potential of educators to educate for life, not for school.

Google the work of John Holt and the growing without schooling philosophy that he evolved (Holt 1977). Can unschooling occur in a traditional school? What do children gain from an unschooling approach? You? Record your takeaways and consider how you might incorporate more choice opportunities for children to pursue their own interests, not just randomly but with your systemic focus on doing so.

Reflective Pause

It's not unusual to read a blog post or follow a Twitter thread about cultural responsiveness in schools. The purpose of schooling across generations has been to homogenize society, to create commonality in what gets learned and how it's taught. This has led to what we call the corporatization of schools through marketing of one-size-fits-all textbooks, programs, and professional training. This quote from Chad caught our attention: "Educating people in only one specific way really robs communities and cultures of the context that they need to bring to learning."

What does this statement mean to you when you think about your own class, your school, or your district? What are implications of abandoning national and state control of education and localizing curricula so that teachers can flex time, content, and pedagogy? How might the curiosities, interests, and background experiences of learners form the context of curricula, pedagogy, and assessment in a school? How would educators and parents understand learning development and growth if standards were not the driver of the work children accomplish? How would we know?

Take Action

Schools have always existed that resist standardization of learning expectations. You know in reading our work that we believe that learning must be flexible, open, and choice-based in as many ways as possible. Private schools, homeschooling, and unschooling all represent spaces where that has been possible outside of public schools. In the public school arena, some charter schools have sought to create more progressive environments for learning from the High Tech High to Big Picture Schools models.

Why wouldn't we want the kind of learning that occurs in those models in all schools? What can we do together to advance a progressive approach?

Four Actions to Increase Learning Biodiversity in Your
School Community

1. "We need more than a genius hour once a week to build learning agency" (Genius Hour n.d.). Analyze how covering content standards for a test at the expense of creating a deep context through exploration of integrated content and experience impacts students in your class, school, district. Write this down and share your perspectives with colleagues. What can you together do to begin to tackle the problem of coverage at the expense of learning?

2. Add a small makerspace in your room or school. It can be anywhere and it doesn't need to have a lot of expensive technology to get it started. Our librarians say that glue sticks, cardboard, and duct tape are a great start to building a makerspace. Ask students "What do you want to make?" Watch them and see what happens.

3. When you use project-oriented learning, break the parameter rules by reducing your own constraints on what students can do. Give choices. Get kids to ask questions about what they want to learn. Teach kids the McCrorie ISearch approach and let them construct projects in first person versus third person (Zorfass and Copel 1995). Accept different media submissions from videos to websites, not just a poster or a written report.

4. Unschool your projects. Abandon an "everyone does the same project" approach. Make more white spaces in your day to move beyond the standards. Begin by asking learners what they are interested in. Grab inspiration from their responses and find connections from their interests to questions they might pursue. Look for curricular intersections as you support them to collaborate with each other in pursuit of learning that's intrinsically interesting to them. If you are tethered to standards, creates spaces every day for students to explore outside of that box using technology including

devices, books, maker and art supplies, and experts in and out of class. Teach your children with their intrinsic drive in mind. Get them talking with each other. Record their questions. Make opportunities to share their work with their parents, the principal, and others in class. Invite parents into the community for learning exhibitions that represent biodiversity.

Resources

Albemarle County Public Schools. n.d.a. "High School 2022." Accessed 30 December 2017. https://www2.k12albemarle.org/acps/division/hs2022/Pages/default.aspx.

———. n.d.b. "Lifelong-Learner Competencies." Accessed 15 December 2017. https://www2.k12albemarle.org/acps/division/Pages/Lifelong-Learner-Competencies.aspx.

———. n.d.c. "Seven Pathways to Lifelong-Learner Competencies." Accessed 14 December 2017. https://www2.k12albemarle.org/dept/dart/edtech/digital-learning/Pages/Seven-Pathways.aspx#&panel1-1.

Alcott, William A. 1832. *Essay on the Construction of School-Houses.* Boston: Hilliard, Gray, Little, and Wilkins.

Aldeman, Chad, Anne Hyslop, Max Marchitello, Jennifer O'Neal Schiess, and Kaitlin Pennington. 2017. "An Independent Review of ESSA State Plans." Bellwether Education Partners. https://bellwethereducation.org/publication/independent-review-essa-state-plans.

Brooks, David. 2011. "Smells Like School Spirit." *New York Times.* 30 June. https://www.nytimes.com/2011/07/01/opinion/01brooks.html.

Brown, Emma. 2017. "Obama Administration Spent Billions to Fix Failing Schools, and It Didn't Work." *Washington Post.* 19 January. https://www.washingtonpost.com/local/education/obama-administration-spent-billions-to-fix-failing-schools-and-it-didnt-work/2017/01/19/6d24ac1a-de6d-11e6-ad42-f3375f271c9c_story.html.

Delisio, Ellen. 2011. "Responsive Classroom Practices Teach the Whole Child." Education World. http://www.educationworld.com/a_issues/schools/schools016.shtml.

E.O. Wilson Biodiversity Foundation. n.d. "The Diversity of Life." Accessed 4 September 2017. https://eowilsonfoundation.org/the-diversity-of-life/.

ETEC 511 DLG 10—Ecology of Educational Technology. n.d. "Zhao and Frank." Accessed 29 October 2017. http://dlg10.weebly.com/zhao-and-frank.html.

Fisher, Roger, William L. Ury, and Bruce Patton. 2011. *Getting to Yes: Negotiating Agreement Without Giving In.* New York: Penguin.

Friedman, Thomas L. 2005. *The World Is Flat: A Brief History of the Twenty-First Century.* New York: Macmillan.

Genius Hour. n.d. Accessed 4 September 2017. http://www.geniushour.com/.

Gray, Peter. 2012. "As Children's Freedom Has Declined, So Has Their Creativity." *Psychology Today.* 17 September. https://www.psychologytoday.com/blog/freedom-learn/201209/children-s-freedom-has-declined-so-has-their-creativity.

Haas, Matt. 2014. "Feedback Doesn't Have to Be Scary." Brain Pan. 2 October. http://brainpanhaas.blogspot.com/2014/10/feedback-doesnt-have-to-be-scary.html.

Holt, John. 1977. "Growing without Schooling." *A Record of Grassroots Movements* 1: 16–23.

Kaufman, Scott Barry. 2017. "Schools Are Missing What Matters About Learning." *The Atlantic,* 24 July. https://www.theatlantic.com/education/archive/2017/07/the-underrated-gift-of-curiosity/534573/.

Landahl, Matt. 2011. "If Your School Teaches to the Test, It's Not the Test's Fault. It's the Leaders of Your School." *Elementary School Leadership.* 3 July. http://elementaryleadershipmattlandahl.blogspot.com/2011/07/if-your-school-teaches-to-test-its-not.html.

Modern History Sourcebook. n.d. "Frederick W. Taylor: The Principles of Scientific Management, 1911." Accessed 15 December 2017. https://sourcebooks.fordham.edu/mod/1911taylor.html.

Moran, Pam. 2016. "Hacking Schools: Getting Ourselves to Yes." https://www.youtube.com/watch?v=_2MtUegl7YI.

National School Boards Association. 2015. "Making It Real at Monticello High School – ASBJ." https://www.youtube.com/watch?v=ilQwPzy6mos.

Postman, Neil, and Charles Weingartner. 1969. *Teaching as a Subversive Activity.* New York: Dell.

Reich, Justin. 2012. "Summarizing EdTech in One Slide: Market, Open and Dewey." *EdTech Researcher.* 30 April. http://blogs.edweek.org/edweek/edtechresearcher/2012/04/all_edtech_summarized_in_one_slide_market_open_and_dewey.html.

Socol, Ira David. 2010. "Constructing Disability: The Second Class Citizen." SpEdChange. 5 March. http://speedchange.blogspot.com/2010/03/constructing-disability-second-class.html.

Steiner, Stephanie. 2013. "Walk Out, Walk On: Learning from Mexico and Brazil." Metta Center. 7 October. https://mettacenter.org/nonviolence-for-daily-living/walk-out-walk-on-2/.

Tatum, L.A. 1971. "The Southern Corn Leaf Blight Epidemic." *Science* 171 (3976): 1113–16.

Wheatley, Margaret J., and Deborah Frieze. 2011. *Walk Out Walk On: A Learning Journey into Communities Daring to Live the Future Now.* San Francisco: Berrett-Koehler.

Woodworth, James L., Margaret Raymond, Kurt Chirbas, Maribel Gonzales, Yohannes Negassi, Will Snow, and Christine Van Donge. 2015. *Online Charter School Study Report.* Stanford, CA: Center for Research on Education Outcomes, Stanford University. https://credo.stanford.edu/pdfs/OnlineCharterStudyFinal2015.pdf.

Zhao, Yong, Gaoming Zhang, Jing Lei, and Wei Qiu. 2015. *Never Send a Human to Do a Machine's Job: Correcting the Top 5 EdTech Mistakes.* Thousand Oaks, CA: Corwin.

Zorfass, Judith, and Harriet Copel. 1995. "Educational Leadership: Strengthening Student Engagement: The I-Search: Guiding Students Toward Relevant Research." *Educational Leadership* 53 (1): 48–51. http://www.ascd.org/publications/educational_leadership/sept95/vol53/num01/The_I-Search@_Guiding_Students_Toward_Relevant_Research.aspx.

Afterword
The Next Generation

He sat in the back of the classroom. Sometimes staring at the fluorescent lights flickering and humming above. Sometimes looking out the window toward the traffic flowing on the street beyond the playground. Sometimes following patterns invisible to others in the woodgrain of his desk or in the tiles of the floor or in the cotton of his jeans.

Beyond him he knew the teacher was usually talking. That other kids were reading or writing, passing notes or hitting each other, talking or rolling pencils off the desk so that they could bend down and pick them up. He knew that numbers and letters and words were being tossed around, but none of it could really touch his attention. He knew that he didn't need them anyway. He told his own stories as he watched his worlds, he added and divided his own sums as he let time wander, he found his own sciences as he watched the earth spin through its day. And he knew that the teacher knew that if she tried to force these things his way, he had very good ways to resist.

So there he sat. Holding an uneasy truce with his captors. Waiting for the best days, the rainy days, when water would streak across the window and the passing cars and trucks would toss spray in the air, and when he was finally paroled at the final bell he could walk slowly home, letting the water from the sky bathe him in its chill embrace.

– Ira Socol (2009b)

As we've considered the work we've shared, we know our story isn't finished, this story isn't finished. But we know our starting point, and we hope we have left much of the nineteenth- and twentieth-century education system in our rear-view mirror. We know many of you have done the same, or begun the process of doing so. We can't begin to document all the incredible ways that we've seen educators inside our district and others across the country make changes in their work.

We've seen the United States Department of Education move in 2009 from not even acknowledging that parents, educators, and children were increasingly fed up with mass standardization of our nation's schools to the White House hosting in 2015 some of the more progressive educators in the country, including a team from our district, to share their work (White House 2015). Just a few years ago, we began to notice the voices of a few radical educators pushing beyond factory schools; sharing ideas, resources, questions, and projects from their schools on Twitter, at fringe educational conferences, and through their blog posts. We watched the maker movement begin to have influence in informal learning environments outside of schools – libraries, museums, and community tech shops (Dougherty 2011).

Over the past decade, educators in our district began to view project work as more normative and less representative of outlier learning work. During that time with leadership of principals, teachers, parents, and our local maker community, we've integrated makerspaces into our schools. Those spaces have allowed our educators to see learners who were disengaged become engaged when given informal and formal opportunities to make to learn and learn to make. We believe that we've made significant progress to integrate a progressive philosophy in curriculum, assessment, pedagogy, and tool uses even as progressive education in this century is only beginning to be more clearly defined.

Even with our success narrative, we know there is so much more to do. The next generation of change in schooling will come not from making teaching and learning more complex but rather from simplifying our approaches. The next generation of leaders who will change schooling must avoid just improving upon the destructive and limiting old paradigms, but rather lead a true reimagination of what educational space, educational time, and teacher-student interaction look like. The cumbersome bureaucratic structures and procedures that evolved over decades will take time to dismantle, but they will be dismantled and replaced with flexible structures that respond to both children and the world.

We know that progressive approaches require more time for teachers to collaborate, to observe and talk with children, to build relationships with parents, and to move beyond one-size-fits-all grade level standards and tests. To make learning a seamless process that never stops and, just as in the beginning of time, is authentic and contextualized across boundaries of home, teacher, and community means we must dismantle all the compliant traditions of factory schools. Breaking through the legacy of Ellwood Cubberley, *A Nation at Risk*, the Presidential and Governor's Summit of 1989, and the federal No Child Left Behind Act will not happen in a year or maybe even a decade.

We know that we live in a data-obsessed society that demands evidence to justify a continuum of educational decisions that will determine the future of learning through interactive technologies, connectivity, agency by design, maker work, project-based learning, and "how to learn" competencies. Education continues to be driven by data to such an extent that even LED lighting color is marketed as positively impacting learners' test results in order to sell this new energy efficient technology in schools (Cree 2017).

To create the conditions for real and deep change inside our educational system, two brilliant thinkers remind us that we need to look beyond "bean counting" student learning data. The twentieth-century management innovator Edwards Deming (1900–1993), who led Japan out of a post–World War II industrial crisis and to a dominant industrial position by the 1970s, wrote in *Out of the Crisis* (Deming 1982):

> But he that would run his company on visible figures alone will in time have neither company nor figures. (p. 121)
>
>   . . . management by numerical goal is an attempt to manage without knowledge of what to do, and in fact is usually management by fear. (p. 76)

And Sir Ken Robinson, British educator and author, wrote:

> Public schools were not only created in the interests of industrialism – they were created in the image of industrialism. In many ways, they reflect the factory culture they were designed to support. This is especially true in high schools, where school systems base education on the principles of the assembly line and the efficient division of labor. Schools divide the curriculum into specialist segments: some teachers install math in the students, and others install history. They arrange the day into standard units of time, marked out by the ringing of bells, much like a factory announcing the beginning of the workday and the end of breaks. Students are educated in batches, according to age, as if the most important thing they have in common is their date of manufacture. They are given standardized tests at set points and compared with each other before being sent out onto the market. I realize this isn't an exact analogy and that it ignores many of the subtleties of the system, but it is close enough. (Robinson and Aronica 2009)

We've chosen to not focus on standardized data in our body of work, in part because we believe that most school districts, schools, and classrooms are swimming in data that measure the outcomes established as important in 1910, not 2017. Our schools, in general, do very well on a continuum of assessments of learning from decontextualized state tests to locally determined and more contextual performance-based assessments.

However, we routinely question in all the assessments our students are required to take: What values are we really measuring? Why should students pass an algebra proficiency test in which they are presented decontextualized theoretical math and asked to use procedural solutions to respond to a question? What matters about reading for a high school junior processing a brief excerpt from *Midnight at the Dragon Cafe*, a novel written in 2004 with 317 pages, when asked to pick from multiple choice options to define what "pensive" means, what a character feels in a particular sentence, or what literary device is being employed in a phrase in order to pass a state test (Commonwealth of Virginia 2015)? Kids, parents, and teachers often ask who cares about the questions that are on such a test? Do standardized tests really measure what matters as learning? When does the purpose of what we do shift to children reading novels for their purposes and using math to understand and solve real problems in their lives, not just pass tests?

The overload of data pumped into schools has created a noisy complexity, actually a jumble of constraints on learning, that defeats the real purpose of education that graduates leave schools ready for all that life has to offer as well as to successfully face challenges placed in front of them. Data drive worksheets in America's schools, a daily overload on children to practice tests or learn test-taking skills. Data drive the use of technology, not to power search, connect, communicate, and make to learn but as devices of rote memory building from multiplication fact practice to fill-in-the-blank sentences in reading passages. Mindless uses of data drive teachers to assign far too much homework to ensure kids are ready for class tests, state tests, and AP exams. Data drive purchases of one-size-fits-all programs that can't possibly fit the needs of all school communities. Data drive professional development so teachers can become better at giving tests and using data to inform what gets taught and tested in preparation for tests.

Collection and analysis of quantitative data have reduced our children to numbers in spreadsheets and plotted points on trend lines. We believe this is wrong, and we are working hard to remember what learning is when at its best for children. We don't believe in the maxim that Pam once saw posted in a 1975 classroom: "If you are having fun, you aren't learning." Or the idea that a first-year teacher shouldn't smile until second semester. We do believe that "All work and no play makes Jack a dull boy." In other words, the preoccupation of educators, politicians, and corporations with numerical data shouldn't get in the way of the curiosities and interests of children that lead to learning. Decontextualized spreadsheets of data should be the least, not the most, of what we do to understand how individual children learn and what we can do to support them.

In this book, we have chosen, instead, to focus on qualitative, indeed *simple* elements of engagement that harken back to how humans learn in natural settings.

Can kids tell stories, learn to communicate how to do things, and think about their own thinking as they solve problems? Can they see math in the world around them and visualize solutions as they make and build with tools, physically and virtually? How do young people research to find out who knows something they need or want to know? How do they learn as they work together and collaborate on creative solutions to thorny problems such as convincing a community to develop sustainable neighborhoods? What happens when play becomes a path to learning about patterns, textures, color, shape, and size? How do Rube Goldberg contraptions get built so that children's experimentation with force and motion moves from concept to real knowledge? In what ways are writing music or poetry similar to coding an app? And, what's the happiness quotient inside a school as measured by smiles and joy in the hallways and spaces of learning?

As we reflect back to the beginning of why we focused on an observational, more emergent design to share what we have noticed about leadership, learning, and life inside our schools, we ask once again:

What do you see when you look at your school?
What do you see when you look in a classroom?
What do you see when you watch children in the playground, or on a street, or in a park?
What does learning look like? What does growing up look like?

In the end it all comes down to knowing how to see. To understanding what we are seeing. And to putting what we learn from our effective vision into action for our children.

> "Can I write 'Dear parent, your son has greatly improved on things not considered important by the school [reporting] system'?" Tomaz Lasic asked on Twitter one day. Mr. Lasic, a teacher in Western Australia, works with "troubled" children, and is a brilliant observer. He sees children, not statistics, he measures learning, not knowledge bits. He continued, in evaluating his "'low achievers' class. Where's 'halted [self]abuse', 'began to smile' [on report card checkboxes]?" Finally, he declared, "Every time a particular kid ([with a] totally socially inept past) walks into our office and says, 'please,' or gives a high-five, we say: 'Evaluate that!'" (Socol 2009a)

So, though this book has covered a great many topics, the primary lesson here is to learn how to be much, much better at seeing children. Because once we are able to see clearly what is happening with our children in our schools and outside of our schools, we will then be able to learn how to take rapid yet deeply considered actions to change the educational system we have inherited.

As we continue this journey, moving forward ourselves along different pathways, we keep in front of us a future destination in which all children will thrive in school because of their diverse interests, range of background experiences, and identities – not in spite of their differences. This means identifying, analyzing, challenging, and revising the dominant narratives of schooling that define some children as competent, capable learners while defining others through a deficit lens because of their family, gender, race, disability, ethnicity, or income level.

To move beyond postcolonial schooling narratives that were built generations ago, educators must question biases and check their filters on children who are not like the educators who mostly serve them. Despite the belief that our nation offers, more than any other, the opportunity to make something of oneself if you live in poverty and are willing to work hard and get an education, bootstrapping is more myth than fact (Pew Charitable Trusts 2014).

Education matters, but not if kids leave schools without the confidence and capability to take on and move past life's challenges. We know how to teach kids to pass tests. We can sort kids out who don't conform in school communities so that they don't disrupt the normative culture; but those actions will not gift all children with the learning they need for success in life. Success in life won't happen without radical changes in the practices and mindsets of the dominant teaching culture. That demands hard questions and hard work.

To reach the learning destination we imagine, educators must replace the current dominant narratives about children who differ from the dominant teaching workforce and that remain static roadblocks to learning. They must begin to see the teacher in their students and the student in themselves as teachers. For, as Columbia University professor and "rachetdemic" educator Chris Emdin says:

> While there is usually an acceptance that media constructs flawed narratives about urban youth, society often overlooks the ways

that schools reinforce these narratives and cause them to fester in the minds and hearts of teachers. . . . When teachers see students like they see themselves, they see the best in students. They see them as heroes that have overcome the challenges of living in communities that have been deprived of resources. Students are not seen as victims, but rather as peers to exchange information with. Once teachers see students as they see themselves, they ask students to give feedback on instruction, consider students' thoughts and opinions on how the school operates, allow students to express their content knowledge in non-traditional ways, and engage with them both inside and outside of the classroom. (Emdin and Lenkei 2016)

Everything we do around children, everything we say, every space we construct, every schedule we apply, every rule we make either opens learning up to all children or creates limitations, filters, and sorting mechanisms. Everything. And perhaps the preface to any change lies in that understanding.

There is something else though: If you do not believe that you can change, or that your system can change – if you do not believe in the possibilities of change – you cannot give children what they need. Children, of course, must believe in their ability to change, because if not, why would education matter at all? Pam and Ira spoke once to a novice teacher who could not imagine that 8-, 9-, 10-year-olds would be different in April than they were in September. Lacking any sense of efficacy, any sense that his very job was to be a change maker, he found himself unable to inspire any sense of the possibility of change in his students. And that meant that for the students from hopeless homes, there was nothing at all. Middle-class children from a classroom like that can fall back on the timeless solution of inspiration at home, but that simply builds our opportunity gaps.

So we must understand ourselves as observers, as people aware of the impact of all we do, and to see ourselves as change-makers in a deeply imperfect world (McElroy 2016). Then we can begin to move.

Our desired state is a world of opportunity and success for every child, but the path to that desired state is a very long, very difficult climb. We are all somewhere on that path, and the universal truth is that, no matter what we have accomplished so far, we are not there yet.

Resources

Commonwealth of Virginia, Department of Education. 2015. "End of Course Reading: 2010 English Standards of Learning." http://www.doe.virginia.gov/testing/sol/released_tests/2015/eoc_reading_released_in_spring_2015.pdf.

Cree. 2017. "How LED Lighting in Schools Improves More Than the Bottom Line." Wesco. 2 August. https://blog.wesco.com/how-led-lighting-in-schools-improves-more-than-the-bottom-line.

Deming, W. Edwards. 1982. *Out of the Crisis.* Cambridge, MA: MIT Press.

Dougherty, Dale. 2011. "We Are Makers." https://www.ted.com/talks/dale_dougherty_we_are_makers.

Emdin, Christopher, and Alex Lenkei. 2016. "Q&A with Christopher Emdin: Reaching Students of Color." *Education Week.* 30 August. https://www.edweek.org/ew/articles/2016/08/31/qa-with-christopher-emdin-reaching-students-of.html.

McElroy, Erin. 2016. "The Makers Movement—What Is a Changemaker?" *HuffPost.* 19 January. https://www.huffingtonpost.com/erin-mcelroy/the-makers-movement-what-is-a-changemaker_b_8982996.html.

Pew Charitable Trusts. 2012. "Pursuing the American Dream: Economic Mobility Across Generations." 9 July. http://www.pewtrusts.org/en/research-and-analysis/reports/0001/01/01/pursuing-the-american-dream.

Robinson, Ken, and Lou Aronica. 2009. *The Element: How Finding Your Passion Changes Everything.* New York: Penguin.

Socol, Ira David. 2009a. "Evaluate That!" SpeEdChange. 13 June. http://speedchange.blogspot.com/2009/06/evaluate-that.html.

Socol, Ira David. 2009b. "Fiction Interlude: Back-to-School." SpeEdChange. 13 August. http://speedchange.blogspot.com/2009/08/fiction-interlude-back-to-school.html

White House, Office of the Press Secretary. 2015. "Fact Sheet: Obama Administration Announces More than $375 Million in Public and Private Support for Next-Generation High Schools." 10 November. https://obamawhitehouse.archives.gov/sites/default/files/docs/fact_sheet_-_white_house_summit_on_next-generation_high_schools.pdf.

Index

A

Access. *See* Equity
Accountability, 33, 39, 157
Ackoff, Russell, 86
Actions, 36–37; biases toward, 89.
    See also Take action
Active learners, 30–31
Adaptation, 216, 269
Adequate yearly progress, 33–35
Adolescence, 203
Adult learners, 83–84
Age-based grade levels, 85
Agency, 9, 26, 143–144; change,
    179–182; democracy and, 55–56;
    from opportunities, 131; with
    poverty, 33; timeless learning and,
    214; voice and, 41
Agriculture, genetic, 247
Alcott, William, 104, 248–249
All means all: assessment and, 36;
    barrier identification about,
    37; collective efficacy for, 36;
    in equity, 25–29; provocation
    and, 33–34; reflective pause in,
    35–36; structured inquiry for,
    34–35; struggles in, 36–37; take
    action in, 36–37

Alliance for Excellent
    Education, 192–193
Alliances, 71–73
Alter, Lloyd, 123
Alternative education programs,
    3–4, 41–42
America, 48–49
Appearances, differences in, 19–20
Apps, design of, 227
Armstrong, Thomas, 202–203
Artificial intelligence, 98, 150–151
Assembly line, 41; "factory school"
    system as, 114, 215, 259
Assessment, 52; all means all
    and, 36; learner-centric,
    111–113; portfolios in, 112; of
    teachers, 78–79
Audio, 102–103
Audio technologies, 133–135
Authenticity, 204
Authors' stories: apology in, 5–6;
    life learners in, 7–11; Special
    Education in, 2–3; teaching
    assistant job in, 3–4
Automation, employment related to,
    141, 147–151
Averages, 53, 249; equity and, 21–22